Bilingualism and Identity in Deaf Communities

Ceil Lucas, General Editor

Bilingualism and Identity in Deaf Communities

Melanie Metzger, Editor

GALLAUDET UNIVERSITY PRESS

Washington, D.C.

Sociolinguistics in Deaf Communities

A Series Edited by Ceil Lucas

Gallaudet University Press
Washington, D.C. 20002

ISBN 1-56368-095-5
ISSN 1080-5494

Cover Design by Joseph Kolb
Interior Design by Richard Hendel
Composition by G&S Typesetters, Inc.

♾The paper used in this publication meets the minimum requirements of American National Standard for Information Sciences—Permanence of Paper for Printed Library Materials, ANSI Z39.48-1984.

Contents

Contributors

Rosa M. Bellés
Institute of Education of the
    City Hall of Barcelona
Barcelona, Spain

Laura Blackburn
Department of Literacy
    Education (Deaf/Hard
    of Hearing Emphasis)
Northern Illinois University
DeKalb, Illinois

Pepi Cedillo
CREDAC Pere Barnils
Barcelona, Spain

Annica Detthow
Division of Student Affairs
Office of Disability Services
Florida International University
Miami, Florida

Rosana Famularo
Argentine Deaf-Mute
    Confederation
Buenos Aires, Argentina

Earl Fleetwood
Language Matters
Silver Spring, Maryland

José González de Ibarra
Institute of Education of the
    City Hall of Barcelona
Barcelona, Spain

Peter C. Hauser
Department of Psychology
Gallaudet University
Washington, D.C.
Department of Psychiatry and
    Behavioral Sciences and the
    Department of Medicine
University of Miami/Jackson
    Memorial Medical Center
Miami, Florida

Verena Krausneker
Vienna, Austria

María Ignacia Massone
Consejo Nacional de
    Investigaciones Cientificas
    y Tecnicas (CONICET)
Buenos Aires, Argentina

Rachel Locker McKee
Victoria University of Wellington
Wellington, New Zealand

David McKee
Victoria University of Wellington
Wellington, New Zealand

Johanna Mesch
Swedish National Association
    of the Deaf
Stockholm, Sweden

Ester Molins
CREDAC Pere Barnils
Barcelona, Spain

José Antonio Noriega
Grupo Tessera
Mexico City, Mexico

Laura Polich
Truesdell Center for Communi-
cation Disorders
University of Redlands
Redlands, California

Claire Ramsey
Special Education and
Communication Disorders
University of Nebraska-Lincoln
Lincoln, Nebraska

Introduction

It has been an honor and a pleasure to serve as guest editor for the sixth volume of the *Sociolinguistics in Deaf Communities* series. The topics contained in this volume include the wide range of sociolinguistic issues that readers of this series have come to expect, including variation, language contact, multilingualism, language policy and planning, discourse analysis, and language attitudes.

In keeping with the series' tradition, the goal for volume six was to include empirically-based work that is international in scope and extends our knowledge of the sociolinguistic issues in deaf communities by building on previous research or breaking new ground with preliminary studies. In keeping with sociolinguistic tradition, this collection of data-based studies follows a variety of research methodologies. I hope that readers of the series who have come to expect these elements will be pleased with the results.

This volume of *Sociolinguistics in Deaf Communities* has two recurring themes. The first pertains to the perception of deaf people and deaf communities. This theme ranges from Laura Blackburn's ethnographic study of a hearing family's view of themselves and their Deaf son to Claire Ramsey and José Antonio Noriega's look at the cultural perceptions of deaf people as revealed through Mexican rituals that focus on "cures" for deaf children. It includes a study by Laura Polich of a Nicaraguan deaf community in which the sociopolitical situation has made it nearly impossible to locate documentation, forcing the researcher to rely on interviews with members of the modern community to understand its emergence. María Ignacia Massone and Rosana Famularo address perceptions as portrayed through the mass media in the semiotic analysis of a videotaped interview, the metamessages within the discourse, and the choices made through the medium that are aimed at changing classic media images of Deaf people. Verena Krausneker describes the perception of signed languages within the European Union. Finally, Rachel Locker McKee and David McKee examine how members of a Deaf community view themselves, as measured by the arbitrary or descriptive nature of name signs.

Bilingualism is a second theme and is central to several chapters. For the past ten years or more, a growing emphasis has been placed on bilingualism or multilingualism for deaf children. How to achieve that, for children whose parents are hearing, has been a topic of great debate. Peter Hauser provides a data-based analysis of one Deaf child in the United States who has been raised bilingually with cued English and ASL, through examination of this child's code switching between the two languages and two distinct visual modes. Rosa M. Bellés, Pepi Credillo, José González de Ibarra, and Ester Molins examine the state of bilingual education in Spain. Earl Fleetwood addresses both the role of interpretation in classes in which deaf children who sign join hearing children who speak and also the effects of policy on services for these children who are expected to acquire aspects of two languages. For Deaf adults who are bilingual, interpretation is also an issue. Annica Detthow analyzes features of transliteration in a spoken Swedish–Swedish Sign Language transliterated text.

In keeping with the tradition of the series, several papers build on previous work, applying the findings of earlier studies to a first-time analysis of another signed language. This is true with the analysis of transliteration, in which Detthow applies the findings of Winston's (1989) analysis of transliteration in the United States to her examination of spoken Swedish–Swedish Sign Language transliteration. Similarly, Locker McKee and McKee extend prior research regarding the role of name signs in signed languages to their analysis of name signs in New Zealand Sign Language. In the same vein, Johanna Mesch builds on the work of Collins and Petronio (in the 1998 volume of this series) in her own analysis of Swedish Tactile Sign Language.

I am extremely grateful to the contributors to this volume, who have increased our knowledge of languages and societies around the globe, from Sweden, Spain, and the European Union to New Zealand, Argentina, Nicaragua, Mexico, and the United States. I would also like to extend my thanks to members of the editorial advisory board and especially to Ceil Lucas, series editor, who made this volume—and all the volumes of this series—a reality for those of us interested in enriching our lives through the growing understanding of sociolinguistic issues in deaf communities. I also would like to acknowledge the support and assistance of Ivey Pittle Wallace (managing editor), Christina Findlay (editor), and Carol Hoke (copy editor). I would be remiss if I did not also extend my gratitude to Jayne McKenzie, Ethylyn DeStefano, Carrie Apple, Shilpa Hanumantha, Claire Klossner, Lauren Tribby, and Earl Fleetwood for assistance with all sorts of tasks associated with the editing of this volume. Thanks also to Eric, Jill, and Dawson.

Part I **Variation**

Name Signs and Identity in

New Zealand Sign Language

Rachel Locker McKee and David McKee

Personal names in any culture are a potential gold mine of information about social relationships, identity, history, and linguistic processes. In Deaf communities around the world, members are commonly referred to by sign names given to them by other Deaf people at various stages of life, which are different from the legal (spoken language) names given by parents at birth. The study of name signs provides a window on the relationship between sign language, social interaction, and identity, in this case within the New Zealand Deaf community. Because they are bestowed by other Deaf peers through a period of close acquaintance, name signs both signal and construct a person's identity as a recognized member of a Deaf community, which is often regarded by members as an extended "family" (Monaghan 1996, 463).

The acquisition of a name sign may mark a person's entry to a signing community, and its use reinforces the bond of shared group history and "alternative" language use (in relation to mainstream society). Thus, using name signs is a linguistically efficient means of personal reference and is culturally important for interactions in a signing community because social networks tend to hinge on connections with other Deaf people rather than one's family of origin (unless the family is also Deaf). Personal identity in the Deaf community is strongly shaped by (and reflected in) language use and by one's relationships with peers—information that is encapsulated in a small way in name signs. Because people in the NZ Deaf community often have several name signs (which are used either at different periods of their life or alternately within different social groups or audiences), their use is somewhat context dependent.

The form of name signs and the particular social values and practices associated with them vary considerably among different signed languages and Deaf cultures around the world. The analysis of name signs contributes to a linguistic understanding of lexical creation and sources in a signed language. This chapter reports on a study that identifies types of name sign structures and derivations and describes their distribution in New Zealand Sign Language (a language used by a community of approximately 7,000 people). The chapter also discusses findings about the acquisition and use of name signs (such as differences between age groups and the use of alternate names) in terms of what these reveal about social norms and values in NZ Deaf culture.

WHAT ARE NAME SIGNS?

Name signs are a distinct category of signs in New Zealand Sign Language (NZSL), which are created as personal names for referring to others, usually members of a signing community.[1] Name signs seem to develop wherever a group of Deaf people have extended contact with each other and use sign language as their vernacular language. They are created for individuals within each generation or social grouping of Deaf people.[2] Most typically, name signs originate in deaf school settings where Deaf children form an autonomous social world beyond the gaze of teachers, which is governed by children's social norms and differentiated from the "authorities" by the use of sign language and a shared sense of Deaf identity. Like the nickname systems of non-Deaf school children

---

1. A *signing community* consists of Deaf people who use sign language as their preferred language of face-to-face communication. Most members have been deaf from infancy or early in their life and identify socially and culturally with other Deaf people. Non-Deaf (hearing) people, such as parents or children of Deaf people, interpreters, teachers, or social workers, may participate in signing communities and have name signs. This study, however, focuses on name signs of Deaf people themselves because their community is the primary reference group for the system of name signs.

2. The capitalization of *Deaf* has become a convention within both the Deaf studies literature and the Deaf community for referring to people who not only have a hearing loss but also identify themselves socially, linguistically, and culturally with other Deaf people who use sign language. This spelling is in contrast to *deaf,* which denotes hearing loss but not necessarily cultural or linguistic identity as part of a signing community. Most people who identify as Deaf have been audiologically deaf since early childhood or birth and have had significant social contact throughout their life with others like themselves.

(Morgan, O'Neill, and Harre 1979, 2), the name signs invented by NZ Deaf children for each other appear to be little affected by either adult or hearing (non-Deaf) influences. Similarly, the name signs that Deaf adults bestow on each other later in life are determined by Deaf social norms and visual language structures rather than those of the "outside" hearing society.

BACKGROUND

A brief sketch of the historical backdrop to NZSL is useful in understanding the social circumstances and linguistic resources from which name signs arise. NZSL was named as a language only in the mid-1980s, although it has been evolving toward its present form since approximately 1880, when the first school for the deaf was opened in Christchurch. NZSL was previously referred to by Deaf people simply as "sign" or "deaf sign" and was not generally viewed as a language per se, prior to research on its structure by Collins-Ahlgren (1989). Negative perceptions of Deaf people's signing were fuelled by the fact that signing was officially banned in the education of deaf children by educational policies enforced from 1880 until 1978. The first scientifically researched *Dictionary of New Zealand Sign Language,* published in 1997 (Kennedy et al.), signals a recent increase in public and academic awareness of Deaf people as a minority language community in New Zealand.

Belonging to the family of British and Australian sign languages (McKee and Kennedy 2000), NZSL is a young language that flourished underground in deaf educational settings (particularly residential) from 1880 onward and also in the adult Deaf community that grew from school networks. It is presumed that in the 1800s a small number of Deaf children with Deaf parents who signed a variety of British Sign Language (BSL), along with Deaf children who had been partly schooled in Britain or Australia using BSL and occasional Deaf adults employed as domestic help at the deaf schools acted as agents of language transmission in the early creolization of NZSL among school children. Because the vast majority of Deaf children enter school without exposure to sign language and generally cannot access adult language models within the school, NZSL is at least in part re-created by each successive generation of children.

Deaf children rapidly acquire schoolyard NZSL from slightly older peers, add to the lexicon and possibly grammar through group invention and usage, and eventually come into contact with mature NZSL signers in the Deaf community as late teenagers or young adults. This pattern has repeated itself for about a century, with the notable exception of Deaf children born to Deaf parents (estimated at around 8 percent in New Zealand), who acquire NZSL natively if their parents sign. This small group of children plays a vital role in the transmission and standardization of NZSL. However, the creation of name signs by Deaf children in New Zealand is an example of spontaneous and systematic language invention arising with limited exposure to conventional models of a signed language.

The majority of Deaf adults in New Zealand who have grown up Deaf and been in contact with other Deaf people during their school years informally acquire and continue to use NZSL as their primary language of communication in the Deaf community. In contrast to middle-aged and younger signers, the older generation of Deaf people prefer to vocalize while signing (although not in standard English) and regard this spoken (voiced and speechread) element of signed communication as very important. NZSL, in whatever form, represents a vital means of social, emotional, practical, and intellectual survival—in other words, a full-fledged language that enables cultural existence. Outside their own language community, Deaf people negotiate communication using combinations of speech, speechreading, gesture, mime, writing, forms of contact signing with those who know some signs, and guesswork.[3]

For Deaf people, having a name sign signals membership in a community that uses NZSL because a name sign is first acquired at the point of contact with, and acceptance by, other signers. Anthropologists and social psychologists have described the cultural and social significance associated with names and naming practices in a range of cultures and social subgroups (cf. Levy-Bruhl 1926; Morgan, O'Neill, and Harre 1979). Given that naming systems are recognized as a subsystem of a language and culture, the existence of a name sign tradition among NZ Deaf people provides evidence that they constitute a subculture that is distinct in many important aspects from the surrounding hearing-speaking society.

---

3. *Contact signing* refers to the type of signed interlanguage that arises between Deaf and hearing (or nonfluent signer) interlocutors. It is often characterized by English word order, increased mouthing of English words, more fingerspelling, and a reduction of sign language grammatical structures. See Lucas and Valli (1992) for a discussion of contact language in relation to Deaf communities.

NAME SIGN SYSTEMS IN OTHER
SIGN LANGUAGE COMMUNITIES

Varying name sign systems have been described in Deaf populations elsewhere, including the United States (Meadow 1977; Supalla 1990, 1992; Mindess 1990), France (Mottez 1985), Sweden (Hedberg 1991), Desrosiers and Dubuisson (1992), Thailand (Nonaka 1997), China (Yau and He 1987), Argentina (Massone and Johnson 1991), and England (Sutton-Spence and Woll 1999). As an example, Deaf Americans have a tradition of two distinct types of name signs: *arbitrary* and *descriptive.* Arbitrary name signs consist of one or more fingerspelled initials of a person's first and sometimes last name, combined with one of a conventional set of movements and locations on the upper body or face. For example, the American Sign Language (ASL) letter *P* may be tapped on the right side of the chin as a possible name sign for "Patrick," or a letter *B* shaken slightly side to side in neutral space could be a name sign for "Betty." Such name signs are called arbitrary because they have no intrinsic meaning connected to the person's identity other than the initial; they simply conform to linguistic conventions about the structure of a name sign.

In contrast, descriptive name signs derive from a physical or behavioral characteristic of a person (such as "curly hair" or "talkative"). In ASL, arbitrary name signs are more numerous than, and generally preferred to, descriptive name signs among the adult Deaf community (Supalla 1990; Mindess 1990). Supalla's (1992) *Book of Name Signs* (a naming guide for parents of Deaf children) advocates arbitrary name signs as the more orthodox system, based on the fact that Deaf parents in the United States traditionally give their Deaf children arbitrary name signs and eschew descriptive ones.

This cultural value differs from the conventions for name signs in Deaf communities such as New Zealand, Australia, England, China, and Thailand, for example, where descriptive name signs are the norm. However, in Australia,[4] France (Mottez 1985), England (Sutton-Spence and Woll 1999), and the United States (Meadow 1977), a different kind of arbitrary system was used in certain deaf schools up until the mid-1900s, in which pupils used and retained their locker numbers as name signs; this system

4. Personal communication with Robert Adam and Adam Schembri, Renwick College, Sydney, and Anne Bremner and Melissa Anderson, Barton Tafe, Melbourne, 1998.

appears to have disappeared with current generations. Anecdotal evidence is that the bearers of locker numbers may have preferred these seemingly impersonal name signs over the alternative of possibly unflattering descriptive name signs.

Supalla (1992) suggests that the arbitrary naming system based on fingerspelled initials probably stems from language planning decisions made by the founding educators of the deaf in the early nineteenth century, one of whom was Laurent Clerc, a Deaf Frenchman. In that period in France, signs incorporating the initial fingerspelled letter of a corresponding spoken word became popular in deaf education, and it is surmised that this influence transferred to the first U.S. school for the deaf, where the teachers probably encouraged the use of initialized name signs among the pupils. This apparently took hold as a tradition in the Deaf community in the United States, with arbitrary name signs becoming a highly conventionalized subsystem of ASL (Supalla 1992, 31–33).

By contrast, the language planning that took place in NZ deaf education proscribed the use of sign language and fingerspelling in classrooms from 1880 until 1978, instead using speech and speechreading exclusively. Although NZ sign language nevertheless flourished on the playgrounds and in the dorms (Collins-Ahlgren 1989), deaf school children were not exposed to a formal fingerspelling system for representing written letters on the hands until after the introduction of Australasian Signed English in 1979.[5]

The oralist tradition was widespread in deaf schools in Western Europe, Asia, and Great Britain's colonies from the late 1800s to the present and has undoubtedly influenced the form of name signs in many places. For example, in Thailand (Nonaka 1997) and China (Yau and He 1987), there is evidence that most name signs are descriptive of appearance, with minimal reference to spoken or spelled names.

Why Do Name Signs Arise?

Name signs develop as alternatives to spoken names (given and family) most obviously because Deaf people perceive and communicate in a vi-

5. In the absence of a formal fingerspelling code, it was (and still is) common among older Deaf people in New Zealand to supplement lip patterns with "air writing," which means tracing letters in the air with the index finger, as if writing on a window. This was used as a means of making words — usually proper nouns — more easily visible than they would be through speechreading alone.

sual rather than an aural modality. People and their identities are experienced and coded visually, thus creating a linguistic need for a signed naming system. The giving, use, and knowledge of name signs also plays an important role in the social cohesion of a group. A Deaf community is no exception to the condition that:

> Any verbal interaction within a group can only be meaningful when explicitly or implicitly, common terms of references are established; otherwise group relations break down. A group can exploit this phenomenon by establishing its own peculiar terms and labels. To function as part of this clique one has to break the "code" —comprehend and utilize the referents—often to acquire one oneself. (Morgan et al. 1979, 110)

Spoken names given by one's family are not especially salient or accessible as identity labels in signed discourse. Spoken names and their social and linguistic significance are not easy for young Deaf children to learn by the usual informal means because they cannot hear their own or others' names called, hear names used in direct address, or overhear others' names used in conversation. Nor can Deaf children necessarily use spoken names easily because speech skills depend on hearing; thus Deaf children often have to be explicitly taught their own spoken/written names (cf. Rottenberg and Searfoss 1993) and the names of others around them.

For example, a Deaf informant recounted that as a child, she was visited at deaf school from time to time by an elderly couple, which she thought was very kind of them. Several years later, at the age of ten or eleven, she inquired about their identity and was surprised to learn that they were her grandparents. This information about personal identity had never been explicitly communicated to her. Another adult Deaf informant from a very large family reported that he does not know the full names of several of his older siblings, let alone cousins, nieces, and nephews. Our observation is that it is not uncommon for some Deaf people in New Zealand to know regular associates in the Deaf community by their name sign or initials only. This is not surprising because a large proportion of name signs in NZSL bear no relationship to the person's legal name, although others are derived either directly or indirectly from the spoken name.

METHODOLOGY

Descriptions of name sign systems in other countries and our own experience of living in the contrasting sign language communities of the United States and New Zealand made us aware that name signs in New Zealand are both similar to and different from those found overseas. The distinctions in form were made abundantly clear to us personally as we moved between the two countries and were promptly renamed "appropriately," according to the conventions of each language community. Our research questions in this study were the following:

1. What linguistic forms and derivations do name signs have in NZSL?
2. How are name signs distributed across these types? What is the dominant or most preferred type?
3. Are there differences in the type of name signs associated with different age groups?
4. When and how are name signs typically acquired and changed?
5. How many name signs do Deaf individuals have?

We videotaped the self-reported name signs of 118 Deaf people from age two years (reported by Deaf parents for their young Deaf children) to approximately seventy years old, in three major regions of New Zealand. Most informants had more than one name sign, so in total we recorded 223 name signs, excluding some that were acquired outside New Zealand. Informants were asked to give their legal name, age, the schools they attended, all the name signs they had had during their life, the date each one was acquired, and the etymology of each name sign. Data were collected by a Deaf researcher who is an immigrant member of the NZ Deaf community. Data were solicited from a cross-section of the community in terms of age, gender, ethnicity, and school background (mainstream/deaf school).

From a preliminary analysis of the data, we made a typology of name signs (that was later expanded) that we used to record the various name signs of each informant. Successive name signs and their etymologies were noted in order to analyze patterns of change in name signs acquired at various junctures in people's lives.

Schooling was noted as an indicator of when informants were likely to have first encountered a Deaf social group and been exposed to signing. The generations of Deaf people over forty years old have been educated mainly in residential schools for the deaf, whereas younger generations are more likely to have experienced a deaf unit class or a fully mainstreamed situation for at least part of their schooling. Each of these settings creates different opportunities for access to sign language, a Deaf peer group, and the acquisition of name signs.

Our data collection approach differs from other studies of name signs in which random examples of name signs have been elicited from third parties. Because name signs are created and used by third parties rather than by the named people themselves, there are valid reasons for seeking name signs and etymologies from others. But because we were interested in linking name signs to personal data such as age, parentage (deaf or hearing), and patterns of acquisition of name signs, we chose to elicit personal profile data directly from informants. In this study we did not specifically elicit data on informants' feelings about their name signs, although frequently this information was volunteered, either explicitly or indirectly.

Our discussion of the data in this chapter, particularly about the usage conventions of name signs, is supplemented by our participant observation in the NZ Deaf community over ten years.

FORMATION OF NAME SIGNS IN NZSL

The formation of name signs highlights the linguistic resources and preferences of the community. The linguistic resources available to the NZ Deaf community for constructing name signs include a wide spectrum of possibilities because NZSL and its users exist in a contact situation with spoken English. Also, given the close historical relationship of NZSL to British and Australian sign languages, it could be expected that the name sign traditions in these language communities would also be quite similar, and this indeed was found to be true.[6] We identified the following potential elements for the construction of NZSL name signs: gesture and mimetic description, the existing lexicon of NZSL, the phonological and morphological building blocks of NZSL (particularly classifiers used for describing size, shape, and movement), spoken English in the form of lip patterns, written English incorporated into NZSL in the form of a

6. For a comparative discussion of name signs in NZSL and Auslan, see Mc-Kee, McKee, Adam, and Schembri (2000).

manual alphabet (two-handed fingerspelling or, more recently, the one-handed alphabet from American Sign Language), and also combinations of these elements.

Name signs in NZSL are not straightforward to describe and categorize, as the NZSL community exhibits a range of ways of creating name signs drawing on these possible resources. Because deaf education in NZ has been dominated by a major emphasis on the teaching of speech articulation and speechreading, the incorporation (or mutation) of information on the lips has carried over into the formation of many name signs. However, the acceptability of signing has increased significantly since the 1980s, and the NZSL community is now experiencing a period of lexical growth and borrowing from American, Australian, and British Sign Languages, which could be expected to affect trends in the formation of name signs.

Types of Name Signs

Our data reveal seven distinct types of name signs in NZSL. Although name signs are the primary means of personal reference in NZSL, they do nevertheless exist in addition to, and often in relation to, a previously given birth name. Bearing this in mind, a typology of nicknames used by Morgan et al. (1979) can be applied to grouping name signs into *internally motivated* types (which are based on the form of the person's spoken name) and *externally motivated* types (based on characteristics of the people themselves or cultural associations). Appendix A shows examples of both types of name signs.

The majority of name signs in this study were externally motivated, being derived from a physical or behavioral description of the bearer. But we also found several interesting ways in which spoken language names interact with signing to produce internally motivated name sign forms. Table 1 shows the types and distribution of name signs in our sample.

Externally Motivated Name Signs

These name signs are unrelated to the form of a person's spoken name, deriving instead from physical or other personal qualities.

TABLE 1. *Types and Distribution of Name Signs in NZSL*

Categories of Name Signs	Types of Name Signs	Distribution of Name Signs ($N = 223$)
Externally-motivated name signs	Descriptive	108 (48%) Appearance 77 Behavior 31
Internally-motivated name signs	Initials (using finger-spelling)	37 (16.5%) 2-handed NZSL: 26 1-handed ASL: 11 (including descriptive signs with ASL initialized handshape)
	English-based (including semantic translation and phonetic analogue)	12 (5%)
	CHILD + lip pattern	10 (4.5%)
Mixed derivation name signs	Generic: name sign generalized from other person(s) of same given name	12 (5%)
	Compound: two-sign sequence. (Most compounds contain one descriptive sign)	32 (14%)
	Other (uncertain origin)	12 (5%)

DESCRIPTIVE NAME SIGNS

These are based on a physical characteristic or behavior of the person. Most name signs in this category (71 percent) describe appearance, including facial features, hair, distinguishing body features, body size, and occasionally national origin. The person's spoken name, or an approximation of it (which might emphasize the visible phonemes), is usually articulated silently on the lips with the descriptive sign. Most often, the lip pattern includes the first and last name articulated quickly with no pause in between, as if the names were one word, although in some contexts only the first name will be mouthed.

Examples of descriptive name signs glossed in English are: POINTY-NOSE, POP-EYES, LONG-NECK, POT-BELLY, SCAR-ON-UPPER-LIP, GLASSES, SIDE-BURNS, MOLE-ON-FACE, CURLY-HAIR, CHOPPED-FINGER, BALD, PLAITS, FRECKLES, EYE-LASHES, TATTOO-ON-NECK, DUTCH, and CHINESE. A smaller proportion (29 percent) of descriptive name signs refers to a characteristic mannerism or trait, for example: FLICK-HAIR-OVER-EARS, RUB-EYEBROW, RUNNER, PUSH-UP-GLASSES-ON-NOSE, JOKER, SERIOUS, FORGETFUL, and RUDE.

Description of physical appearance or behavior is perhaps the most universal means by which people identify each other in the absence of labels for known names or relationships. This would describe the situation of Deaf school children, who not only experience each other visually but who also may not yet have developed a common language, either spoken or signed. This may be a factor in the common tendency of Deaf children to name each other descriptively because descriptive gestures are logically the most easily accessible visual language resource. However, the nicknames of non-Deaf children in many cultures also show a relatively high degree of reference to physical appearance and other personal qualities, indicating that these are quite important in the perceptions and social hierarchy of children in general, regardless of language form (cf. Morgan et al. 1979).

Occasionally, descriptive name signs refer to a particular incident from which a person's behavior or utterance is captured. For example, one informant's name sign derives from a gesture of straightening his hair. This originated from a windy boat trip in which he was supervising a group of young Deaf students who noticed he was having trouble keeping his flyaway fringe in place and mischievously created a new name sign that mimicked his gesture. Descriptive name signs such as this one usually undergo phonological change by a reduction in movement and/or a slight shift in location of the original sign, as the original productive morpheme (i.e., a sign or gesture) becomes frozen into a name sign. This phonological change was apparent in our data by the contrast between the way that informants demonstrated their name signs and the way in which they described the actual signs or circumstances from which it was derived.

In a Chinese school for Deaf children, Yau and He (1987) observed that lengthy descriptive sequences that were initially devised by new children to refer to each other were quickly reduced to two-gesture forms and that older Deaf children adapted all name signs to a standard format consisting of: FACE (meaning appearance) + descriptive gesture + a gender-appropriate pronoun equivalent to "younger sister" or "younger brother." In our data, no name signs contained sequences of more than two gestures, and all purely descriptive name signs consisted of a single sign. It would be necessary to observe the name signs used by young Deaf children to determine whether any of the adult forms were reduced from longer descriptive sequences, but none of our informants mentioned this in their own explanations.

Internally Motivated Name Signs

In English, internally generated nicknames play on the proper name through processes such as alliteration, rhyming, contractions, or verbal analogue (Morgan et al. 1979, 136). In NZSL, internally motivated name signs are based on a feature of the spoken name, such as the initials, a semantic translation, or word play on speechreading.

INITIALS

Some name signs consist of the fingerspelled initials of the person's legal name. Initials are signed using either the two-handed NZ manual alphabet or in a few cases the one-handed ASL alphabet. The spoken name is articulated silently on the lips while the initials are signed. NZ fingerspelling is used twice as frequently as ASL fingerspelling in name signs. In a few cases, an ASL one-handed fingerspelling handshape is combined with an NZSL descriptive morpheme to form a descriptive name sign: for example, the ASL handshape A (for Andrea) made with a movement back across the head to depict a streak of white hair, or the handshape K (for Kellye) made with the movement and location of the sign VOMIT in reference to a drinking incident. In this manner, signers have grafted ASL phonology onto NZSL morphology to generate a new kind of name sign form.

Although borrowing from ASL into NZSL appears to be on the increase, the one-handed ASL alphabet still has foreign-language status in relation to NZSL.[7] It is interesting that although the one-handed ASL alphabet is not used in NZSL discourse, it does appear in young people's

7. Lexical borrowing from ASL is evidenced in some of the entries in the 1997 *Dictionary of NZSL*, and we have personally observed it in the NZ Deaf community over a number of years. (It is apparent to the authors because we are both NZSL/ASL bilinguals.) Sources of ASL borrowing include a growing number of younger Deaf people who have been to the United States as exchange students in high school or at Gallaudet University and returned to New Zealand, become active participants in their local communities, and, through codeswitching in their own language use, have become inadvertent agents of language transmission. A rise in Deaf New Zealanders' contact with the international Deaf scene through sports events and conferences over the last decade has also increased exposure to

name signs. Our observation in the community is that the incorporation of ASL fingerspelling into name signs is currently popular in the teenage and early twenties age group, who (perhaps like hearing young people) enjoy the novelty value and in-group marking achieved by borrowing words and expressions from elsewhere—especially American media.

SEMANTIC TRANSLATION

Some name signs translate a meaning extrapolated from a spoken language name or part of a name, for example, BROWN from the surname Brown, ANGEL from Angela, FISHING from Fishlock, BELL from Campbell, BAT from Batten, PAT-HEAD from Patty, ANT + ON from Anton, and even the elaboration NORTH + SOUTH from Southern. Semantic translations occur more often in relation to surnames than first names, probably because surnames are more likely to have obvious semantic content.

PHONETIC ANALOGUE

Phonetic analogue is the term we use to describe name signs that are sign transliterations of a speechreading "rhyme" that looks similar to the given name pronounced on the lips. For example, the sign RABBIT is a name sign for Robert, BATTERY for Patrick, BORING for Maureen, WATER for Walters, BRA or BARBER for Barbara, SNOT for Scott, TAIL for McPhail, and PANTS for Pat. This group of name signs provides an interesting example of the interplay between speech and sign in NZSL. In fact, this is not unique to name signs; NSZL has some other signs in the standard lexicon that apparently derive from a lip pattern or spelling look-alike (for example, the sign ONION is also used for UNION).

This play on speechreading is possibly one of the outcomes of Deaf people using NZSL in school and home environments in which oral communication is valued and where codeswitching is considered a linguistic norm even in Deaf-to-Deaf communication. In our sample, it appears that all the name signs in this category were devised by children, although many were retained into adulthood. These name signs form a visual parallel to the unorthodox nicknames created by hearing children as they verbally play with names, routinely mutating names into related forms through rhyme and other processes.

ASL (which tends to predominate as a second language in international Deaf events).

CHILD + LIP PATTERN

One unusual form of name sign that exists in the NZSL community is a generic combination of the sign denoting CHILD, performed simultaneously with a silent lip pattern specifying the person's proper name. The lip patterns demonstrated in these name signs were articulated very rapidly (to match the length of time it takes to articulate the single movement sign), with exaggerated features, and in a manner that was clearly specific to its use in a name sign. In other words, the lip patterns appear to have undergone reduction or phonological change, like the signs in descriptive name signs, to increase their efficiency as a frozen referent.

This generic kind of name specifier was reported mainly by informants over the age of about forty and was used at deaf schools in their childhood. It is not coincidental that oralism prevailed in the educational era when this pattern developed and thus the use of silent lip patterns for coding useful spoken information, combined with one general sign, was clearly a viable adaptation or compromise between speech and sign, given the linguistic resources available.[8] Australian Deaf informants report that the same system existed among Deaf children in Australia in the same era. Some middle-aged informants who reported previously having this name sign at school recounted it with some amusement and wonderment, in retrospect, that it really worked to distinguish one person from another. Apparently it did because it was widely used for some time, but by today's NZSL norms this form of name sign is considered somewhat unsophisticated, particularly now that the manual elements of sign language are more openly valued than in the past.

Mixed Derivation Name Signs

Two groups of name signs in the data could not be categorized by a single type of derivation. These included *compound name signs,* which are formed by two signs, and *generic name signs,* which take various

---

8. This phenomenon is not unique to name signs in NZSL. There is a small class of "old" signs (as they are now referred to by Deaf people) that functioned as "indicators" and were specified by information on the lips, including a generic sign for all place names, all colors, and all ranks of people of high status (boss, prime minister, chief, etc.). Many other polysemous signs in modern NZSL are also specified by lip patterns.

forms but compose a set because they are generalized from one person to another.

COMPOUND NAME SIGNS

Compound name signs formed a relatively large category. They consist of two signs in a fixed sequence, sometimes corresponding to first and last names. The first and second signs in compounds are normally of contrasting types or derivations. For example:

PAUL (generic) + WATER (phonetic analogue of Walters)
PAUL (generic) + "pot-belly" (descriptive)
S (first name initial) + SPEED (sign describing a fast runner)
M (first name initial) + KING (translation of surname).

Of 32 compound name signs, the first sign in 29 of these was more arbitrary (such as an initial or generic name sign), with the second element specifying personal information either through physical description or semantic derivation from the spoken surname. For example, one Paul has a name sign consisting of a generic sign for PAUL (depicting a dimple, but exact origin unknown), followed by a personally descriptive sign for "pot-belly." The "pot-belly" sign distinguishes him from several other Pauls who share the generic PAUL name sign. He reported that the second part of the name sign was added as an adult, to differentiate him when another Paul came into the community. Similarly, a Noeline who inherited her name sign from a previous pupil at school with the same name was always referred to with the addition of a sign translating her last name (until she acquired a different name sign later in her life).

However, it is not always the case that people with generic name signs have a second sign added; this seems to happen mainly when a distinction becomes socially necessary through proximity or when both people participate in the same immediate social network. This practice is similar to the origin of some English surnames, which derived from the addition of descriptive information such as White-Head or Son-of-John, as the need arose to distinguish between two people of the same name in a village (Bryson 1990, 195).

GENERIC NAME SIGNS

Generic name signs originate as a name sign for one Deaf person (usually descriptive) and are later generalized to other Deaf persons with the same spoken first name. For example, in our data we had generically name-signed Johns, Andrews, Tonys, Pauls (with different southern and northern versions), Roberts, Peters, Maureens, and Susans. In our data, generic name signs were more common for males than females. Some of these generalized name signs can be traced directly to one namesake, usually of an age group or locale different from the informant's. For example, Susan had a descriptive childhood name sign consisting of two simultaneous gestures of thumb sucking and eyebrow rubbing, which was later simplified by dropping the thumb-sucking gesture. As an adult, she acquired an entirely different name sign but not before a younger Susan in another town inherited the modified eyebrow rub as her permanent name sign, which in her case was not descriptive, but arbitrary.

This kind of name sign generalizing is akin to being named after someone but in this case is based purely on the coincidental overlap of a spoken name rather than on any particular relationship or shared characteristic of the individuals concerned. The specific descriptive (or other) etymologies of the most widely used generic name signs (such as PAUL or JOHN) have been lost, so they now have merely a conventional association with the name. These name signs form a parallel to what Morgan et al. (1979) classified as *traditional nicknames* associated with British surnames, such as "Dusty" for Miller and "Nobby" for Clark, which are assigned purely on the coincidence of name rather than on personalized or transparent meaning. Once they have been "borrowed," generic name signs are thereafter assigned on the basis of a signed to spoken name association within the community.

The existence of generic name signs in NZSL dispels the idea that name signs are unique to, or descriptive of, each person's particular identity. Interestingly though, at least one informant was unaware that his name sign was generic even though there were several other individuals with the same name sign in his community. A generic NZSL name sign for people named Robert is the sign RABBIT—a phonetic analogue based on the similarity of "rabbit" and "Robert" on the lips. But this particular Robert suggested that he had probably behaved like a little rabbit as a child at school and thus acquired the name sign. Although the name sign is a common generic one and fairly obviously related to the form of the word *Robert*, he tried to devise a descriptive explanation for it based on his cultural assumption that name signs are both descriptive and unique.

The generalizing of name signs can be seen as an efficiency in the system, where the need for constant invention is reduced by the availability of some fixed translations into NZSL for certain given names. It seems that the efficiency of generalizing name signs would be offset by the increased ambiguity created when referring to different people sharing the same name sign. But this is often solved by the addition of a second element to the name sign to form a compound that differentiates these individuals. Shared name signs may serve to preserve historical links, at least in naming traditions, among different generations and social groups in the wider Deaf community.

"Other" name signs are those for which neither we nor the informant could determine a clear derivation. Some of these probably had undesirable descriptive origins that have been disguised as the form of the sign has altered over time through a slight change of location, movement, or handshape of the sign.

USE OF NAME SIGNS IN NZSL DISCOURSE

Name signs in NZSL are used only to refer to others in the third person, rather than as a form of address. This convention appears to be common to signed languages even in countries where polite address in the surrounding hearing culture emphasizes the use of proper names (e.g., the United States) or kinship terms (e.g., Japan; cf. Peng 1974). Because strategies for getting attention in NZSL discourse are visual and not aural, signers do not use names in direct address to call someone's attention, initiate a turn, or index intimacy, politeness, or anger, as might be done in English. Instead of using a name, an interlocutor's attention is attracted by visual or tactile means such as a small tap on the shoulder or waving slightly in peripheral vision. Once eye contact is established, it is considered redundant and indeed unusual to use a name in direct address. An exception to this is that several informants reported that their childhood name sign was originally used in a teasing, name-calling way, just as hearing children use nicknames to taunt or challenge each other. However, many such name signs persist long beyond the name-calling situation, lose their original pragmatic force, and continue to be used only for normal third-person reference.

Name signs in NZSL are used for third-person reference in both informal and formal discourse (such as awards ceremonies, speeches, and meetings) in the Deaf community and also situations in which shared context is minimal (such as job interviews, meetings, or courtrooms) and at which an interpreter is present. Naturally this can present some challenges for the sign language interpreter who needs to know, or be able to elicit, the spoken language name for the referent, or else must resort to vague pronouns in order to make sense in English.

People who are mentioned regularly by Deaf people, regardless of whether they are Deaf, are likely to be referred to by name signs, with or without their awareness. For example, Deaf people typically refer to their former school teachers (none of whom were Deaf) by a name sign — often unflattering, as might be expected given the context. Public figures such as politicians and sports people are also referred to by name signs; for example, a former prime minister of New Zealand, Robert Muldoon, has a descriptive name sign depicting an unusual facial feature, while another former prime minister, Jenny Shipley, has the name sign J + SHIP because her surname has obvious potential for translation.

Sign language interpreters are another category of non-Deaf people who are usually assigned name signs, which are regarded by interpreters as an essential social asset. In the case of hearing people in general, having a name sign does not necessarily signify participation in or acceptance by the signing community but indicates at least being known to a group of Deaf people. By contrast, most hearing children of Deaf couples in our observation do not seem to have name signs unless they later take up some socially significant role in relation to the Deaf community, at which point they acquire one. This may be because their parents do not see their children's primary social identity in relation to the Deaf community because they know they will participate in the hearing social world. But perhaps more important, the hearing children do not enter a Deaf peer group, which in the NZ context would be the natural source of a name sign. Of course, exceptions to this generalization exist.

The use of name signs reveals something about norms for how to talk about others and how to present oneself to others. For example, in Deaf-to-Deaf introductions in NZSL, name signs are routinely proffered either by the introducer or the person being introduced, usually with the spoken name articulated simultaneously on the lips. Occasionally the spoken name will also be fingerspelled, especially by younger signers. The origin of a name sign is typically explained in the course of an introduction as part of an exchange of personal information. Most Deaf informants can explain the etymology of a large proportion of name signs of people known to them in the community, indicating that a name sign and its origin is a salient piece of information in identifying and knowing other people. Perhaps the information contained in a name sign also serves as a mnemonic aid for placing names and faces. Deaf people we have asked about this say it is easier to recall people and their names if they have been introduced with a name sign, as opposed to remembering names that are finger-spelled, written, or spoken.

Our observation is that introduction protocol in NZSL differs from that in the Deaf community in the United States, where a name sign is not typically given in an introduction unless asked for; instead, the person's legal name is likely to be fingerspelled in full. This is undoubtedly related to the fact that fingerspelling is used more extensively and apparently val-ued more positively in ASL than in NZSL. Also, because the majority of name signs in ASL do not have a descriptive origin, a discussion of the et-ymology is less relevant.

ACQUISITION OF NAME SIGNS

At the beginning of a fresh epoch in his life, at his initiation, for in-stance, an individual receives a new name, and it is the same when he is admitted to a secret society. A name is never a matter of indifference; it implies a whole series of relationships between the man who bears it and the source from which it derives. (Levy-Bruhl 1926, 51)

Although referring to so-called primitives in a past anthropological era, this observation has some resonance with the acquisition of name signs. The giving of a first name sign usually coincides with a Deaf person's en-try into either the child or adult society of other Deaf people, and new name signs often mark junctures in life such as moving to a new school or adult community, moving into a new social group, or undergoing a change in physical appearance.

The Deaf world of sign language is not, of course, a secret society in Levy-Bruhl's sense, but the use of name signs and sign language are indeed of a "secret" nature insofar as they were not a recognized activity of the institutions (schools) in which they flourished and existed as part of an underground, alternative culture.[9] Name signs are a matter of personal in-terest and cultural significance in the NZ Deaf community precisely be-cause they signify how Deaf people are connected to and perceived by

9. This situation is different for the current generation of children, now that NZSL has been recognized and used as a language of instruction in an increasing number of congregated deaf education settings since approximately 1993.

each other, which is usually considered a more relevant identity factor than family origin, in the context of Deaf culture.

The language and subculture of Deaf people are unusual in that they are transmitted mainly across a generation of peers, rather than between generations, because most Deaf children have non-Deaf parents (about 92 percent). This intragenerational construction of a linguistic community is illustrated by the fact that name signs are the invention of each generation of Deaf people, custom-made for each individual. Name signs are not typically bestowed by parents or extended family but almost invariably by the same age or slightly older peers, often in a school setting with other Deaf children. For the small percentage of Deaf children born to Deaf parents in New Zealand (approximately 8 percent), there is some variation in whether they acquire name signs within or outside the family.

Acquiring a name sign first occurs when a Deaf person comes into regular contact with other Deaf people and NZSL. For most informants, this was soon after entering a school for the deaf or a deaf class, at whatever age this occurred (between four and sixteen years). For boarders at deaf schools, name signs were generated through close knowledge of each other in dorms and classrooms and on playgrounds. For day pupils, name signs were given by others in the context of playground relationships. For the younger generation of informants who have been schooled mainly in mainstream settings (the predominant pattern since the 1970s), their first name sign was acquired when, as young adults, they found a Deaf peer group, perhaps in a transition year with a Deaf high-school class, or when they joined the adult Deaf community through a Deaf club or sports group.

CHANGE OF NAME SIGN

Most Deaf individuals have more than one name sign during their life. Normally only one or two of the name signs are current at any time, although some people are referred to variously by different groups of people. Table 2 shows the number of name signs our informants reported having during their life to date.

This table shows that 69 percent of a cross-section of Deaf people in New Zealand have had two or three name signs. It is unusual to have more than three, while almost a quarter have had only one. Informants in this study were of various ages, so the younger ones probably still have

TABLE 2. *Frequency of Multiple Name Signs*

Number of Name Signs	Percentage of Informants
One	22%
Two	39%
Three	30%
Four	7%
Five or more	2%

additional name signs in store. But all except one of the informants under twenty already had two name signs at the time of reporting (in all except one case, the first one was a fingerspelled initial), with the second name sign generally being given around eleven to fifteen years of age. Changes in name signs around this stage may coincide with the emerging adolescent interest in sorting out new norms for social acceptability and establishing personal identity (cf. Turner and Helms 1979).

Although it is normal for individuals to have more than one, name signs are clearly more enduring than the usual nicknames and epithets of childhood, when compared to nicknames studied in hearing boarding school settings, in which each boy averaged between four to seven nicknames in one school year (Morgan et al. 1979, 94).

Changes of name sign may occur as individuals and their peers mature and are perhaps prompted by new perceptions of personality traits: the appearance of physical characteristics, such as changes in body size and shape at puberty, or unusual body mutations such as the loss of a limb or digit (one informant has a name sign meaning "chop-finger," given after a finger was lost in a childhood mishap with an axe), teeth (one informant's descriptive name sign dates from an accident resulting in missing front teeth, which have long since been disguised by a dental plate), acquisition of facial tattoos, or baldness. But descriptively derived name signs do not automatically change with a change in physical appearance. Many name signs based on a hairstyle, appearance, or habit are retained long after the physical evidence has disappeared or become nonnotable.

Changes of name sign may arise when a Deaf person moves to a different community or takes on a new role in relation to a group of signers (such as a job in a Deaf school as a teacher or residential social worker or as a teacher of sign language classes in a hearing community). Sometimes a period of intensive social contact in a situation that results in some shared personal history (such as a holiday, sports team, or class) may motivate a new name sign. In such situations, it is common to be "tagged" by a new social group with a new name sign that encodes shared meaning. In this sense, name signs are like nicknames that develop in closed social groups and mark in-group, out-group, and a range of other social statuses and relationships (cf. Morgan et al. 1979).

However, unlike most nicknames, name signs remain the primary identity symbol for Deaf people throughout life because participation in the "closed" social system of the sign language community is likely to continue and to remain of primary significance in Deaf people's identity. This is more parallel to village society in Arabia, where nicknames are almost universally given, originating in descriptive (often impolite) appellations of childhood and remaining in continual use within the village for life. In this society, seemingly pejorative nicknames are accepted as a cultural norm, with the names losing much of their offensive power and connotation through constant use (Morgan et al. 1979, 124). This also seems to be true of the name sign system in the NZ Deaf community.

WHO CAN CHANGE NAME SIGNS?

According to our informants, changes of name sign in NZSL are nearly always initiated by others and accepted (or borne) by the recipient. It is difficult for the bearer of an unwanted name sign to do anything about it once the name sign becomes established in the community. The general expectation for naming new (and previously unnamed) arrivals in the Deaf community is that the individual will be observed through an initial period of acquaintance until a name sign is spontaneously ascribed by someone and settled on by the group.[10] Informants reported being given name signs by people older than themselves (e.g., older children at school, older adults in the community, Deaf parents or siblings), people of the same age (classmates or friends), and sometimes by people younger than

10. This study did not examine the question of specifically who gives name signs to whom. Morgan et al. (1979) observed that in the world of children, at least, the roles of leader and name-giver are often synonymous. Supalla (1990) noted that in the Deaf community in the United States, the giving of name signs is most often done by the Deaf children of Deaf parents, who naturally tend to have more linguistic power (and associated status) because of their native language command of ASL and its cultural traditions.

themselves (e.g., younger people at a Deaf club or by students to a Deaf teacher). In other words, our data did not suggest a clear hierarchy of who is qualified to give name signs to whom, with the exception that established members of the group invariably name the newcomers, usually by informal consensus.

Among adults at least, our observation is that the creation of name signs is generally approached with reasonably good humor (on the part of givers) and resignation (on the part of recipients), even when an apparently unflattering name sign is bestowed, because within the context of NZ Deaf culture, this does not necessarily imply social stigma or disrespect. However, a handful of informants in our data did report successfully shedding a name sign that they considered offensive (e.g., SLANT-EYE for a person of Chinese origin) or unattractive (for example, one person had been called BUCK-TEETH, which had been generalized from one Deaf person with buck teeth to our informant, who happened to have the same given name as the original BUCK-TEETH). Naturally enough, he actively rejected this label because his own teeth were quite straight. In the Chinese case, the person happened to move to another city for a period of time and, on her return, used the opportunity to introduce a new name sign that had been bestowed by the Deaf community elsewhere, which was seen as an acceptable change by the original community. In the case of BUCK-TEETH, the individual encouraged others to use his initials instead of the offending sign until a new name sign based on his own characteristics spontaneously arose. Self-initiated changes were occasionally achieved by individuals who let it be known that they were unhappy with a name sign and encouraged cooperative friends to invent and spread a replacement name sign.

Not surprisingly, in a couple of cases in which informants reported to us that an offensive name sign had been replaced, we observed from our interactions in the community that the offending name sign is still in use but out of sight of its referent. Common sense says that in any social group, self- and others' representation of one's identity do not always match and do not necessarily change at the same rate; this can sometimes be seen in the disparity between the way Deaf individuals might introduce themselves and the way they might be introduced or referred to by someone else.[11]

11. As an illustration of this, after presenting a version of this paper at a Deaf Studies Research Symposium in Australia, during question time one well-known Deaf audience member mentioned that she does not have a name sign and does not want one (instead she said her name is fingerspelled). At the tea break after

An interesting contrast with American name sign preferences emerged from our investigation of changes in name signs. In ASL, adults are reported as more likely to have an arbitrary, initialized name sign than a descriptive one—descriptive name signs being more strongly associated with children (Mindess 1990; Supalla 1992). In the reverse direction from the American pattern, our study found that using fingerspelled initials (the least descriptive form of name sign) is regarded by NZ signers as a temporary and uninteresting measure, usually adopted only until a descriptive name sign evolves. Fingerspelled initials are typically described by the owner as "not really having a name sign," even when this is the usual way of referring to that person.

When we asked members of families with Deaf parents and children about name signs used within their family, many simply said "we don't have any." When the question was rephrased to "how do you talk about your child/brother/sister?" and so on, the most common response was the initial of the first name, until a descriptive name sign was given by Deaf people outside the family or by Deaf siblings (although a few parents had either initiated or adopted descriptive name signs for their children).

From such responses we conclude first that naming in the NZ Deaf community is perceived primarily as a descriptive process (even though in reality there is a wider range of acceptable types) and second that the peer group or the community are the expected source of "real" name signs, even where the parents are Deaf and have the linguistic and cultural knowledge to create a name sign. This may reflect the fact that for the vast majority of the Deaf community (except for those of Deaf parentage), one's identity as a Deaf person originates in the community rather than the family, and this cultural norm is so pervasive that it has influenced naming practices within Deaf families. Another possible interpretation is that Deaf parents choose not to bestow descriptive name signs because they do not like them, but this feeling was not clearly expressed by our informants. Further investigation of attitudes to different types of name signs and naming specifically in Deaf families may shed more light on cultural preferences about name signs.

---

the session, a couple of Deaf people hastened to tell us what her names signs are, according to community usage.

Kinship and naming systems in many languages often have alternative subsets of terms for people's identity, depending on contextual dimensions such as formality, intimacy, presence or absence of the named person, age relationships, humorous reference, or the current reference group for the relationship (cf. Gumperz and Hymes 1986, 253). Some Deaf informants reported being called by alternate name signs in different groups of people simultaneously, whereas others did not necessarily acknowledge that alternate name signs were used to refer to them. One informant commented that occasionally an individual may remain unaware of an alternate name sign that the community uses to refer to them behind their back and which usually makes fun of the person or their name in some way.

Multiple name signs can encode various perceptions of a person's identifying characteristics and may map their personal history of relationships to particular subgroups in the community. A clear example of this in our data was that informants with Deaf parents generally had one name sign used by parents and family and another (or others) used by friends. Some Deaf parents adopt the name sign given by peers, whereas others stay with the system originally used within the family (usually initials).

Some people with alternate name signs may have one maintained by school friends, while also being identified by a different name sign by a more recent set of friends. When a new name sign is bestowed within the same community, there is often a period during which the old and the new forms overlap in use, sometimes continuing indefinitely, although one usually becomes dominant through popular usage. Relocating in a new city and community sometimes results in a new name sign, so that a person may have a Christchurch name sign and an Auckland name sign in alternate use. In this vein, even Deaf sojourners on a working or study trip overseas may acquire a name sign from each set of Deaf companions that they form a significant connection with, even if it is temporary. Sometimes a traveling name sign may be carried back to the home community (if the bearer likes it and others accept it), whereas others are left behind.

Thus, the notion of a name sign as a representation of one's identity appears to be flexible rather than fixed in the NZ Deaf community, even though name signs are regarded as "core" names (as opposed to many spoken nicknames). The acceptability of alternate name signs highlights their symbolic function in representing valued social ties with other Deaf people, over and above their linguistic function of personal reference.

Our data revealed some differences between age groups in the distribution of their current name sign types (table 3). Although the numbers are too small to be statistically significant, the proportions in our data are shown as percentages for ease of comparison.

Descriptive name signs are the most common type across all age groups. The dimension on which name sign types differ most across the age groups is the extent and manner in which they incorporate aspects of the spoken/written name, through fingerspelling or lip patterns. The oldest cohort (51+ years) has a heavy concentration (50 percent) of name signs based on the spoken name, and the next age group down (41–50) has the next highest proportion of English-related name signs (26 percent). This is consistent with a higher degree of codeswitching of spoken English and signs in the discourse style of the older age groups in the NZSL community. The overlapping use of two languages is particularly marked in signers over about 55 years, and their name signs reflect this greater use of speech. It is interesting to note that the most "oral" of all the name sign forms (CHILD + lip pattern) is not found at all in signers under the age of 30 but accounts for almost a quarter (24 percent) of the name signs of the 51+ group.

On the other end of a spectrum in which fingerspelling can be seen as the "manual" alternative to the lips for coding spoken names, NZ fingerspelling is not found at all in the name signs of signers over 51. The overall use of fingerspelled initials in name signs is most prevalent in the

TABLE 3. *Current Name Sign Types by Age Group*

Name Sign Type	< 20 yrs (*n* = 12)	< 30 yrs (*n* = 28)	< 40 yrs (*n* = 33)	< 50 yrs (*n* = 25)	50+ yrs (*n* = 20)
Descriptive	67%	50%	51%	44%	50%
Compound	8%	18%	15%	12%	0
Initials N.Z.	17%	7%	9%	12%	0
Initials U.S.	8%	14%	0	0	12%
English-based (semantic translation and phonetic analogue)	0	0	6%	8%	14%
Generic	0	3%	0	4%	0
CHILD + lip pattern	0	0	9%	12%	24%
Other	0	7%	9%	8%	0

under-20 group and next most frequent in the 21–30 age group; again this corresponds with the introduction of fingerspelling into Deaf education (and thus the wider language community) from 1978.

The under-30 age group have also been exposed indirectly to ASL fingerspelling through the one-handed fingerspelling shapes incorporated into initialized Australasian Signed English vocabulary, which most have used in school.[12] The use of ASL fingerspelling is concentrated in the 20–30 year old group, although table 3 shows that two (12 percent) of the 51+ group have name signs using the ASL fingerspelled letters *V* and *L*. This seems to be an anomaly in light of the fact that this age group uses fingerspelling in their NZSL the least of all age groups and is generally least familiar with the ASL alphabet. However, the handshapes for *V* and *L* are among the most iconic of the ASL fingerspelled letters, which may account for their adoption into these name signs.

As well as simply reflecting the availability of fingerspelling as a recently adopted linguistic tool in NZSL, the high proportion of fingerspelled initials in the youngest group (25 percent) may also indicate that they have not yet acquired descriptive name signs and are likely to do so later. Six of the subjects in this age group are children of Deaf parents, and five of these acquired descriptive name signs after infancy, during which their parents simply used their first initial to refer to them. A progression from a more arbitrary to a more personalized descriptive name sign appears to be common in Deaf children of both Deaf and hearing parents. This contrasts with what has been reported in the Deaf community in the United States (e.g., Supalla 1992), as does the overall predominance of descriptive name signs. Notions about what constitutes suitable semantic content and linguistic structure for a mature name sign are clearly not universal across signing communities but are shaped instead by different sociolinguistic histories and circumstances.

Compound name signs occur most frequently in the 21–40 age group. It is possible that the one-sign-per-word mode of signed English that the younger generations (under 30 in particular) have experienced in the

12. For example, some signs in the Australasian signed English system are "initialized" by forming the sign with a letter handshape from the ASL alphabet, such as PARENTS, formed with a P handshape, or SEA, formed with an S handshape. These handshapes did not previously have morphological meaning in NZSL, and many did not naturally occur in the language prior to the introduction of signed English in 1978.

classroom may have influenced a word-for-word approach in forming name signs (i.e., two signs corresponding to the first name and last name). But because compound name signs first appear in the 41–51 age group, two-part name signs may instead have become favored as a supplement or alternative to the lip patterns used by older signers to disambiguate similar names or name signs.

Generic name signs account for a small proportion of name signs overall, appearing only in the 40–49 and 21–30 age groups in this sample. Apparently the practice of generalizing some name signs emerged during a particular era and has carried over to a lesser extent in giving generic name signs to some younger people. The 40–49 age group, in which generic name signs emerge, almost universally attended large residential schools for the Deaf, before Deaf classes and mainstreaming became more widespread in the 1970s. We speculate that within the large community of children living together in a Deaf school and a history of known "old pupils," the recycling of name signs was a possible and even efficient system, whereas those Deaf children socializing with a limited number of Deaf peers (in a deaf or mainstream class) would be less likely to reuse name signs and indeed would be less likely to encounter repetitions of the same given name within a small social group.

In general, the greater diversity of name sign forms found in the groups under the age of 51 reflects a wider range of lexical resources and linguistic structures becoming available to the Deaf community as NZSL has evolved naturally, been influenced by changes in Deaf education, and borrowed from other signed languages.

ARE THERE FAMILY NAME SIGNS IN NZSL?

In general, name signs in NZSL do not carry information about family relationships. Occasionally Deaf couples share part of their name signs and transform the married surname into the second element of a compound name sign (e.g., [husband's name sign] + BIRD and [wife's name sign] + BIRD). This is more the exception than the norm, as most spouses do not share a family name sign. Sometimes a Deaf person is referred to in relation to the better-known spouse or partner (e.g., [man's name sign] + WIFE, or [woman's name sign] + HUSBAND). This occurs usually during the period or in a social context in which the spouse is a relative new-comer (as happens in the hearing world as well, in the form of "so-and-so's husband"). This is usually a temporary identity until the spouse's own name sign becomes known or a new one is assigned. This manner of referring applies also to siblings or children of a Deaf person.

The Deaf children of Deaf parents that we have observed do not seem to share a specific element in their name signs, except that Deaf parents tend to give all their children the same basic type of name sign: either descriptive or fingerspelled initials. In the Deaf community, Deaf offspring of Deaf parents are frequently identified in relation to their parents, especially by the parents' peers, rather than by their own name sign, which is more likely to be used by the child's peers. For example, one of our adult informants who has Deaf parents and does have a name sign said his parents' friends often refer to him as: KNOW RICHARD JENNIFER SON, SECOND-ONE, DEAF, CHILD + lip pattern "Steven"—which is a rather elaborated way of identifying him but indexes all the important elements of his identity—who his Deaf parents are, that he is the second of their three sons, that he is Deaf, and his given name (mouthed).

Another informant with an older Deaf sister told us that she was known throughout his childhood at Deaf school (which his sister also attended) as CHILD + lip pattern "Ava, Paul," which translates as "Ava's younger-one, Paul." This second example was a short enough compound to become frozen into an actual name sign that was used continually by her peers, whereas the previous example functions as a more longhand way of contextualizing Steven's identity in relation to his parents and family.

In a similar way, a hearing person with three older Deaf siblings, who grew up among her Deaf siblings' friends in England, recounts having three different name signs used by her brother and two sisters' sets of friends respectively. The names were formed thus: [brother's name sign] + SISTER YOUNGER, [first sister's name sign] + SISTER YOUNGER, and [second sister's name sign] + SISTER YOUNGER, depending on who was talking about her and to whom (i.e., which sibling the participants knew best). Not until she had left England in her thirties and resettled in New Zealand was she was given her own descriptive name sign by the local Deaf community because she entered this group as an individual rather than in relation to known family members. She further reported that, at the age of 45, when revisiting her brother's and sister's Deaf clubs and friends, she was still introduced by the "little sister" name signs even though she let it be known that she now had a different name sign; apparently this was not seen as relevant in the original community. We loosely call these examples "relational name signs." Although they provide a functional name referent for the person, they also carry important social information about the person's kinship status and identity in the community because biological family relationships to other Deaf people are relatively rare and generally positively valued.

CONCLUSIONS

Linguistic Aspects of Name Signs in NZSL

Name signs in NZSL are formed according to seven types of structure or derivation that we have categorized as descriptive (of appearance or behavior), compound (two signs of different derivations), initials (fingerspelled), semantic translation (of a morpheme in a spoken name), phonetic analogue (translation of a speechreading "rhyme" with a name), generic (generalized from others of same name), and CHILD + lip pattern (general sign for child, with spoken name simultaneously formed on the lips).

Over half of all name signs in NZSL are descriptive in origin, including signs in compound name signs. If generic name signs, most of which originated as descriptive name signs, are added to the descriptive category, the proportion is even higher. Other types of name signs are derived in various ways from the linguistic form of the person's spoken name. This analysis of name signs into consistent types shows that although name signs in NZSL are first created by children largely in the absence of adult sign language models, they nevertheless reveal patterning in the selection and combination of available linguistic resources to create an effective system of personal reference. Evidence of a long-standing linguistic tradition in name signs is also found in the fact that the most common forms of name signs in NZSL mirror those described for BSL, which is the mother language of NZSL (cf. Sutton-Spence and Woll 1999, 235–36).

The high frequency of descriptive name signs reflects gestural and classifier-based sources of lexical creation in NZSL, whereas the range of other types derived from spoken names reflects a relatively high degree of contact and codemixing between spoken English and NZSL. Oral education methods have left clear traces in the structure of name signs in the form of lip pattern incorporation and the transliteration of English names. Fingerspelling has gradually been adopted by the NZSL community in the last twenty years to code words (usually nouns) from English into NZSL and even now is scarcely used by many older signers who prefer to mouth a word rather than fingerspell it. These linguistic factors mitigate against the development of a more arbitrary name sign system such as the ASL one, which relies on fingerspelling and the transmission of adult name sign conventions to younger generations through regular contact with Deaf adults.

The distribution of name sign types across age groups indicates that although the basic sources of name derivation may remain similar, the types of name signs favored in NZSL are moving away from oral-based and toward more manual-based forms. Generational differences in name sign types appear to be linked to more general changes in NZSL use over the last thirty years or so.

Sociocultural Aspects of Name Signs in NZSL

The naming system in NZSL is informative for cultural and social reasons because, like nicknames in other cultures, name signs encapsulate rites of entry to socialization in the signing community. They also contain information about the way a person is perceived by others and how they are related to others in the group through shared history. The use and choice of name signs in discourse may be influenced by contextual factors such as the audience (e.g., whether the named person is present) and the historical relationship between the speaker and the named person, as shown by the existence of alternate name signs.

Unlike nicknames, name signs have a primary linguistic function of enabling Deaf people to refer to others in NZSL. But in addition, the cultural significance of having a name sign is that it indexes membership in a signing Deaf community, as a Deaf person is christened with, and known by, a name sign only within a Deaf social context. Name signs are normally acquired from a peer group rather than from family, even, in many cases, when the parents are also Deaf and use NZSL. In some cases the type of name sign a person has may signal the generation they belong to and possibly the context in which the name sign was acquired. For example, the CHILD + lip pattern name sign is used by middle-aged and older generations who attended deaf schools, whereas name signs incorporating ASL fingerspelling are associated with the younger generation.

Descriptive name signs representing physical or other personal characteristics did not generally appear to be a cause for concern or comment among most informants in this study. NZSL users in general do not share hearing cultural taboos about making direct reference to a person's appearance because in sign language, detailed visual description is an essential way of identifying things and people in the environment.

Another important factor in the greater tolerance for frankly descriptive name signs must be simply that it is the norm in the Deaf community to be identified in this way, and thus the stigma is insignificant compared to the effect on a hearing person of being given an unflattering nickname that specifically marks them as different from others. Relatively speaking, it is not such a disadvantage to be known as POP-EYES, LONG-NECK, BUCK-TEETH, or MOLE when other acquaintances are known by names such as FAT-FACE, BALDY, or POINTY-NOSE. In fact, glossing these name signs into written English completely transforms their semantic impact from something quite mundane and acceptable in NZSL into words that are negatively loaded or downright offensive by English speakers' standards.

In working at the cross-cultural interface between Deaf and hearing people, sign language interpreters instinctively know never to literally translate name signs into spoken English as this would not render a culturally equivalent sense of the person's name. The Deaf person's legal (spoken) name (if known) would always be substituted. The cultural and linguistic difference in personal names becomes especially salient for interpreters in formal contexts (such as meetings or legal situations), where spoken/legal names must be ascertained because they are of pragmatic and factual importance, and alternative forms of names are not considered context appropriate.

Some informants reported that they did not appreciate descriptive name signs they had been given that were obviously pejorative, such as UGLY, BIG-BOOBS, CRAZY. The informants who had been given these name signs in school years had succeeded in changing their name sign later in life to something more neutral, such as fingerspelled initials or a milder descriptor. On the other hand, others in the Deaf community retain such name signs with apparent equanimity or at least forbearance. Although the acceptability of explicit reference to physical appearance is apparently greater in Deaf culture than in hearing Anglo culture in New Zealand, it would be interesting to further investigate perceptions of taboo or undesirable name signs in the Deaf community and any effects of having such a name sign.

Deaf communities and the way they interact can be described as high-context cultures, (Smith 1996), in which much shared knowledge about referents in discourse is assumed, due to a high degree of shared personal history and experience. In such a culture, it would seem logical that a naming system may utilize quite personalized aspects of peoples' identity (e.g., appearance, traits, incidents) and that such descriptors would be highly recognizable to other members of the community in a system of in-group reference.

Possibly as a Deaf community gets larger or as it interacts more extensively with "outsiders," the amount of shared context is reduced, in-group norms are likely to be influenced by the dominant contact culture and language, and the naming system may become less descriptive and more arbitrary. The NZ Deaf community is small and relatively close-knit, and NZSL is still mainly confined to Deaf-to-Deaf interaction, although this is changing rapidly as the language becomes more publicized. From this study it appears likely that the descriptive basis for name signs will continue to predominate, particularly as name signs are still created by Deaf children who are nonnative signers, for whom visual description is the most obvious source of identification.

Finally, the name sign system in NZSL illustrates first how Deaf people, often at a very young age (or from the time they enter a Deaf group), co-construct their personal identities and social reference system quite independently from those imagined and ascribed for them by non-Deaf family or teachers. Signed names ascribed by others, as well as changes in personal names, are accepted as a natural function of belonging to a close network of people whose primary mode of perceiving and classifying the physical and social world is visual. The linguistic resources upon which Deaf people have drawn in creating name signs in NZSL through various generations and social circumstances reflect shifting influences in the "linguistic mosaic" (cf. Branson and Miller 1998) in which all signers and signed languages inevitably exist. For a member of a Deaf community, having a name sign is linguistically necessary and socially indicative of identity; its form is determined by the linguistic and cultural preferences of a particular sign language community and the subgroups within it.

REFERENCES

Branson, J., and D. Miller. 1998. Nationalism and the linguistic rights of Deaf communities: Linguistic imperialism and the recognition and development of sign languages. *Journal of Sociolinguistics* 2 (1): 3–34.

Bryson, B. 1990. *Mother tongue: The English language.* London: Penguin Books.

Collins-Ahlgren, M. 1989. *Aspects of New Zealand Sign Language.* Ph.D. diss., Victoria University of Wellington.

Desrosiers, J., and C. Dubuisson. 1992. Name signs in Quebec Sign Language (LSQ) and what they tell us about Quebec Deaf culture. In *Proceedings of the Fifth International Symposium on Sign Language Research,* ed. I. Ahlgren, B. Bergman, and M. Brennan. England: Durham.

Gumperz, J., and H. Hymes, eds. 1986. *Directions in sociolinguistics: The ethnography of communication.* New York: Blackwell.

Hedberg, T. 1991. Name signs in Swedish Sign Language: Their formation and use. In *Equality and Self-Reliance. Proceedings of the XI World Congress of the World Federation of the Deaf,* ed. World Federation of the Deaf, 792–800. Tokyo: Japanese Federation of the Deaf.

Kennedy, G., R. Arnold, P. Dugdale, S. Fahey, and D. Moskovitz, eds. 1997. *A Dictionary of New Zealand Sign Language.* Auckland: Auckland University Press with Bridget Williams Books.

Levy-Bruhl, L. 1926. *How natives think.* London: George, Allen and Unwin.

Lucas, C., and C. Valli. 1992. *Language contact in the American Deaf community.* San Diego: Academic Press.

Massone, M., and R. Johnson. 1991. Kinship terms in Argentine Sign Language. *Sign Language Studies* 73:347–60.

McKee, D., and G. Kennedy. 2000. Lexical comparison of signs from American, Australian, British, and New Zealand Sign Languages. In *The signs of language revisited: An anthology to honor Ursula Bellugi and Edward Klima,* ed. H. Lane and K. Emmorey, 49–76. Mahwah, N.J.: Lawrence Erlbaum.

McKee, R., D. McKee, R. Adam, and A. Schembri. 2000. Name signs in New Zealand Sign Language (NZSL) and Australian Sign Language (Auslan). In *Proceedings of the XIII World Congress of the World Federation of the Deaf, July 25–31, 1999.* Brisbane, Australia: World Federation of the Deaf.

Meadow, K. 1977. Name signs as identity symbols in the Deaf community. *Sign Language Studies* 16:237–46.

Mindess, A. 1990. What name signs can tell us about Deaf culture. *Sign Language Studies* 66:1–24.

Monaghan, L. F. 1996. *Signing, oralism and the development of the New Zealand Deaf community: An ethnography and history of language ideologies.* Ph.D. diss., University of California, Los Angeles.

Morgan, J., C. O'Neill, and R. Harre. 1979. *Nicknames: Their origins and social consequences.* London: Routledge and Kegan Paul.

Mottez, B. 1985. Aspects de la culture sourde (extended version). *Sante Mentale* 85 (April): 13–16. Cited in Yau and He 1987.

Nonaka, A. 1997. Name signs in Thai Sign Language. Paper presented at the Deaf Studies Research Symposium, May, at La Trobe University, Melbourne.

Peng, F. C. 1974. Kinship signs in Japanese Sign Language. *Sign Language Studies* 5:31–47.

Rottenberg, C. J., and L. J. Searfoss. 1993. How hard of hearing and Deaf children learn their names. *American Annals of the Deaf* 138 (4): 358.

Smith, T. B. 1996. *Deaf people in context*. Ph.D. diss., University of Washington.

Supalla, S. 1990. The arbitrary name sign system in American Sign Language. *Sign Language Studies* 67:99–126.

———. 1992. *The book of name signs: Naming in American Sign Language*. San Diego: Dawn Sign Press.

Sutton-Spence, R., and B. Woll. 1999. *The linguistics of British Sign Language: An introduction*. Cambridge: Cambridge University Press.

Turner, J. S., and D. B. Helms. 1979. *Life span development*. Philadelphia: W. B. Saunders.

Yau, S., and J. He. 1987. How do Deaf children get their name signs during their first month in school? In *SLR '87: Papers from the Fourth International Symposium on Sign Language Research,* ed. W. Edmonson and F. Karlsson, 243–54. Hamburg: Signum.

Examples of Name Signs

1. Descriptive

"POINTED NOSE"

"JOKER"

"LONG-NECKED"

"FRECKLES"

"DUTCH"

"CREW CUT"

1. Descriptive (*continued*)

"BEARD"

"BIG BELLY"

2. Generic

"PETER"

"PAUL"

3. CHILD classifier + lip pattern

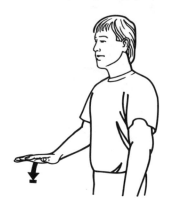

Part 2 Languages in Contact

An Analysis of Codeswitching:

American Sign Language and Cued English

Peter C. Hauser

Sociolinguistic studies on the codeswitching that occurs when American Sign Language (ASL) and English come into contact have claimed that the codeswitching is qualitatively different from spoken language codeswitching (e.g., Davis 1989, 1990; Lucas and Valli 1989, 1992). These studies have focused on the contact between users of ASL and users of spoken English. However, the codeswitching between English in a visual modality—cued American English (hereafter cued English)—and ASL has not been studied. This chapter focuses on the codeswitching of a ten-year-old bilingual deaf girl who is fluent in ASL and cued English.[1]

This chapter provides descriptive examples of ASL–cued English codeswitching as well as a discussion on social motivations for and functions of codeswitching. In the first section of this chapter, studies on spoken language codeswitching are introduced, followed by a second section discussing codeswitching in the Deaf community.[2] The third section includes a description of cued English and a review of previous studies on cued languages. Following the review of literature, evidence of ASL–cued English

I wish to thank Hilary Franklin, Angela Hauser, Claire Klossner, and Melanie Metzger for their help in various parts of this study. I also thank the participants and their family for permission to videotape their interactions and for sharing information and providing previous video clips and documentation used in this study.

1. Some authors use the term *code-mixing* when referring to intrasentential codeswitching or *borrowing* when referring to single morpheme/lexeme switches from one language within an utterance to another language. (Additionally, some authors use *code switching* as two separate words, whereas others use *codeswitching* as one word or use *code-switching*.) In this chapter, I use *codeswitching* to refer to both intrasentential and intersentential codeswitches as well as borrowing.

2. In this chapter *deaf* refers to the audiological condition of hearing loss and *Deaf* to social collectivities; Woodward (1972) first made this distinction.

codeswitching is demonstrated and compared with examples of code-switching in spoken languages. The results of this chapter's study demonstrate that codeswitching between ASL and cued English follows a similar pattern found in spoken language codeswitching.

CODESWITCHING

Codeswitching occurs when a bilingual or multilingual individual switches from one language to another. The term is used when identifying alternations of linguistic varieties within the same conversation (Myers-Scotton 1993). Romaine explains that codeswitching occurs when "the items in question form part of the same speech act. They are tied together prosodically as well as by semantic and syntactic relations equivalent to those that join passages in a single speech act" (1995, iii). Codeswitching is commonly found in bilingual communities and has been studied by anthropologists, psychologists, sociologists, and linguists. Codeswitching can be a communicative resource because it reveals the speakers' sensitivity to both formal and functional aspects of language (Grosjean 1982; Gumperz 1982; Heller 1988; Lanza 1992; Poplack 1981; Romaine 1995).

Codeswitching has been found to be used by children (two years old or older) who are from bilingual families (Boeschoten and Verhoeven 1987; Fantini 1985; Lanza 1992; McClure 1981; Zentella 1997). Children in bilingual communities do not only learn two languages but also the social rules regarding when and where the languages may be used and how to codeswitch within a single utterance (Zentella 1997). Numerous studies have demonstrated that there are no qualitative differences between children's and older bilinguals' codeswitching patterns (e.g., Lanza 1992), whereas others have found developmental patterns of codeswitching (e.g., Zentella 1997).

Codeswitching can occur at the boundaries of complete sentences *(intersentential)* or within sentence boundaries *(intrasentential)*. The following are examples of intersentential (example 1) and intrasentential (example 2) Spanish–English codeswitching from Zentella (1997, 80):

EXAMPLE 1

Si, pero le hablo en español. When I don't know something, I'll talk to her in English.
("Yes, but I talk to her in Spanish.")

EXAMPLE 2

You know they walk *que ellas se comen el* aisle *completo.*

("in such a way that they take up the whole")

It is generally held that an individual must know at least two languages in order to be able to codeswitch. Breitborde (1983, 5) stated that "the principal behavior through which bilingualism is expressed is code switching." Grosjean describes the everyday nature of a bilingual as follows:

> In their everyday lives, bilinguals find themselves at various points along a situational continuum, bilinguals are in a total monolingual mode in that they are speaking (or writing) to monolinguals of one-or-the-other of the languages that they know. At the other end of the continuum, bilinguals find themselves in a bilingual language mode in that they are communicating with bilinguals who share their two languages and with whom they normally mix languages (i.e., code switch and borrow). (1982, 309)

When referring to bilinguals (or multilinguals), most researchers do not consider them to have native fluency in both languages (Baetsens-Beardsmore 1986; Grosjean 1982, 1992; Hakuta 1986; Haugen 1969; Myers-Scotton 1993; Romaine 1995; Zentella 1997). It is rare to find a bilingual who can pass as a native user of both languages (Grosjean 1992; Zentella 1997). Zentella (1997) claims that it is more accurate to speak of a "bilingual/multidialectal repertoire" that consists of a spectrum of linguistic codes. The linguistic spectrum ranges from standard use to non-standard dialects and from the language in which an individual is most fluent to other languages the individual may use only with specific inter-locutors or for specific purposes. Zentella defined bilingualism as the ability to produce meaningful utterances in two languages (which is also the definition used in this chapter). As in other codeswitching studies, native fluency in both languages was not a prerequisite.

Language proficiency influences an individual's ability to codeswitch. Zentella found that the overall pattern of her subjects' language choices were related to their language proficiency; however, "the choice of language in a particular setting depends on a myriad of factors involving the participants, the setting, and the social and communicative goals" (1997, 87). Children in her study who were Spanish-dominant often would start their utterances in Spanish and move to their weaker language (English) with bilinguals. For example, a six-year-old (Paca) who was talking to Zentella (Z) changed from her dominant language to English (88):

EXAMPLE 3

PACA: *Dame una cura.* ("Give me a Band-Aid.")
Z: ¿Pa(-ra) qué? ("For what?")
PACA: For my hand.

Zentella pointed out that Paca codeswitched to English for several possible reasons: (a) for emphasis, (b) to recognize Zentella's U.S.-born identity, or (c) to show off her knowledge of English—the "prestige language" (1997, 88).

Codeswitching can also occur because one language has an advantage over the other. For example, in some situations, one language has a more suitable term for what the speaker is trying to express, and this motivates the speaker to codeswitch. Clyne (1967) studied German–English bilinguals and observed that sometimes a speaker switches to the other language before the particular term is used. He named this type of codeswitching *anticipational triggering* because the need for a specific term in the other language triggers the switch before the term is reached. In other situations, a speaker may codeswitch when the particular term is reached and then continue using that term's language. Clyne named this type of triggering *consequential triggering.*

Bentahila (1983) studied codeswitching in Morocco, where it is common among those who are fluent in both French and Arabic (e.g., Lahlou 1989; Heath 1989). In informal conversations in which all participants were bilingual, codeswitching often occurred both intersententially and intrasententially. Bentahila observed that both anticipational and consequential triggering occurred with the Moroccan bilinguals. Bentahila identified some external factors that provoke codeswitching. He found that Moroccans who have lexical access to many of the same terms in both French and Arabic often use terms from one language rather than another when referring to certain topics. For example, the Moroccan bilinguals codeswitched to French when using technical terms and concepts associated with Europe and codeswitched to Arabic for numbers, dates, times, insults, and swearing. The Moroccan bilinguals also switched to Arabic for stereotyped phrases that serve as fillers to avoid a pause.

Codeswitching has also been observed in pauses when the speaker is unsure how to continue. Gumperz and Hernandez-Chavez (1975) also observed that Spanish–English bilinguals switched to Spanish for idiomatic pauses. In Zentella's (1997) study, many community members stated that they codeswitch when they were at a loss for words. She termed this type of codeswitch a *crutch* because, just as crutches can help a mobility-impaired individual to keep walking, a codeswitch can help speakers to keep talking when they are at a loss for words in one language (98).

Kachru (1977) noted that Hindi–English bilinguals codeswitch to repeat their utterances in order to avoid possible vagueness or ambiguity. Bentahila (1983) observed situations in which the speaker attempted — with difficulty — to explain something in one language before codeswitching and start explaining again in the other language. Bentahila claimed that repeating utterances in another language is not always used for adding clarity; instead it often occurs because the speaker wants to achieve a certain effect, such as emphasis. This type of codeswitching was also observed in Spanish–English bilinguals (Gumperz 1976; Redlinger 1976; Timm 1975; Zentella 1997) and in Hindi–English and Slovenian–German bilinguals (Gumperz 1976). Zentella (1997) found codeswitching for clarity and for emphasis was most frequent among the children in her study.

Codeswitching can also occur within utterances when one wants to make a comment unrelated to the main topic (Bentahila 1983; Zentella 1997), or to recite a quotation (Bentahila 1983; Gumperz 1976; Timm 1975). The following example of a topic shift is found in Zentella (1997, 103): "She works a lot. *Ay, tengo que ir pa(-ra e-)l baño*" ("[Ugh] I have to go to the bathroom"). Zentella also found codeswitching to be used to check for approval, gain someone's attention, or verify the interlocutor's knowledge of what they were about to refer to. Gumperz (1976) found examples of codeswitching for attention from four language groups around the world. When Puerto Rican children in New York asked a question and then answered it themselves, the answer sometimes was in their other language (Zentella 1997). Data from Bentahila's (1983) observations of different types of codeswitching of Arabic–French bilinguals in Morocco can be found in the "Evidence of Codeswitching" section of this chapter.

CODESWITCHING MODELS

Situational and Metaphorical Codeswitching

Blom and Gumperz (1972) identified two types of codeswitching in the 1960s while they were studying linguistic variation and use in a small town in Norway. They claimed that codeswitching occurs for social reasons and depends on (a) who the speakers are, (b) their social identities and social relations with others when speaking, (c) how the two codes are used, and (d) how the social identities are brought into the social relationship. They noticed that the northern Norwegian standard language, Bokmal, was used in social relationships characterized by regional values and that the local dialect, Ranamal, was used in social relationships characterized by local values. The merchants were linked to both the locals and nonlocals and were found to codeswitch often. The two types of codeswitching they identified were *situational codeswitching* and *metaphorical codeswitching*.

Situational codeswitching depends on a situation. On the other hand, metaphorical codeswitching is independent of the situation and tends to be a short codeswitch between languages. In situational codeswitching, one language is used in one social situation, and the other language is used in another social situation. In metaphorical switching, the switching occurs in the same situation with the same individuals. Blom and Gumperz (1972) stated that metaphorical switching allows one speaker to share two or more different values with the same interlocutor.

An example of situational codeswitching from Zentella (1997) involved a situation in which an eight-year-old Puerto Rican girl (L) in New York pushed a five-year-old boy (T) off her bike. The boy tells the nearby adults about what L did:

EXAMPLE 4

L to T: Get off, Timmy, get off.
T to adults: *Ella me dió!* ("She hit me.")
L to T: *¡Por que TU me diste!* ("Because YOU hit me!")
T to L: Liar!
Adult to L: *¿Por qué?* ("Why?")—[interrupted by L]
L to adult: *Por que él me dió, por eso. El siempre me está dando cuando me ve.* ("Because he hit me, that's why. He's always hitting me whenever he sees me.")

The interlocutors L and T were able to speak both English and Spanish. In this situation, the language they used depended on the dominant language of those they were addressing. When T and L spoke to each other, they used English unless they wanted to involve an adult in the conversation. In other words, when the situation involved only the two children, the language was English; when the situation involved adults, the language was Spanish. On the other hand, the conversation between Paca and Zentella (mentioned earlier in the chapter) is an example of metaphorical codeswitching (1997). Two bilinguals were communicating with each other in the same situation using two languages.

Myers-Scotton (1993) stated that the work of Blom and Gumperz had an enormous impact on codeswitching research because it has provided researchers a suitable framework for analyzing codeswitching. Myers-Scotton observed that the majority of codeswitching literature mentions and/or follows Blom and Gumperz's framework and that "much of the work done on [codeswitching] would not have been done at all without the stimulation of [Blom and Gumperz]" (1993, 55). However, she points out that it is difficult to pin down exactly what is intended by situational and metaphorical codeswitching. She claims that it is "especially unclear how many and diverse might be the motivations included under metaphorical code switching . . . [and] situational code switching is never really very well defined" (1993, 52). Auer (1984, 91) also criticized Blom and Gumperz' model:

> [T]he distinction between situational and metaphorical code switching must be criticized from both ends; at the "situational code switching" end, the relationship between language choice and situation features is less rigid, more open to renegotiation, than a one-to-one relationship, at the "metaphorical code switching" end, things are less individualistic, less independent of the situation. The distinction collapses and should be replaced by a continuum. (1984, 91)

Myers-Scotton (1993) also finds fault with the writing of Blom and Gumperz, Gumperz (1982), and other studies that have followed Gumperz's lead in that they use primarily a descriptive approach, such as the better-taxonomy approach, to analyze different functions of codeswitching. She argues that a theory that can be generalized across different interactions would be more beneficial than viewing each social interaction independent from others. She claims that codeswitching "serves the same general sociopsychological functions everywhere" (Myers-Scotton 1993, 3), and she developed a markedness model that attempts to explain social motivations for codeswitching across different languages and situations.

Markedness Model

Myers-Scotten developed a *markedness model* with an eye to providing a framework for describing sociopsychological motivations for codeswitching in all languages and situations. The theory behind this model proposes that speakers have a *markedness metric* that "enables speakers to access all code choices as more or less *unmarked* or *marked* for the exchange type in which they occur" (Myers-Scotton 1993, 80). Although the markedness metric is considered a universal cognitive ability, the markedness of a code has a normative basis within a community. In other words, speakers are conscious of what code is expected *(unmarked)* or unexpected *(marked)*. If the marked code is used, it has a shock value not just because of the language used but also because of the change from the unmarked choice.

The markedness of a code depends on the rights-and-obligations sets (RO sets) between participants in a given interaction type. "Rights-and-obligations sets are salient cultural biases that are associated with a specific language in a specific situation. The language choice itself exposes cultural and/or personal values/biases, in other words, the language choice (or code switch) indexes to a specific RO set" (Myers-Scotton 1993, 84). Myers-Scotton illustrates the concept of markedness and RO sets by describing conversations between a guard in IBM's Nairobi head office and visitors to the office:

> With no other information than the visitor's appearance, the most salient factor determining the guard's selection of an unmarked choice for enacting this encounter is whether the visitor appears to be a Kenyan African. The guard decides this is the visitor's identity and so he speaks Swahili, the unmarked choice for the unmarked RO set between two Kenyan Africans in their respective roles. . . . Had the visitor been a *Mzungu* ("European"), the guard would have tried English. . . . Since the guard's apparent motivation is to convey nothing more than "business as usual" and a very neutral RO set between himself and the visitor, Swahili is his choice to open the conversation. . . . By switching from Swahili to Luyia [unmarked code indexing the unmarked RO set

for intraethnic-group encounters in Nairobi], the guard acknowledges (and makes salient) their shared ethnic-group membership. But when a second visitor appears, the guard addresses him in Swahili, indexing again the more neutral RO set for such encounters. (1993, 87)

The markedness model postulates that codeswitching is not influenced by situations as found in Blom and Gumperz (1972). Instead, codeswitching is a choice that a speaker makes. The guard did not have to switch to Luyia even though he recognized the visitor was from his ethnic group. He switched to Luyia because he chose to use the unmarked code for intraethnic-group encounters to acknowledge their shared ethnic membership. Under the markedness model, all code choices can be explained in terms of speaker motivations. There are four codeswitching types:

1. *Sequential unmarked codeswitching:* codeswitching as a sequence of unmarked choices
2. *Unmarked codeswitching:* codeswitching itself as the unmarked choice
3. *Marked codeswitching:* codeswitching as the marked choice
4. *Exploratory codeswitching:* codeswitching as an exploratory choice

Sequential unmarked codeswitching and unmarked codeswitching ultimately have related motivations; however, sequential unmarked codeswitching is triggered by changes in the situation factors, whereas in unmarked codeswitching, the situational factors remain more or less the same. Myers-Scotton uses the guard conversation to illustrate sequential unmarked codeswitching: "[W]hen the security guard discovers that the enquirer comes from his own ethnic group, the content of the factor 'ethnicity' changes from 'unknown' to 'shared,' and the unmarked RO set changes from that holding between strangers to that between ethnic brethren" (1993, 114).

On the other hand, unmarked codeswitching occurs in a conversation of at least two bilinguals (or multilinguals) in which the switching is often intrasentential. Myers-Scotton claims that "the interaction has to be of a type in which speakers wish to symbolize the dual memberships that such [codeswitching] calls up" (1993, 119). Many of the codeswitching examples found in Zentella's study involved unmarked codeswitching, which Zentella described as the creation of "a style of discourse that is emblematic of their dual identity" (1997, 101). Poplack (1988) also studied Puerto Rican communities in New York and found similar evidence of unmarked codeswitching.

Marked codeswitching involves making an unexpected code choice that does not index to the expected RO sets. Myers-Scotton (1993) postulates that marked choices are made when a speaker is attempting to increase or decrease the expected social distance between participants. Marked codeswitching can be used to express authority or anger, to exclude others from a different ethnic group, or to simply add a stylistic effect. By moving away from the expected RO sets, the usage of a marked choice has a message of its own. On the other hand, exploratory codeswitching is used when speakers are unclear of the unmarked RO sets. When exploratory codeswitching is used, a speaker may attempt to be neutral by avoiding committing to a single RO set. In situations in which a speaker does not have adequate proficiency in the unmarked choice, the speaker might switch codes while apologizing for needing to switch.

LANGUAGE CONTACT: AMERICAN SIGN LANGUAGE AND SPOKEN ENGLISH

Almost all deaf individuals who use ASL also use written English to communicate with others (e.g., via e-mail or TTY). Also, many have been exposed to oral English through speech training and when communicating with hearing individuals who have minimal or no sign language knowledge. Therefore, most deaf individuals who sign are bilingual (Grosjean 1992). When two ASL and English bilinguals interact (deaf–deaf, deaf–hearing, or hearing–hearing), their signing might be in ASL or in another form such as Pidgin Sign English (PSE; Woodward 1972, 1973), manually coded English (MCE; Lee 1982), or contact sign (Lucas and Valli 1989, 1991, 1992). When ASL–English bilinguals interact,

> [D]epending on such factors as their knowledge of the two languages, the person(s) being addressed, the situation, the topic, the function of the interaction, etc., they choose a base language — usually a form of sign language (the natural sign language of the community or a signed version of the spoken language). Then, according to various momentary needs, and by means of signing, fingerspelling, mouthing, etc., they bring in the other languages in the form of code switching or borrowings. (Grosjean 1992, 312)

The language contact situation when ASL and English meet is qualitatively different from patterns found in spoken language contact (Lucas and Valli 1989, 1991, 1992). Studies have shown that PSE does not follow the same linguistic patterns that are found in spoken pidgin languages (Lucas and Valli 1992; Mühlhäusler, 1986; Reilly and McIntire 1980). MCE is a signing system that is claimed by some to express English via a signed medium. Studies have shown that MCE signs are not English words because they do not share the same phonological structure and do not equivalently present English morphology or syntax (Davidson, Newport, and Supalla 1996; Fleetwood and Metzger 1991, 1998; Johnson and Erting 1989; Johnson, Liddell, and Erting 1989; Kluwin 1981; Stack 1996; Supalla 1991; Swisher 1985).

Lucas and Valli (1989, 1991, 1992) studied sociolinguistic factors that influence ASL–English bilinguals' language use. They found a number of situations in which deaf signers change their signing so that it is more "English-like" (1992, 18). They termed this type of signing *contact sign*. Contact sign is what many have referred to as PSE in earlier studies. Its lexical forms are ASL signs with ASL semantics and functions; however, sometimes the signs use English semantics and functions, such as the English use of conjunctions and prepositional phrases. Mouthing of English lexical items (sometimes with voice) occurs. Lucas and Valli's analysis demonstrated that contact sign involves a drastic morphemic and syntactic reduction of both ASL and English. In their data (which involved recordings of interactions among ASL–English bilinguals), English inflectional and derivational morphology was nonexistent, and ASL inflectional and derivational morphology was virtually absent.

Lucas and Valli (1989) claimed that contact sign and spoken language pidgins involve different features and that contact sign is not a pidgin form of English. In their study, contact sign did not involve codeswitching; instead it involved an unusual type of mixing that is not observed in spoken languages. English codes and ASL codes were observed to often mix simultaneously in contact signing. The results might be different if one studied codeswitching between two signed languages (for example, between ASL and French Sign Language). Unfortunately, to date there are no empirical or qualitative studies of sign-to-sign codeswitching.

As already mentioned, signed English does not preserve the linguistic features of English. As the next section explains, the phonetic features of English phonemes are replaced with visual phonetic features in cued English, and the morphology and syntax of English remain intact. This leads to our central question: Is the codeswitching pattern in ASL and cued English similar to that found in spoken-spoken language contact? A discussion on cued English is necessary before we can answer our question.

CUED ENGLISH

Cued Speech was developed by Cornett (1967) when he was a vice president at Gallaudet College (now Gallaudet University).[3] He noticed the difficulties deaf undergraduate students were having in developing adequate English literacy skills. He believed that the use of Cued Speech would provide deaf readers the linguistic (phonological) foundation necessary to develop successful literacy skills. In 1975 Cornett stated that in order for deaf individuals to live life to the fullest, they should be bilingual (English and American Sign Language) and bicultural (Deaf culture and hearing culture). He believed that the cue system would enable them to become true bilinguals by helping them gain fluency in English as their second language. The Cued Speech system has since been adapted for use with over fifty-six different languages and is now used in many countries (Cornett and Daisey 1992).

Fleetwood and Metzger (1998) conducted a linguistic analysis of the use of cued English. They used the term *cued language* because cues are visible allophones representing consonant and vowel phonemic values of a language (Fleetwood and Metzger 1991, 1998). For example, there are spoken languages (e.g., spoken Spanish), signed languages (e.g., ASL), written languages (e.g., written French), and cued languages (e.g., cued English). The cues themselves are not a language, just as the articulation of both spoken languages and signed languages is not a language. The cues

3. Cornett (1967) called the system Cued Speech because its purpose is to make spoken language visible through the use of cues. The name has created misunderstandings from the general public, who often assume that it has something to do with speaking skills. Therefore, it is necessary to clarify some misunderstandings here. Cued Speech was not developed to improve deaf individuals' speech. It does not require the use of speech (Fleetwood and Metzger 1991, 1997, 1998). The National Cued Speech Association's position statement makes this point clear: "[T]he primary goal of Cued Speech use is to enable the deaf person to become as literate as he/she would be without a hearing loss. Cued Speech was created to enable deaf children to absorb the same phonemic/phonological language base as hearing children as a foundation for reading."

TABLE I. *Phonetic Differences Between the Word* Cat, *Spoken and Cued*

	Spoken			Cued	
/k/	/æ/	/t/	/k/	/æ/	/t/
+ consonantal	− consonantal	+ consonantal	+ index	+ contact	+ index
− sonorant	+ low	− continuant	+ middle	+ neck	+ middle
− continuant	− back	− voice	+ open	+ open	+ ring
− voice	− tense	+ coronal	− round	− round	+ little
+ back	− round	+ anterior	− spread	− flat	+ thumb
		− d.r.			+ tongue
					− tip

Note: The notation system for the phonetic features of cued language was borrowed and modified from Fleetwood and Metzger (1998).

are systematized sets of arbitrary features that represent the phonemes used to express a language. The phonemes of signed languages are represented via the articulation of languages such as ASL, French Sign Language, and British Sign Language. The phonemes in spoken languages are represented by the articulation of different languages (e.g., English, French). The phonemes of cued languages are represented via the articulation of different languages (e.g., cued English, cued French). Cues are visual allophones that reference the phonemes of a traditionally spoken language (see Fleetwood and Metzger 1998 for a comparison of spoken language and cued language linguistic structure).

Cued Speech uses eight handshapes, four hand locations, and ten nonmanual signals (NMS). The NMS that are phonetic features of the cues are mouth NMS. A combination of one handshape and one NMS produces each consonant, and each vowel is produced by a combination of one hand location and one NMS. The production of cued English words follows the same consonant and vowel syllables used to produce spoken English words. The differences between a spoken word and a cued word are at the phonetic level. To illustrate this point, the word *cat* is used in table 1. The table demonstrates that when the word *cat* is spoken or cued, it represents the same phonemes; however, the segments of phonetic features representing each phoneme are different.

To illustrate the adequacy of the Cued Speech system in creating a visual modality of English, let us consider a few studies that have demonstrated the success of this system in providing deaf children access to English (see Kipila and Williams-Scott 1988 for a more thorough review).

Berendt, Krupnik-Goldman, and Rupp (1990) used the Rhode Island Test of Language Structure (RITLS) with deaf children from ages six to sixteen who had used cued English for at least two years. The study found that the children's mean English reading comprehension scores were at the 92nd percentile when compared to the norms for those with hearing loss. Wandel (1989) compared the Stanford Achievement Test's (SAT) Reading Comprehension subtest scores of deaf oral, cued English, Total Communication, and hearing students. There were 30 students in each group that were carefully matched from a sample of 213 students. All students had prelingual, bilateral hearing loss. In each group, 15 students had severe hearing loss (except the hearing students), and 15 had profound hearing loss. The researchers found no significant differences in the reading comprehension subtest scores between the deaf cuers and the hearing controls. The oral and Total Communication students' scores were significantly lower. The structure of cued English gives cuers access to English's phonological codes, and this is most likely why the cuers have demonstrated successful English literacy skills (Beaupré 1986; Cornett 1967; Fleetwood and Metzger 1998; Hauser 1997; Leybaert and Alegria 1990; Leybaert and Charlier 1996).

THE PRESENT STUDY

Methodology

A ten-year-old bilingual Korean-American girl who has been profoundly deaf since birth was used in this study to determine whether code-switching occurred between ASL and cued English. The participant was involved in another case study (Hammes 1995) and was selected for this study for several reasons: (1) it was reported that she was fluent in both ASL and English (Hammes 1995), (2) her family and Hammes have had her academic and language skills assessed annually and have been keeping records of all evaluations, and (3) they had videotapes of her early language use. The same pseudonym, "NQ," used by Hammes for the participant will be used here.

A state-certified cued-language transliterator (who also uses ASL) and I visited the family. I am a Deaf nonnative user of ASL and have intermediate skills in cued English. My native language is English, and I used English orally before learning ASL during late adolescence. I did not use cued English with NQ until the end of the day—after four hours of video data of NQ's language use. The transliterator provided interpreting from ASL to cued English and vice versa. I did not use cued English because I was the only Deaf ASL-user present during the study, and I wanted at least one person to be present whom NQ felt she could communicate with only via ASL.

During the home visit, NQ had a deaf friend visiting. Her friend (referred to hereafter with the pseudonym "CP") was a ten-year-old deaf girl who had learned cued English when she was three years old. She had learned signed English when she was in preschool but was not exposed to sign in school again after preschool. She mainstreamed kindergarten and first grade with cued language transliterators and then continued the rest of her schooling without any support services. At the time of the study she was in fifth grade. CP's sign vocabulary was limited. CP's mother and sister (three years older) communicate with her via cued English. CP usually spends much of her free time with NQ.

Upon arrival, I set up a video camera in the family's living room, where NQ and CP were present, and left it on for most of the day. As soon as the video camera was set, NQ and CP decided to put on a show. They created a skit in which they pretended to be news reporters who performed "commercials" between their "news reports." The transliterator and I were in another room with NQ's mother conducting an interview to collect background information. After the interview, NQ's mother and I joined the girls. NQ's mother, who has adequate ASL fluency to engage in a signed conversation, used only cued English during this conversation; I used ASL.

The rest of the video data consisted of more play by NQ and CP as well as normal interactions between NQ, CP, and other family members. CP's mother was present later in the day and was also interviewed for background information. When CP returned home with her mother, I administered the Woodcock Johnson-Revised (WJ-R) Tests of Achievement (Mather 1991) to NQ. The word–letter identification and passage comprehension subtests from WJ-R measured her English knowledge and reading achievement.

With the help of a research assistant who is a deaf, native user of cued English, I reviewed the six-hour video footage from the home visit and a one-hour tape that consisted of video clips of NQ at different ages. Most of the clips on the one-hour video were made when NQ participated in other studies. During the review, all of the situations in which NQ code-switched were identified and transcribed. English glosses were used for

ASL signs and were typed in capital letters; cued English utterances were typed in lowercase letters. In each transcribed conversation, the addressee was noted. This was important for the analysis of the situations in which codeswitching occurred. The research assistant, the cued language transliterator, and I transcribed NQ's utterances, and a certified ASL interpreter translated NQ's mother's spoken English when she was out of the camera's view (NQ's mother used spoken English simultaneously while she cued English).

Background

Because NQ was adopted, only limited information on her birth history is available. She lived in a foster home in a different country before she was adopted at five-and-a-half months of age by her current family in the United States. Her adoptive mother (who is referred to as "mother" in this chapter) suspected NQ's hearing loss almost immediately when she noticed that NQ was copying her mouth movements but was not making any sounds. NQ was first exposed to sign language when she was fifteen months old through a hearing babysitter who was a special education teacher. Concurrently, her mother, father, and older brothers attended ASL classes for a year. When NQ was two years old, she had a full-time babysitter who was deaf and signed to her. The babysitter continued to work for the family until NQ was five years old.

NQ's mother decided to use ASL with NQ after she read literature about deafness and deaf culture. Reading *Unlocking the Curriculum: Principles for Achieving Access in Deaf Education* (Johnson, Liddell, and Erting 1989) convinced her to choose ASL as the language to use to communicate with her daughter. During that time, she heard about cued English and decided that it would be an effective means to expose her daughter to English. However, a misinformed teacher told NQ's mother that nobody uses this communication mode anymore. NQ's mother continued to use ASL but still wanted to find a way to introduce her daughter to English.

When NQ was four years old, she was placed in a self-contained preschool classroom for deaf students that emphasized instruction in ASL. During that time, she started to write words and use fingerspelling. NQ's mother started to realize the need for English phonological awareness in order for NQ to be able to read. She began to wonder how her daughter could learn to read English through ASL and fingerspelling alone. During that time, a deaf girl who used cued English moved into NQ's area. When

NQ's mother heard of this, she contacted the girl's teacher to learn more about cued English. She learned that there was a teacher who used both cued English and ASL and that locally there were two cued language transliterators and two ASL interpreters who also knew how to cue. NQ's mother had the teacher and one of the transliterators teach her how to cue.

When NQ was five years old, she had three different babysitters. One was a Deaf native ASL user from a Deaf family, one was hard of hearing and used ASL, and the other one was a deaf person who used cued English and knew some ASL. Hammes (1995) reported that at that time NQ had a good ASL foundation and her parents felt that it was time to introduce her to English via cueing. The school administrators would not allow cued English to be used in the kindergarten classroom because they were afraid it would influence the other children's use of ASL. As a result, NQ mainstreamed kindergarten with two ASL interpreters who also knew how to cue.

Hammes (1995, 21) reported that NQ's parents felt that cueing "would give NQ equal access (visually) to all of the languages her siblings and classmates in the mainstream routinely heard." Her parents said "all of the languages" because NQ's kindergarten class was learning Spanish. Also, NQ's father is a native of Denmark and sometimes speaks Danish at home. NQ's parents value cultural diversity and wanted to expose NQ to a number of different languages and cultures, including Deaf culture. The family has brought NQ to different Deaf cultural events and ASL family camps. At the time of this study, the family reported that they were continuing to bring her to such events.

In kindergarten the pupils often switched between cued English and ASL; the interpreters and the teacher tried to give NQ information in both languages, using one language at a time. For example, the teacher would read stories to her twice, and the interpreters used one language during the first reading and another language during the second reading. When the teacher introduced Spanish to the class, the interpreters transliterated spoken Spanish to cued Spanish.

NQ's mother continued to use ASL at home except when she wanted to use an English word. She used to fingerspell when she used English words but then began cueing the English words instead. When NQ at first thought cued English was a different fingerspelling system, her mother explained to her that it was "handshapes that show the 'sounds' of English." NQ's mother knew that the cues did not actually represent sounds and that they really represented the phonemes of English, but she did not know how to explain that to NQ without using the word *sounds.*

NQ started to understand the relationship between the English phonemes and written English. For example, she once asked her mother, "BLUE SPELL" ("how do you spell 'blue'?").[4] Her mother replied in cued English, "blue." And NQ wrote *bloo.* This was the first time NQ's mother noticed NQ develop a phonological awareness of English. Her mother gradually used more cued English. When NQ was seven years old, her mother started to cue English more than she signed ASL.

From first grade to her current fifth-grade class, NQ remained at the same school. She is the only Deaf child in her school and has been using cued language transliterators for all of her classes. There are several hard of hearing students in the school. When NQ was in first grade, she loved to write and often would spend a lot of her free time writing to others. The school has brought different deaf adults and teenagers into the classroom to introduce the children to other deaf people and to ASL. NQ has been involved in extracurricular activities such as soccer, ice skating, gymnastics, and diving. She attends an ASL Sunday school on the weekends at a local church. Many of NQ's classmates have learned how to cue and are able to communicate with her directly. Some of them also know how to fingerspell.

American Sign Language Fluency

Standardized tests with normative data used to measure ASL development in children are not yet available; however, some are currently in development (Hoffmeister et al. 1997; Strong and Prinz 1997). Thus it was necessary to rely on qualitative data to judge NQ's fluency in ASL. The language environment had to be taken into consideration in order to qualitatively analyze NQ's signing skills. In the home visit, no native ASL users were present; there were two hearing nonnative users of ASL who also knew cued English (NQ's mother and the cued language transliterator); a deaf girl (CP), NQ's friend, who uses cued English and has a limited sign vocabulary; and a Deaf nonnative user of ASL (the author).

4. Transcription conventions in NQ's utterances: SMALL CAPS = American Sign Language glosses, noncaps = cued English, CL = classifier, G = Gesture, 2h = two hands, x-x-x = fingerspelled utterance, and . . denotes a pause over 1.5 seconds.

TABLE 2. *Achievement Scores from Stanford Achievement Test –*
Hearing Impaired (Allen, White, and Karchmer 1983)

Subtest	Age	Grade	Grade Equivalent	Percentile Rank
Reading vocabulary	8	3rd	2nd	n/a
	9	4th	4th	n/a
	10	5th	5th	99th
Reading comprehension	7	2nd	2nd	72nd
	8	3rd	3rd	87th
	9	4th	4th	n/a
	10	5th	5th	96th

Note: Grade equivalents were based on hearing norms; percentile ranks were based on the SAT-HI hearing-impaired norms, all levels of hearing loss.

NQ's signing consisted of many of the features that are characteristic of ASL, such as the use of nonmanual signals, classifiers, space, role shifting, and gesture. Often her signing resembled contact signing (Lucus and Valli 1992) rather than a more ASL-like form of signing. For example, when she signed to me in her mother's and her friend's presence, she used less space and fewer classifiers than when she was alone with me. Her mother reported that NQ's signing during the visit was not like the "usual ASL" she used when she signed with her Deaf friends who are native ASL users. Although NQ used some signs from MCE such as IS and THE, most of her signs were not in the initialized form introduced by MCE. Overall, her signing style in this situation was similar to what is normally found among native ASL signers when they are in contact with English users (cf. Lucas and Valli 1992).

English Fluency

I used standardized English achievement tests to measure NQ's English proficiency. Although a thorough discussion on reading is beyond the scope of this chapter, a brief look at NQ's reading achievement helps to illustrate her English knowledge, including her knowledge of English phonology. NQ has taken a number of standardized English achievement tests since she entered second grade. Table 2 shows her scores from the Stanford Achievement Test — Hearing-Impaired (SAT-HI; see Allen, White, and Karchmer 1983).

During the home visit, I gave NQ the WJ-R letter–word identification subtest, which measures ability to rapidly and automatically recognize letters and words by sight (Mather 1991). However, it does not require knowledge of word meanings. This is an important skill for reading because it indicates that the reader does not have to attribute conscious energy attending to words and is therefore able to use the mental energy to process and understand written materials (Mather 1991). This subtest was used here to measure her awareness of English phonology.

The standard administration procedure for this subtest is for the participant to read lists of words aloud. To get a correct score, a hearing reader has to pronounce the test items correctly, which demonstrates his or her ability to use phonetic encoding. Therefore, this test is usually not used with deaf readers (or is used with modifications of the standard procedures) because they often do not have a way to demonstrate that they use phonemic encoding. For example, if the test is administered to an oral deaf child, the examiner would not be able to distinguish between errors in phonemic encoding and speech errors. However, with NQ, no modification of the standard procedures was necessary—NQ was able to cue the words because their phonemes can be shown with cues rather than spoken allophones.

I videotaped NQ's responses, and the cued language transliterator was present during the testing. The transliterator determined whether the correct sequence of cues (English phonemes) was used when NQ read the test items. The transliterator reviewed the videotape to confirm the results. For example, for the word *expostulate,* NQ cued /ɛkspɑstʃəleɪt/, which is a correct phonological sequence for that word. Using the standardized norms of the WJ-R, NQ's scores were equivalent to a 5.4 grade hearing child who was ten years and nine months old. The results of this test indicated that she is able to use English phonemic encoding and that her phonological awareness of English was at her age and grade level.

I also administered to NQ the Passage Comprehension subtest of the WJ-R, which measured her ability to use contextually based word-recognition skills and semantic and syntactic cues to comprehend written text. The test items were short passages with one word missing from each passage. The test required her to read a passage, understand its main idea, and respond with the missing word. To be able to respond with the correct word, NQ had to understand the meaning of the entire passage. Using the norms from the WJ-R, NQ's reading comprehension skills were at the 5.6 grade-equivalent level and the ten-year, ten-month age level. The results of this test can also be generalized to cued English conversations: NQ's understanding of English semantics and syntax is equivalent to that of a hearing native speaker of English at her age and grade level.

EVIDENCE OF CODESWITCHING

This section consists of two parts: first, examples of codeswitching for different functions, and second, a discussion of NQ's sociopsychological motivations for codeswitching. The first section illustrates the manner in which NQ switched from signing ASL to cueing English and vice versa and also some of her reasons for doing so. For this analysis I used data from video clips taken when NQ was younger as well as the videos from the family visit.

In ASL, repeating a sign two to three times creates a durational inflection that can be added to some root morphemes to show that an event is recurring (Klima and Bellugi 1979). For example, the sign AGAIN can be repeated three times to indicate that something occurs frequently. Interestingly, NQ cued "again" and repeated the word three times in a video clip taken when she was seven years old, as illustrated in this example:

EXAMPLE 5

One day, I make again, again, again.

She was talking about making peanut-butter-and-jelly sandwiches and was trying to say that she makes them quite frequently. This is a syntactic form of intrasentential dynamic interference in which the ASL durational inflection influenced her cued English utterance. Dynamic interferences are short-lived intrusions of one language on another language (Grosjean 1992). This type of syntactic intrasentential dynamic interference was not observed in the data of NQ when she was ten years old. However, more naturalistic data are necessary in order to claim that it occurred only during the period in which she started to acquire her second language (cued English).

At seven years of age, NQ codeswitched to ASL during cued English utterances when she appeared unsure how to cue an English word or was unsure of an English morpheme/lexeme. This type of codeswitching was most frequent in the video clips of NQ when she had had only two years of experience with English. In example 6, NQ did not know how to cue the word *toast* or did not know the word in English. As a result, she code-switched intrasententially to her dominant language for the sign TOAST:

EXAMPLE 6

. . . but I do TOAST and butter and jelly almost everyday

This crutch is similar to what Zentella observed in some of the children and adults in her study (1997, 98). NQ wanted to continue to tell her story but was at a loss in English when she wanted to use "toast," so she used codeswitching as a crutch to help her continue. Three percent of the codeswitches in Zentella's (1997) data of Puerto Rican children consisted of crutches employed when a child did not know a word. For example (Zentella 1997, 98):

EXAMPLE 7

Look at her *lunar*. My brother's got one on his *nalga*.
    ("mole")   ("buttock")

In the video of the family visit, sometimes NQ began an utterance in one language and switched to another language because a term was more readily available in it. After the switch, she continued in that language. This is what Clyne (1967) referred to as *consequential triggering*. In the following example, NQ was describing the results of a football game:

EXAMPLE 8

MINNESOTA WON AND . . AND . . Timberwolves lost because . . .

Instead of codeswitching to cued English, NQ could have fingerspelled T-I-M-B-E-R-W-O-L-V-E-S, which would have been equivalent to saying each letter of the word in English (unless she used lexicalized fingerspelling). It is possible she switched to cued English because she did not know how to fingerspell the name of the team but knew how to cue it in English.

Bentahila (1983) also observed consequential triggering from Arabic to French in Moroccan bilinguals. In the following example from Bentahila's article (1983, 236), the speaker began an utterance in Arabic and switched to French for the term *weekend* because Arabic has no equivalent term. The conversation continued in French. The italicized utterances are in French, and the romanized utterances are in Arabic. An English translation follows in quotation marks:

EXAMPLE 9

ana maʕrftš fugaś jžI raši:d qalk *l weekend je ne sais pas quand est-ce que le weekend d'après lui.*
("I don't know when Rachid is coming; he said at the *weekend, I don't know when the weekend is according to him.*")

As mentioned earlier in the chapter, the Arabic–French bilinguals borrowed terms from one language intrasententially while using another language as the matrix language because the speakers preferred to use some terms in a specific language. For example, in Bentahila (1983, 236) the Moroccan bilinguals frequently switched from Arabic to French for medical terminology:

EXAMPLE 10

min ħi:t tatSwwab *le vaccin* baš jšuf l *réaction positive.*
("as soon as he has *the vaccination* in order to see the *positive reaction.*")

When using ASL, NQ often switched to cued English for proper names and names of places. This was illustrated in example 8, in which she codeswitched to cued English for the name of a football team. Another example of this type of codeswitching is:

EXAMPLE 11

. . . GO TO Heidi's HOUSE . . . PRO.1 CAN GO TO Kilpher FOR MY BIRTHDAY

NQ also switched from cued English to ASL for some adjectives that can be produced with facial expressions to add descriptive information to a verb (e.g., WAKE-UP) or an adjective (e.g., TIRED). Codeswitching sometimes imparts a stylistic effect (Zentella 1997). In example 12, NQ used facial expressions in addition to ASL signs to show that her brothers woke up restless and were extremely tired:

EXAMPLE 12

. . . brothers are WAKE-UP so woke up so TIRED so I said . . .

In this example, the codeswitching did not seem to add a stylistic effect. Instead, ASL appeared to have an advantage over English because ASL permits the incorporation of dramatic facial expressions during a role switch to illustrate affect. By signing TIRED, she was able use ASL features such as putting her head and shoulders down, closing her eyes, and making a facial expression that suggested fatigue.

When NQ was unsure whether her utterance was clear, she codeswitched and repeated her utterance. In example 13, she wanted to say "Tornadoes are scary."

EXAMPLE 13

HURRICANE . . . CL:1 (tornado) . . . tornado SCARY

She did not know a sign for tornadoes and signed HURRICANE. Realizing that it was the wrong sign, she then used a classifier to show what she was talking about. Still unsure whether her meaning was clear, she switched to cued English and cued "tornado." Kachru (1977) also observed this type of codeswitching in Hindi–English bilinguals, and Zentella (1997) observed codeswitching for clarification in the Puerto Rican children's conversations.

During pauses, while NQ was thinking of how to finish her utterance, she sometimes codeswitched to fill in the pause and then returned to the matrix language:

EXAMPLE 14

AND NOT HAVE-TO PAY BECAUSE . . my . . MY FRIEND FATHER WORK FOR
AIRPLANE

Bentahila (1983) also observed codeswitching by the Arabic–French bilinguals to fill in a gap while thinking and then returning to the matrix language. This is another crutch that can be used to "cover a momentary lapse of memory" (Zentella 1997, 98). Three percent of the codeswitches in Zentella's study consisted of this type of crutch that was used to aid the flow of an utterance.

Bentahila (1983, 240) also found the Arabic–French bilinguals codeswitched while making comments that were unrelated to the topic they were discussing. The following example illustrates this point:

EXAMPLE 15

f lluwl kanu gaʕ ma kajbanu. *Tu veux un peu de coca?*
("at the beginning they weren't seen at all. *Do you want some Coke?*")

A similar example was mentioned earlier in which a speaker codeswitched when the topic shifted (Zentella 1997). This type of codeswitching was also observed in NQ's conversations. In example 16, NQ stopped cueing to get a drink, and in the second example, she was trying to remind herself of what else she needed to say:

EXAMPLE 16

(a) upstairs to kitchen EXCUSE-ME and I said . . .
(b) that is why I like that . . . SECOND THING MORE SAY

The examples discussed here demonstrate that it is possible to codeswitch between ASL and cued English. More important, NQ's codeswitching illustrates that ASL–cued English codeswitching functions in a manner similar to spoken language codeswitching.

Eight types of codeswitching were identified in this study:

1. A form of syntactic intrasentential dynamic interference in which the syntax of one language appeared in another language being used. This appeared in the data of NQ only when she was seven years old.
2. When NQ appeared at a loss for words in her matrix language, she switched to the other language for the word and then continued in the matrix language.
3. She switched from one language to another for specific words, such as proper names and names of places.
4. In situations in which she felt she did not have the words she wanted in the language she was using, NQ switched to the other language, then continued to use that language for the rest of her utterance.
5. NQ switched to another language when she felt that the other language could better describe what she was trying to say.
6. NQ codeswitched when she was not sure if what she said in one language was clear.
7. Codeswitching was used to fill in a gap while thinking.
8. Codeswitching was used to make a comment unrelated to the topic.

Sociopsychological Motivations

NQ used both situational and metaphorical codeswitching (Blom and Gumperz 1972). In situations in which she was communicating directly with her friend CP, the only person in the room who had a limited sign vocabulary, NQ used cued English. And in situations in which NQ was communicating directly with me, the only person who NQ thought did not know how to cue, she used ASL. In these two social situations, NQ had to choose the language to match the situation—this is what Blom and Gumperz (1972) refer to as situational switching. The following conversation is an example of situational switching. In that situation, NQ's mother (MQ) and NQ were talking about an amusement park. NQ was explaining an amusement park ride to me (PH), and CP wanted NQ to tell me about another ride. NQ codeswitched from ASL when she was communicating with me to cued English when communicating with CP:

EXAMPLE 17

1. MQ [to NQ]: and the monster that one was really bad too
2. NQ [to PH]: PRO-3 GO TO MONSTER WITH ME
3. PH [to NQ]: MONSTER
4. NQ [to PH]: KNOW RIDE CL:2h (round object) CAN SIT THREE O-R SIX PEOPLE IN CL:2h (round object) MANY CL:G (there and there) CL:G (pull seat bar) CL:G (move in large circles) . . LOOK-LIKE GO HIT OTHER CL:2h (round object)
5. MQ [to NQ]: I like the water park
6. CP [to NQ]: remember
7. NQ [to CP]: monster
8. CP [to NQ]: remember
9. NQ [to CP]: Excalibur
10. CP [to NQ]: NO . . YES . . Excalibur
11. NQ [to PH]: E-X-C-A-L-I-B-U-R

Blom and Gumperz (1972) also observed metaphorical switching, in which codeswitching occurred in utterances with the same individual. For example, in the previous conversation CP used some of the ASL signs she knew when she was talking to NQ, and she completed the utterance with a word cued in English (line 10). CP has limited sign vocabulary; nevertheless, she was able to demonstrate some codeswitching. Blom and Gumperz (1972) also observed metaphorical switching in bilingual individuals who had a greater fluency in both languages than CP had in ASL. A better example of metaphorical switching is between two bilinguals, and this was observed in example 18, when NQ was communicating with her mother (an ASL–cued English bilingual):

EXAMPLE 18

12. MQ [to NQ]: who all went snowboarding that time . . it was Jen, that's right
13. NQ [to MQ]: SECOND TIME because because ONE TIME she GO TO Heidi's HOUSE and she hiding out and HAVE snowboard and she . . her . . no . . no . . she HAVE a neighbor THAT HAVE CL:(big hill)
14. MQ [to NQ]: she tried it in her back yard
15. NQ [to MQ]: G: (over there) IT HARD because there . . IT HARD

Using the markedness model (Myers-Scotton 1993), I was further able to analyze the social motivations of NQ's codeswitching. However, I did so with caution because the markedness model is based on the premise that speakers operate within a normative framework specific to their community. Although the model postulates that codeswitching occurs because speakers make choices and not because norms direct them to do so, it is necessary to understand the community's pattern of use to identify what could be considered marked or unmarked codes. With this in mind, I attempted an analysis of the social motivations of NQ's codeswitching. Again, unlike the purpose of the markedness model, the analyses cannot be generalized to other ASL–cued English codeswitching situations until community norms have been investigated.

When I first arrived at NQ's home, NQ opened the door and her mother was behind her. NQ looked at me and was not sure what the unmarked RO set was for a conversation with me. She turned to her mother, who signed WELCOME. Immediately, NQ signed WHO YOU? She chose to use ASL with me apparently because she believed that her mother's WELCOME in ASL indexed to the unmarked RO set for a conversation with me. From her mother's use of ASL to greet me, NQ realized that I was a member of her community and started to converse with me in the language used in Deaf culture.

When NQ was alone with CP, she used cued English, which was the unmarked code in conversations between them. I cannot claim here that the use of cued English is the unmarked code within the cueing community; a study is needed to investigate the markedness of cued English within that community. However, within the microcommunity (i.e., the family and CP) the unmarked code for conversations with CP was apparently cued English. This was understandable because cued English was the only language CP was able to use fluently. As noticed in the dialogue about the amusement park ride, NQ used ASL with me and cued English

with CP. NQ codeswitched to maintain the unmarked RO set for interactions with a perceived ASL-only monolingual and a cued English
monolingual. Similarly, the Spanish–English bilingual children in Zentella's (1997) study were most responsive to the dominant language of
their addressee.

When NQ conversed with her mother, a bilingual, as in the conversation about snowboarding, she used unmarked codeswitching. It is possible that she was switching between two unmarked RO sets with her
mother as a way of showing her bilingual identity (as Paca might have done
in example 3). It is more likely that NQ codeswitched between ASL and
cued English when she was conversing with her mother in front of me and
CP because she did not want to exclude us from the conversation. Therefore, it is possible to claim that NQ was codeswitching in order to be neutral by avoiding committing to a single RO set and excluding one of the
individuals in the room.

CP appeared to attempt to be neutral as well by speaking English
rather than cueing or signing. This could be termed *mode switching* because she switched from cueing English to NQ to speaking English to
both NQ and me. She apparently hoped that this would be an effective
means of communicating with both of us and that we would be able to
speechread her. When I did not understand her, she switched to the unmarked code between herself and NQ to tell NQ what she wanted to say,
and then NQ used the unmarked code between NQ and me to tell me
what CP had said. An example of this situation occurred when NQ's pet
bird flew onto my shoulder:

EXAMPLE 19

CP [to PH]: (speaking—unclear what was said)
CP [to NQ]: it might poop (laughs)
NQ [to PH]: MIGHT POOP (laughs)

Earlier in the chapter, I mentioned that within some linguistic communities, individuals codeswitch to change the topic or to check for clarification. Example 20 illustrates that NQ was using ASL to converse with
me and switched to cued English to check something with her mother:

EXAMPLE 20

NQ [to PH]: YES AND MY MOTHER GO AND THE TRIP IS FREE
NQ [to MQ]: right, it's free? Becky told me.

This type of codeswitch is similar to the codeswitching that occurred between L and T in example 4, in which they were talking with each other and nearby adults (Zentella 1997). L and T spoke English with each other when they apparently did not want to involve the adults in the conversation and spoke in Spanish to involve the adults. It is possible to claim that L and T chose to use the marked code (English) when they wanted to maintain distance from the expected RO set for a conversation with Spanish-dominant speaking adults and switched to the unmarked code to include the adults in the conversation. Similarly, in example 20 when NQ codeswitched from ASL to cued English to check something with her mother, it is possible that she used the apparent marked code for a conversation with an ASL monolingual so that she could momentarily distance herself from the expected RO set between herself and me.

DISCUSSION

The examples from this section illustrate three main points: (1) it is possible to codeswitch between ASL and cued English, (2) the functions of ASL-cued English codeswitching are found in spoken language codeswitching, and (3) it is possible to analyze the sociopsychological motivations of codeswitching between ASL and cued English. However, it is *not* possible to generalize the markedness of cued English or ASL within specific communities based on these very limited data. Additionally, frequencies of specific codeswitching functions were not tallied because more naturalistic data are necessary before we can make any such generalizations.

It would be interesting to investigate the markedness of ASL within the cueing community and of cued English within the signing community. Based on my experience with those two communities, I can hypothesize that using cued English within a signing community would be a marked code choice because it is most likely the unexpected RO set. However, the cueing community is more used to being around cued English and ASL bilinguals and witness conversations in ASL more frequently than members of the signing community witness cued English conversations. Therefore, I assumed that signing within the cueing community would be less marked than cueing in a signing community. In some bilingual communities, unmarked codeswitching is often not predicted (Myers-Scotton 1993; Scotton 1988). In those communities, codeswitching presents intergroup competition or conflict. These are communities in which intergroup tension exists, and language loyalty expresses that tension. I assume that this is also the case within the deaf community. However, these assumptions need to be tested with qualitative studies.

NQ usually codeswitched to the language the addressee understood best. Although this practice was prevalent in the community that Zentella (1997) studied, NQ's experiences were different from those of the Puerto Rican children. In the New York community, parents counseled their children to speak the language that an addressee understands best. NQ's mother did not explicitly teach NQ when and where to codeswitch. However, her mother and other bilingual members of her community did function as codeswitching models. As mentioned earlier, NQ depended on her mother to identify the unmarked RO sets for a conversation with me when I first arrived at their house.

NQ's mother reported that NQ codeswitches frequently at home even though her mother now primarily uses cued English. This is not an unusual situation. In Zentella's (1997) study, immigrant mothers who were Spanish-dominant and knew only a little English and rarely codeswitched often had children who codeswitch frequently at home. For example, in one two-hour recording of a bilingual child and her mother in their home, the child codeswitched fifty-seven times, whereas her mother switched with her only twice.

NQ is aware that she is fluent in two languages. She uses ASL to communicate with members of the Deaf signing community. She uses cued English to communicate at school (via transliterators) and with others who know cued English. She considers herself a member of both the Deaf World and the Hearing World. Although this was self-reported, it was also evident through her codeswitching. Codeswitching is a way of showing that a person has a bilingual identity (Zentella 1997). One summer NQ's family went to the National Association of the Deaf's biennial convention. During the convention, a Deaf adult approached NQ and asked her why she was cueing. At the age of eight, she laughed, "I know two languages, and you only know one!"

Some studies on codeswitching include a structural analysis. For example, Zentella (1997) found that Spanish–English bilinguals do not favor switches between a pronoun and an auxiliary or between an auxiliary and an infinitive; they also do not omit a "personal *a*" (Zentella 1997, 116) or indirect objects. The Puerto Rican children in New York switched primarily at the boundaries of a restricted variety of syntactic categories. Their switches occurred in English and Spanish in every category and subcategory of constituents. It would be interesting to analyze the structural constraints of ASL and cued English to determine the permissible loci for codeswitching.

Although this chapter is not a study of applied linguistics, the findings should be of interest to linguists involved in education and language planning. Most educational programs that use cued English in the classroom are mainstream programs. Only a few use cued English along with ASL or manually coded English. It would be interesting to investigate whether the use of ASL and cued English in the classroom is a successful method for strengthening deaf children's bilingual skills.

CONCLUSION

The results of this case study demonstrate that the codeswitching functions in ASL and cued English are similar to those found in spoken language codeswitching. Cueing enables people to express English in a visual mode and to use English phonology, morphology, and syntax. This study demonstrates that, when used by a bilingual who is fluent in ASL, codeswitching between ASL and cued English exhibits sociolinguistic characteristics similar to those found with people who are bilingual in spoken languages. This study provides additional support that cued English — as another natural form of English and when used in natural interaction — is influenced by similar sociolinguistic factors.

Further studies are needed before the results of this study can be generalized to other cued English bilinguals. In addition, a future study is necessary to investigate the patterns of codeswitching with cued English and ASL native monolinguals present. It would also be interesting to explore the codeswitching patterns of deaf individuals who are fluent in more than one cued language. Additionally, studies on codeswitching between two or more signed languages are much needed. Similar results may be found for deaf bilingual signers who are fluent in two or more signed languages.

REFERENCES

Allen, T., C. White, and M. Karchmer. 1983. Issues in the development of a special edition for hearing-impaired students of the seventh edition of the Stanford Achievement Test. *American Annals of the Deaf* 128:34–39.

Auer, J. C. P. 1984. On the meaning of conversational code-switching. In *Interpretative sociolinguistics: Migrants – children – migrant children,* ed. J. C. Auer and A. Di Luzio, 87–108. Tübingen: Niemeyer.

Baetens-Beardmore, H. 1986. *Bilingualism: Basic principles.* Clevedon, U.K.: Multilingual Matters.

Beaupré, W. J. 1986. Cued Speech as a phonologic model. *Cued Speech Annual* 2:22–33.

Bentahila, A. 1983. Motivations for code-switching among Arabic-French bilinguals in Morocco. *Language and Communication* 3:233–43.

Berendt, H., B. Krupnik-Goldman, and K. Rupp. 1990. Receptive and expressive language abilities of hearing-impaired children who use Cued Speech. Master's thesis, Colorado State University, Fort Collins, Colo.

Blom, J., and J. J. Gumperz. 1972. Social meaning in linguistic structure: Code switching in Norway. In *Directions in sociolinguistics,* ed. by John J. Gumperz and Dell Hymes, 407–34. New York: Holt, Rinehart, and Winston.

Boeschoten, H., and L. Verhoeven. 1987. Language mixing in children's speech: Dutch language use in Turkish discourse. *Language Learning* 37:191–215.

Breitborde, L. B. 1983. Levels of analysis in sociolinguistic explanation: Bilingual code switching, social relations, and domain theory. *International Journal of Social Language* 39:5–43.

Clyne, M. G. 1967. *Transference and triggering.* The Hague: Martinus Nijhoff.

Cornett, R. O. 1967. Cued Speech. *American Annals of the Deaf* 112:3–13.

———. 1975. Cultural and social orientation: Implications in Cued Speech. In *Proceedings of the First Gallaudet Symposium on Research in Deafness: The role of research and the cultural and social orientation of the Deaf.* Washington, D.C.: Gallaudet University.

Cornett, R. O., and M. E. Daisey. 1992. *The Cued Speech resource book: For parents of deaf children.* Raleigh, N.C.: National Cued Speech Association.

Davidson, M., E. Newport, and S. Supalla. 1996. The acquisition of natural and unnatural linguistic devices: Aspects and number marking in MCE children. Paper presented at the Fifth International Conference on Theoretical Issues in Sign Language Research, McGill University, Montreal, Canada.

Davis, J. 1989. Distinguishing language contact phenomena in ASL interpretation. In *The sociolinguistics of the Deaf community,* ed. C. Lucas, 85–102. San Diego: Academic Press.

———. 1990. Interpreting in a language contact situation: The case of English-to-ASL interpretation. Ph.D. diss., University of New Mexico, Albuquerque.

Fantini, A. 1985. *Language acquisition of a bilingual child: A sociolinguistic perspective.* Clevedon, U.K.: Multilingual Matters.

Fleetwood, E., and M. Metzger. 1991. Signed English and cued English: A contrastive analysis. Paper presented at the Deaf Awareness Conference, Dothan, Ala.

———. 1997. Does Cued Speech entail speech? A comparison of cued and spoken information in terms of distinctive features. Manuscript. Washington, D.C.: Gallaudet University.

———. 1998. *Cued language structure: An analysis of cued American English based on linguistic principles.* Silver Spring, Md.: Calliope Press.

Grosjean, F. 1982. *Life with two languages: An introduction to bilingualism.* Cambridge, Mass.: Harvard University Press.

———. 1992. The bilingual and the bicultural person in the hearing and Deaf world. *Sign Language Studies* 77:307–21.

Gumperz, J. J. 1976. The sociolinguistic significance of conversational code switching. In *Papers on language and context* (Working Paper 46), ed. J. Cook-Gumperz and J. J. Gumperz, 1–46. Berkley, Calif.: University of California Language Behavior Research Laboratory.

———. 1982. *Discourse strategies.* Cambridge, Mass.: Cambridge University Press.

Gumperz, J. J., and E. Hernandez-Chavez. 1975. Cognitive aspects of bilingual communication. In *El lenguaje de los Chicanos,* ed. E. Hernandez-Chavez, A. Cohen, and A. Beltramo. Arlington, Va.: Center for Applied Linguistics.

Hakuta, K. 1986. *Mirror of language: The debate on bilingualism.* New York: Basic Books.

Hammes, D. M. 1995. Auditory training and speech production procedures and outcomes: A case study of a child cochlear implant candidate. Master's thesis, University of Minnesota, Minneapolis.

Haugen, E. 1969. *The Norwegian language in America: A study in bilingual behavior.* Bloomington, Ind.: University of Indiana.

Hauser, P. C. 1997. Cued Speech and its role in bilingual education. Paper presented at the Convention of American Instructors of the Deaf/Conference of Educational Administrators of Programs and Schools for the Deaf, June 28–July 2, 1997. Hartford, Conn.

Hauser, P. C., and C. M. Klossner. 1998. Prosody and cued English. Paper presented at Visions '98, May 5, 1998, Gallaudet University, Washington, D.C.

Heath, J. 1989. *From code-switching to borrowing: A case study of Moroccan Arabic.* London: Routledge and Kegan Paul.

Heller, M. 1988. *Code switching: Anthropological and sociolinguistic perspectives.* Berlin: Mouton de Gruyter.

Hoffmeister, R. J., M. Philip, P. Costello, and W. Grass. 1997. American Sign Language Assessment Instrument (ASLAI): Impact of ASL on reading skills in deaf children. Paper presented at the Convention of American Instructors of the Deaf/Conference of Educational Administrators of Programs and Schools for the Deaf, Hartford, Conn.

Johnson, R. E., and C. Erting. 1989. Ethnicity and socialization in a classroom for deaf children. In *The sociolinguistics of the Deaf community,* ed. C. Lucas, 41–84. San Diego: Academic Press.

Johnson, R. E., S. Liddell, and C. Erting. 1989. Unlocking the curriculum: Principles for achieving access in deaf education. Gallaudet Research Institute Working/Occasional Paper Series, 89-3. Washington, D.C.: Gallaudet Research Institute.

Kachru, B. B. 1977. Code switching as a communicative strategy in India. In *Linguistics and anthropology,* ed. M. Saville-Troike. Washington, D.C.: Georgetown University Press.

Kipila, E. L., and B. Williams-Scott. 1988. Cued Speech and speechreading. *Volta Review* 90:179–89.

Klima, E., and U. Bellugi. 1979. *The signs of language.* Cambridge, Mass.: Harvard University Press.

Kluwin, T. 1981. The grammaticality of manual representations of English in classroom settings. *American Annals of the Deaf* 126 (4): 417–21.

Lahlou, M. 1989. Arabic–French codeswitching in Morocco. Paper presented at Annual African Linguistics Conference, University of Illinois, Urbana.

Lanza, E. 1992. Can bilingual two-year-olds code switch? *Child Language* 19: 633–58.

Lee, D. M. 1982. Are there really signs of diglossia? Reexamining the situation. *Sign Language Studies* 35:127–52.

Leybaert, J., and J. Alegria. 1990. Cued speech and the acquisition of reading by deaf children. Paper presented at "De Zevende Sociolinguistiedagan" Brussels, Belgium, 1998. *Cued Speech Journal* 4:24–38.

Leybaert, J., and B. Charlier. 1996. Visual speech in the head: The effect of Cued Speech on rhyming, remembering, and spelling. *Journal of Deaf Studies and Deaf Education* 1 (4): 234–48.

Lucas, C., and C. Valli. 1989. Language contact in the American Deaf community. In *The sociolinguistics of the Deaf community,* ed. C. Lucas, 11–40. San Diego: Academic Press.

———. 1991. ASL or contact signing: Issues of judgement. *Language in Society* 20:201–16.

———. 1992. *Language contact in the American Deaf community.* San Diego: Academic Press.

Mather, N. 1991. *An instructional guide to the Woodcock-Johnson psycho-educational battery, revised.* Brandon, Vt.: Clinical Psychology Publishing Company.

McClure, E. 1981. Formal and functional aspects of code switching discourse of bilingual children. In *Latino language and communicative behavior,* ed. R. Duran, 69–94. Norwood, N.J.: Ablex.

Mühlhäusler, P. 1986. *Pidgin and Creole linguistics.* Oxford: Blackwell.

Myers-Scotton, C. 1993. *Social motivations for code switching: Evidence from Africa.* Oxford: Clarendon Press.

National Cued Speech Association. 1990. Position statements of the National Cued Speech Association. Cleveland, Ohio: National Cued Speech Association [Available: http://web7.mit.edu/cuedspeech].

Poplack, S. 1981. Syntactic structure and social function of code switching. In *Latino language and communicative behavior,* ed. R. Duran, 169–84. Norwood, N.J.: Ablex.

———. 1988. Language status and language accommodation along a linguistic border. In *Language spread and language policy,* ed. P. Lowenberg, 90–118. Washington, D.C.: Georgetown University Press.

Redlinger, W. E. 1976. A description of transference and code switching in Mexican-American English and Spanish. In *Bilingualism in the bicentennial and beyond,* ed. G. D. Keller, R. V. Teschner, and S. Viera, 174–89. New York: Bilingual Press.

Reilly, J., and M. McIntire. 1980. American Sign Language and Pidgin Sign English: What's the difference? *Sign Language Studies* 27:151–92.

Romaine, S. 1995. *Bilingualism,* 2d ed. Oxford: Backwell.

Scotton, C. M. 1988. Codeswitching and types of multilingual communities. In *Language spread and language policy,* ed. P. Lowenberg, 61–82. Washington, D.C.: Georgetown University Press.

Stack, K. 1996. The development of a pronominal system in the absence of a natural target language. Paper presented at the Fifth International Conference on Theoretical Issues in Sign Language Research, September 19–22, 1996, McGill University, Montreal, Canada.

Strong, M., and P. Prinz. 1997. The relationship between ASL skill and English literacy. Paper presented at the Convention of American Instructors of the Deaf/Conference of Educational Administrators of Programs and Schools for the Deaf, Hartford, Conn.

Supalla, S. 1991. Manually coded English: The modality question in signed language development. Master's thesis, University of Illinois, Urbana-Champaign.

Swisher, M. 1985. Characteristics of hearing mothers' manually coded English. In *SLR '83: Proceedings of the Third International Symposium on Sign Language Research, Rome, June 22–26, 1983,* ed. W. Stokoe and V. Volterra, 38–47. Silver Spring, Md.: Linstok Press.

Timm, L. 1975. Spanish–English code switching: *El porque y* how-not-to. *Romance Philology* 28:473–82.

Wandel, J. E. 1989. The use of internal speech in reading by hearing and hearing-impaired students in oral, total communication, and Cued Speech programs. Ph.D. diss., Teachers College, Columbia University.

Woodward, J. C. 1972. Implications for sociolinguistic research among the deaf. *Sign Language Studies* 1:1–7.

———. 1973. Some characteristics of Pidgin Sign English. *Sign Language Studies* 3:39–46.

Zentella, A. C. 1997. *Growing up bilingual: Puerto Rican children in New York.* Malden, Mass.: Blackwell.

Transliteration between Spoken Swedish

and Swedish Signs

Annica Detthow

Interpreting is the process of conveying the meaning of a message from one language into another. Transliteration is the process of representing the discourse of a language in a different form. There is no standardized form of transliteration, but certain strategies used by sign language interpreters have been identified (Winston 1989, Siple 1995).

In Sweden, transliteration is referred to as *Svenskt påverkat teckenspråk* ("Swedish-modified Sign Language"). Utilizing its awareness of the parties' knowledge of Swedish Sign Language, an agency can request that an interpreter use this technique. To my knowledge there are no previous studies of Swedish transliteration. The purpose of this study was to determine whether the strategies found by Winston could also be found in Swedish transliteration.

LITERATURE REVIEW

Interpreter programs in Sweden do not formally address transliteration. Indeed, in Swedish the definition of transliteration is not compatible with the definition of interpretation. For transliteration to be successful, the "receptor" has to know the "base" language (a language's vocabulary and structure). Sign language transliteration is neither standardized nor does it use two natural languages. Siple suggests that there are three reasons that transliteration is a critical skill for interpreters in the United States. The first reason is that "practitioners and consumers have identified transliteration as a key competency needed by Sign Language interpreters." The second reason is that "transliteration responds to the communication preference or needs of a large number of deaf community members." The third reason is that "federal legislation has opened up educational opportunities for deaf people and as a result there is an increased demand for interpreters skilled in transliterating at all educational levels" (1995, 11).

Humphrey and Alcorn define transliteration as "the process of changing a message expressed in a language into a code of the same language" (1995, 397). They discuss the term *transliteration* as it is used in music: "The term is used to refer to the transcription of words from one written language into a phonetic form of English, allowing a singer who doesn't read Italian, for example, to sound out the Italian words by reading them in the transliterated or phonetically based form" (1995, 133).

Frishberg describes transliteration used in a written form as a "transcription of a written text from a non-Roman print or script form to Roman letters" and states that "transliteration permits the reader of Roman print to pronounce but not necessarily understand the source language message" (1986, 18). Transliteration for spoken language interpreters seems to be used primarily to impart a flavor of the source language.

As Larson points out, certain words "are often transliterated in order to retain a sense of time in history. This is often done in novels and short stories. For example, in translating Spanish novels into English, words like plaza and patio are often used as 'token' words to give a Spanish flavor to the translation" (1984, 181).

Cokely suggests that "for spoken language interpreters it is quite obvious that there are two distinct languages involved in their interpreting and hence, it is relatively easy to distinguish the two" (1980, 152). He further states that this distinction is not so clear-cut for sign language interpreters, who "most often function in a situation where there are not two languages involved but rather two forms of the same language" (1980, 152). Cokely likens transliteration to "a spoken language interpreter hearing an English sentence and simply substituting German words for the English words, but retaining English grammatical patterns" (1980, 152).

Frishberg defines sign language transliteration as "the process of changing an English text into manually coded English (or vice versa). An interpreter who transliterates, also called a 'transliterator,' gives the viewer English in a visually accessible form" (1986, 19). However, it is important to note that manually coded signing systems are not the only ways in which deaf and hearing communities come to sign something other than a natural signed language.

For example, Lucas and Valli discuss the outcome of language contact between ASL and English (1992). Their study suggests that language contact between Deaf bilingual people and hearing bilingual people creates a sign variation they call "contact signing." [1] Contact signing has many features that could relate to the process of transliteration, including English mouthing and signing in English word order.

Regardless of the nature of the signing being performed, McIntire suggests that there are problems with transliteration, that it "is often the case that the transliterated message lacks sufficient grammatical information to accurately convey the intent" (1986, 94). Perhaps it is the features of contact signing as opposed to those of manual codes that are behind her observation that "accurate transliteration often requires certain modifications or adjustments to the source message" (1986, 96).

Cokely suggests that "in the early years of the Registry of Interpreters for the Deaf (RID) there was an overt attitude of linguistic superiority and language chauvinism. This attitude did not result from a conscious attempt to suppress the language of the Deaf community, but rather from a lack of knowledge about the complex linguistic situation within the Deaf community and the unique task facing Sign Language interpreters" (1980, 152–53).

Despite the somewhat unique sociocultural context in which deaf and hearing communities interact, Fleetwood and Metzger (1997) propose that transliteration and interpretation in the sign language interpreting community are much like the notion of free versus literal translation that has been an issue for translators for centuries.

Larson points out that translations fall into two main types: *form based* and *meaning based*. She explains that a form-based, or literal, translation may sometimes be of interest, for example, in a study of the linguistic features of a source text. However, as Seleskovitch maintains, generally "a word-for-word translation would only render the primary meaning of the word; the message would not come through clearly and would be little short of incomprehensible" (1978, 7).

Larson suggests that a "literal translation sounds like nonsense and has little communication value" (1984, 15). If a sign language transliteration is a more literal interpretation, and if literal translations tend to be nonsensical, then more research is needed to understand transliteration, both the process and the product.

1. In this chapter *deaf* refers to the audiological condition of hearing loss and *Deaf* to social collectivities; Woodward (1972) first made this distinction.

Winston (1989) discusses the lack of transliteration standardization output and the difficulty of describing the variations in the target form. Her study was the first of a transliterated event, and she found that the interpreter was using identifiable strategies. She also found that the interpreter used "conceptual choice of signs" (meaning-based rather than form-based signs), mouthing patterns of English, addition, omission, and restructuring.

Siple (1995) expanded the concept of Winston's addition strategy by identifying additional categories within this strategy. These include cohesion (such as spatial referencing), clarification (such as fingerspelling and signing for a single word), and modality adaptations (such as the incorporation of visual strategies to convey cultural information).

These preliminary studies of transliteration provide the foundation for further research and a better understanding of transliteration for sign language interpreters in the United States. However, transliteration occurs in other countries, also. One cannot automatically assume the raison d'etre for transliteration is the same in different countries. For that reason it is worth comparing the history of transliteration in the United States with that in other countries such as Sweden.

Quigley suggests that the goal of sign transliteration is not to give a flavor of the source language but rather to clarify the concepts contained in the source material (1965). He says that the term *translating* (which is now called transliterating) refers to Deaf–hearing communication, in which the interpreter recognizes that the "Deaf interlocutors are highly literate individuals who prefer to have their thoughts and those of the hearing people expressed verbatim" (1965, 1). He also suggests that Deaf people need to have their message interpreted because "the lower the verbal ability, the greater is the need for simplification of the presentation" (1965, 1). This view of Deaf people was prevalent in educational institutions in Sweden. The National Board of Education states that "Sign Language is different for the speech of hearing people by the difference in syntactic structure. This hinders and prevents the child from learning speech. . . . Sign Language is only to be used for children with less intellectual ability" (Bergman 1977, 9).

Bergman also discusses Signed Swedish as a tool to enhance the Deaf child's abilities to learn Swedish (Bergman 1977, 157). This idea is endorsed by the Swedish National Association of the Deaf (SDR), which selected a committee to develop a second sign dictionary. In the introduction, two ways of signing are discussed: genuine sign language and Signed Swedish. Genuine sign language combines signs with concepts, and these signs exhibit a word order that is different from that of spoken Swedish. Another way to use signs is to speak and sign at the same time. The signs must accompany the spoken language and follow the same word order as spoken Swedish.

This variation of Signed Swedish is used in the schools for the deaf and in sign language classes for hearing people. The purpose of Signed Swedish is to teach adult hearing people a means of communication that can be acquired in a short time, but above all it purports to help Deaf people learn Swedish (Fondelius 1978, 2).

This brief historical background makes it clear that transliteration in Sweden shares some of the evolution as transliteration in the United States. For this reason it is viable to apply Winston's preliminary findings regarding transliteration in the United States to transliteration in Sweden.

SWEDISH SIGN LANGUAGE

Swedish Sign Language is a language spoken by Deaf, hard of hearing, and hearing individuals in Sweden. The approximate number of Swedish Sign Language speakers is 10,000. Swedish Sign Language is considered to be the native language of Deaf people in Sweden and has been recognized by the government as the primary language in deaf education. Written Swedish is taught as a second language. The existence of Swedish Sign Language can be traced through historical documents to the mid-eighteenth century.

SIGNED SWEDISH

In 1971 the Swedish National Association of the Deaf charged a group of nine people (three Deaf and six hearing) with developing a dictionary of signs to be used in Sweden. The goal was to produce materials for courses in Swedish Sign Language taught throughout the country. Other objectives were to standardize variations of signs used in different parts of Sweden and to adjust signs using the principal of "one word-one sign" (Bergman 1977, 15). A prevalent notion at that time was that Deaf students would learn Swedish if the "one word-one sign" method of signing was used instead of Swedish Sign Language. Research at the Swedish Sign Language Institute at Stockholm University has provided a greater understanding of Swedish Sign Language as a complete language.

The findings from such research on Swedish Sign Language seem to have pushed signed Swedish into disfavor. The current philosophy is to use sign language in schools, TV programs, interpreting, and other settings in which Deaf people participate.

Swedish Sign Language Interpreting

Although sign language interpreting is a service provided throughout Sweden, there is a national shortage of interpreters. The Swedish government has made a substantial number of funds and grants available for interpreting services and interpreter education programs. The goal of all programs is to ensure an adequate level of skills necessary to interpret between spoken Swedish and Swedish Sign Language. Some programs require students to be fluent in Swedish Sign Language before they are admitted to a program, and others do not. Some programs provide extensive language development and continue teaching interpreting skills.

Swedish Sign Transliteration

Transliteration is a concept that is not addressed formally in educational programs of interpretation. One reason for this is that the country's Deaf population and the SDR are gaining respect and recognition. As a result, there is growing support for natural Swedish Sign Language. Another reason is that people do not regard interpretation as a respectable field of study; and so, of course, they do not have interest in one of the "subfields" within interpretation.

In the early days of interpreter training in Sweden—in the 1970s and 1980s—Signed Swedish was considered the appropriate choice for interpreting. However, some hard of hearing and deaf people have an oral, mainstreamed background or became deaf late in life. For various reasons they use a transliterated form of Swedish, and they are provided with transliteration services by interpreting agencies. The concept and the English word *transliteration* is sometimes used by Swedish interpreters to discuss this phenomenon, but when it is referred to in the service sector, it is usually described as "Svenskt påverkat teckenspråk" (Swedish-modified Sign Language). The term *transliteration* has been used in Swedish literature in a study of the psychological and social work environment of sign language interpreters (Lundberg 1981). Transliteration services are usually determined by knowledge of the individual consumer's needs and self-identification.

THE TRANSLITERATION STUDY

Methodology

The data for this study were collected from an informant who is an experienced Swedish interpreter. The informant is Caucasian, male, and fully bilingual. He has been a professional interpreter for 15–20 years. The informant was given the task of transliterating a spoken Swedish text to Swedish signs. The informant had not had formal training nor had he studied transliteration techniques. The source text was a recording of a Swedish radio program that was broadcast in Sweden. The text included a monologue, a narrative text describing the "Deaf President Now movement," and a dialogue with a sign language researcher discussing language use in hearing and Deaf communities.[2] The data were collected using a video camera in a home setting during the informant's visit to the United States.

The informant had not heard this particular text before but was familiar with the subject. The speed of the text presented to the informant was somewhat fast, and the informant addressed this problem. This did not affect the overall data collection except for the omission of certain passages, which can be attributed to the speed and density of the text.

Data

The recorded data were transcribed in three segments: the source language text, transcription of the manual signs, and the mouthing pattern. A non-idiomatic English translation is provided for better understanding of the source text.

2. Ideally, the data would have been gathered in a more formal setting and with a live audience. Due to the very small number of Swedish Sign Language users in the United States and the lack of Swedish Sign Language interpreters there, however, data could not be collected in that manner.

The transliterated Swedish signs are glossed using small capital letters (BESÖKA OLIKA LEKTIONER). The Swedish mouth movements (besöker olika lektioner), are in upper and lowercase, and are shown with or without an existing sign equivalency.

RESULTS

This preliminary study indicates that the same strategies identified by Winston appear in Swedish Sign transliteration. In both studies sign choices are consistent with the interpreter's goal of conveying a more accurate meaning. In both studies source language words are mouthed (to preserve their form) while a sign conveys the meaning. Both studies have instances of mouthing patterns related to the sign rather than mouthing the word from the source language. Features of signed language, such as space, negations, and indexing, were also found in the Swedish transliterations.

Comparison of Sign Choice Strategies in ASL and Swedish Sign Language Transliteration

Winston's definition of a conceptual sign choice is the use of a sign — rather than a literal translation of the source language words — to convey a meaning. Winston found that transliterators used this strategy of matching meaning in individual signs rather than using a lexical correspondence (1989, 156). Table 1 shows examples of conceptual sign choice found in both sets of data.

Mouthing

Another strategy Winston found was the use of mouthing associated with the sign, rather than the spoken word. Mouthing was identified in the Swedish transliteration data as well; as shown in table 2, the mouthed words could correspond with either the signed or spoken utterance.

Grammatical Additions

Another strategy Winston discusses is the use of ASL features that the transliterator adds to render the output more grammatical. Some of the

TABLE I. *Transliteration Techniques: Conceptual Sign Choice*

	Signed	Mouthed
Spoken English		
"for speech varieties that correspond *to* solidarity"	WITH	
"it looks like *everyone*"	YOU-(plural) A-L-L	
"because it doesn't *work* as well as"	SUCCEED	
"could you *make it up?*"	INVENT	
"and *turn it in* so you can get credit for it"	GIVE-TO-ME	
Spoken Swedish		
som meddelade sig med varandra **genom** *tecken*	MED	
("who communicated with each other **through** signs")	("with")	
men alla **nyttjade** *sign, teckenspråket*	ANVÄNDA	
("but all **used** sign, sign language")	("use")	
det erkänt **framför** *allt*	SPECIELL	
("it is recognized especially")	("especially")	
att forskning har **bidragit** *till*	HJÄLPA	
("research has **contributed** with")	("help")	
Source word (spoken)		
"brilliant"	SMART	brilliant
"wonder"	PUZZLE	wonder
Source word (spoken)		
universellt	INTERNATIONAL	universellt
("universal")	("international")	("universal")
med	OCH	med
("with")	("and")	("with")

Note: Spoken and signed English are examples from Winston (1989, 156–57).

additions are space, directional verbs, and negations using headshaking; these are shown in table 3. Other additions found in the Swedish data were sentence boundaries indicated by eye-blinking and role-shift in the dialogue part of the text.

Omission

Winston suggests omission as a fourth strategy, in which portions of the source text are omitted in the sign output. Examples of this strategy

TABLE 2. *Transliteration Techniques: Mouthing*

Source word (spoken)	Sign	Mouthed
"appear"	SHOW-UP	show up
"data sheet"	DATA PAPER	data paper
"normally"	MOST TIME	most time
välvillig	POSITIV	positiv
knöt an	ANKNYTA	anknyter
komplext	KOMPLICERAD	komplicerat

Note: Spoken and signed English are examples from Winston (1989, 156–57).

are the consistent omission of conjunctions, prepositions, and pronouns that are not important to the message. Examples of such omissions were found in the Swedish data (see table 4), although the Swedish informant was inconsistent in the use of this feature. A possible explanation could be the speed of the source text. Certain parts of the data indicate that the source message is redundant, and omitted passages are obviously due to the lack of processing time. Other omitted segments might be explained by the code switching to the English lexicon in the source text. The code switching is perceived by the interpreter as language interference and requires additional processing. Winston's study discusses the omission of

TABLE 3. *Transliteration Techniques: Grammatical Additions Identified in the Swedish Data*

Type of Addition	Source Text	Swedish Mouth Movements	Swedish Trans-literation
Space	*ledningen, dessa tjänst-män och de övriga* ("officials, these officers and the others")	ledningen andra	LEDNIGNEN ("left") ANDRA ("right")
Directional Verb	*min medicinska syn-punkt på dövhet* ("my medical opinion on deafness")	jag då med min medicin syn	JAG DÅ MED MIN MEDICIN SYN *
Negation (by Headshaking)	*de är inte alls barnsliga* ("they are not [negation by headshaking] at all childish")	de är inte alls barnsliga	DE (negation by head-shaking) BARNSLIG

* SYN = directional verb

Type of Omission	Source Text	Swedish Mouth Movements	Swedish Trans-literation
Conjunction	*döv president nu. Sökte* *och fick stöd* ("deaf president now tried **and** got support")	döv president nu dom sökte kontakt	DÖV PRESI-DENT NU DE SÖKTE KONTAKT
Preposition	*love, som att hålla tal* *med som **för** flört eller* ("love which to hold speech with which **for** flirt or")	som tal flört eller	SOM TALA FLÖRT ELLER
Pronoun	*åsikt och inte anlägga* ***min** medicinska syn-* *punkt på dövhet* ("opinion and not attach **my** medical view on")	åsikt och inte ha medicinsk syn på döva	ÅSIKT INTE HA MEDICIN SYN PÅ DÖVA

pronouns. Although some of the data demonstrate such omissions, I found that in most cases the pronouns are retained.

Restructuring

"Restructuring" is the fifth strategy Winston found. The purpose of restructuring is to make the message more explicit, and it is used to replace one grammatical structure with another. This can be a combination of the previously discussed features of strategies or changes of longer utterances. The mouthing patterns follow the reconstructed parts of the output rather than the source text. Restructuring was also found in the Swedish data (see table 5). The mouthing strategy — found in the Swedish data — for disambiguating signs that have several possible meanings is also consistent with the Winston study.

Mouthing

The sixth strategy mentioned by Winston occurs when a sign has several possible meanings, and the mouth pattern is used to disambiguate the output. The purpose then is to convey the intended meaning of the sign.

TABLE 5. *Transliteration Techniques: Restructuring*

Spoken	Restructured to
English	
"which is **voiced 'th'**"	T-H WITH VOICE
"I'm giving you a **week from today** off"	NEXT-WEEK MONDAY
"more friendly and more **trustworthy**"	CAN TRUST MORE
Swedish	
som ett tillstånd, condition som måste botas	HAR BRIST MIN MEDICIN SYN HAR NÅGON BRIST
("as a condition that has to be cured")	(HAS DEFICIENCY MY MEDICAL VIEW HAS SOME KIND OF DEFICIENCY)
nyhets bulletiner	TIDNING MED NYHETER
("press releases")	(PAPER WITH NEWS)
Vad spelar ett öra för roll om bara sinnet hör?	OM BARA SINNET HÖR DÅ SPELAR HÖRSEL ROLL VAD?
("How important is the ear if the mind can hear?")	(IF ONLY MIND HEARS HOW IMPORTANT IS THE HEARING WHAT?)

Note: Spoken and signed English are examples from Winston (1989, 161).

TABLE 6. *Transliteration Techniques: Mouthing*

English		Swedish	
Signed Utterance	Mouthed Translation	Signed Utterance	Mouthed Translation
RELATE-TO	correspond/associated	ACCEPTERA	godkänd/erkänd/acceptera
SITUATION	situation/domains	ANVÄNDA	använda/nyttja/utnyttja
MUST	will/should/have to	BILDA	etablera/bilda/skapa

Notes: Multiple mouthed words in both English and Swedish data show variations used by the informants. Spoken and signed English are examples from Winston (1989, 161).

This also requires speech-reading skills and a good command of the source language. Fingerspelling and mouthing of the same word spelled is another way of providing the form of the source language.

CONCLUSION

It is indeed significant that the same strategies found by Winston also appeared in the Swedish transliterations, although the data show that they are used inconsistently. The reason for this inconsistency may be due to the informants' lack of understanding of the process of transliteration. To draw any definite conclusions, future studies should modify the data collection to include an appropriate audience and expand the data with transliteration samples from several informants.

Suggested research areas for the future include an in-depth study of the differences between transliterated and interpreted text. An expanded study might not only reveal the obvious differences in the output but also contribute to a more detailed description of both processes.

Another area of study would be an investigation of the comprehension of an interpreted and a transliterated text. Researchers might also attempt to determine whether these approaches to transliteration are used in other countries or explore how these findings might be used in interpreter education programs.

Interpretation and sign language interpretation are still unexplored activities in many regards. It is important to find facts and definitions based on research. Findings need to be made available to the interpreting community, both nationally and internationally, which should then invite individuals to undertake advanced studies so that further learning can take place.

REFERENCES

Bergman, B. 1977. *Tecknad Svenska*. Stockholm: Rosenlundstryckeriet.

Cokely, D. 1980. Sign language: Teaching, interpreting, and educational policy. In *Sign language and the Deaf community: Essays in honor of William C. Stokoe,* ed. C. Baker and R. Battison, 137–58. Silver Spring, Md.: National Association of the Deaf.

Fleetwood, E., and M. Metzger. 1997. What is transliteration, anyway? Paper presented at the Florida Registry of Interpreters for the Deaf, Tampa, Fla.

Fondelius, E. 1978. *Teckenordbok*. Borlänge, Sweden: Sveriges Dövas Riksförbund.

Frishberg, N. 1986. *Interpreting: An introduction*. Silver Spring, Md.: RID Publications.

Humphrey, J., and R. Alcorn. 1995. *So you want to be an interpreter: An introduction to sign language interpreting*. Amarillo, Tex.: H and H Publishers.

Larson, M. 1984. *Meaning-based translation: A guide to cross-language equivalence*. Lanham, Md.: University Press of America.

Lucas, C., and C. Valli. 1992. *Language contact in the American Deaf community*. San Diego: Academic Press.

Lundberg, J. 1981. Att vara teckenspråkstolk: En studie av teckenspråkstolars psyko-sociala arbetsmiljö. Stockholm: Stockholms Universitet, Psykologiska Instutionen.

McIntire, M., ed. 1986. *New dimensions in interpreter education: Task analysis, theory, and application.* Silver Spring, Md.: RID Publications.

Metzger, M. 1999. *Sign language interpreting: Deconstructing the myth of neutrality.* Washington, D.C.: Gallaudet University Press.

Quigley, S., ed. 1965. Interpreting for deaf people: A report of a workshop on interpreting. Washington, D.C.: U.S. Department of Health, Education, and Welfare.

Seleskovitch, D. 1978. *Interpreting for international conferences: Problems of language and communication.* Washington, D.C.: Pen and Booth.

Siple, L. 1995. The use of addition in sign language transliteration. Ph.D. diss., University of New York, Buffalo.

Winston, E. 1989. Transliteration: What's the message? In *Sociolinguistics of the Deaf community,* ed. C. Lucas, 147–64. San Diego: Academic Press.

Woodward, J. C. 1972. Implications for sociolinguistic research among the deaf. *Sign Language Studies* 1:1–7.

Part 3 **Multilingualism**

The Education of Deaf Children in Barcelona

Rosa M. Bellés, Pepi Cedillo,

José González de Ibarra, and Ester Molins

HISTORY OF DEAF EDUCATION IN BARCELONA

The history of the education of deaf people in Spain is little known both within Spain and abroad. For example, the Scientific Commission on Sign Language of the World Federation of the Deaf (1993) reports that even the inception of deaf education in Spain is unknown.

Sixteenth, Seventeenth, and Eighteenth Centuries

Deaf education in Spain is generally believed to have begun in the six-teenth and seventeenth centuries with the tutoring of deaf children of roy-alty and the aristocracy. Two noted teachers of that time were Pedro Ponce de León and Juan Pablo Bonet; Bonet also created the fingerspelling alpha-bet (Bonet [1620] 1992). Documents archived in large educational cen-ters assist us in reconstructing the history of deaf education and the Deaf community because those centers contributed to the appearance of sign language and with it the characteristics of that signing community.[1]

In the eighteenth century, deaf education in Spain was similar to that in other European countries. Fundamental questions regarding language were asked: Is language innate or acquired? Are those who are deprived of language human? After infancy, is it possible for a human to learn lan-guage? If so, under what circumstances can it be learned? These issues were debated in scholarly centers and in the philanthropic societies of the Age of Enlightenment, and they fostered the patronage of studies and charity work intent on proving either the innatist or environmentalist position. Wild children, not uncommon at that time, became important subjects of study for demonstrating both of these arguments (Itard 1801; Lane 1984).

1. In this chapter *deaf* refers to the audiological condition of hearing loss and *Deaf* to social collectivities; Woodward (1972) first made this distinction.

Religious questions were also asked: Is one who has no language worthy of God? Will one who has never heard the word of God (and is therefore unable to confess) be able to achieve salvation? With a relationship between language, mind, and faith thus established, humanitarian institutions were created to attain the salvation of deaf people by educating them.

The archives of the old school of the deaf in Barcelona indicate that in the late eighteenth century, canon Joan Albert Martí initiated the education of the deaf citizenry in order to attain their salvation (Bellés 1993; Llombart 1991; Perelló and Tortosa 1978). Martí asked City Hall for a location in which to set up his school. On February 4, 1800, the government agreed to provisionally cede part of the Saló de Cent and to cover the expenses of sheltering the deaf children who attended Martí's school.[2] The education of deaf people was thus begun in Barcelona by city government and has been linked to it ever since by its perceived civic nature.

Nineteenth Century

On March 27, 1802, the Real Escuela de Sordomudos de Madrid (Royal School of the Deaf-Mute in Madrid) was founded (Perelló and Tortosa 1978). By 1817 the Barcelona school had been named the Instituto de Sordomudos de Barcelona (Barcelona Deaf-Mute Institute). Public interest in achieving salvation for deaf people via education was obvious and in agreement with other institutions of the time, even those in other European countries. Public presentations were arranged to demonstrate the capacities and abilities of both the pupils and their teachers. For instance, an advertisement in the newspaper *Diario de Barcelona* on March 5, 1817, informed readers that "admittance to the [exhibition in] City Hall will be granted only on Saturdays that are not a holiday" (Perelló and Tortosa 1978). Similarly, a document in Barcelona City Hall reflects the impact on the audience of such public demonstrations: "[T]here were shed tender tears by many of those present, for the joy of witnessing how those poor destitutes showed a degree of instruction and culture that seemed achievable for them" (Llombart 1991). Throughout the nineteenth century a similar beneficial-religious approach was the rule.

2. The Saló de Cent is the royal hall in the Barcelona City Hall.

In the two centuries since its foundation, the center for the deaf in Barcelona has changed its location and name several times. It has been called the Instituto de Sordomudos; Escuela Municipal de Sordo–Mudos de Barcelona; Escuela Municipal de Ciegos, Sordomudos, y Anormales de Barcelona; Centro Municipal Fonoaudiológico; and other names. Obviously, there have been significant changes in the curriculum and methodology employed, but it was the Milan Congress of 1880 that had the most profound impact on not only the Barcelona educational institution but those of other Mediterranean countries as well.

Oralist teaching prohibits the use of sign languages in educating deaf children and causes sign language to become hidden within the schools. In the late-nineteenth century, educators often refused the status of "language" to sign language, spitefully calling it "mimicry." The establishment and acceptance of oralism led to a perception of deaf people as people without a language or, at the very least, as people suffering language disorders. Such a clinical rehabilitation model was generated from the Milan Congress, but its influence was and still is very strong in Spain. Having serious consequences for deaf people, the oralist model played a pivotal part in the evolution of sign language and the development of the Barcelona Deaf community. Similarly, even the devaluation of sign language has influenced the Deaf community, which used the term "mimicry" until just recently.

PRESENT-DAY SIGN LANGUAGE AND THE DEAF COMMUNITY

Nowadays both the Deaf community and its language have a social presence in Barcelona. In the city there is a burgeoning perception of Deaf people as a bilingual and bicultural minority whose heritage and culture are expressed by a visual–gestural language. The cultural–anthropological model (Skliar et al. 1995), in radical contrast to the clinical–rehabilitation model, is beginning to show some vitality. Let us consider a few examples.

One or Two Sign Languages?

For several years now, the existence in Spain of two sign languages has been promoted. One of them is the Catalán Sign Language (LSC); the other is Spanish Sign Language (LSE). The former is signed in the autonomous community of Catalonia, where Barcelona is located, and the latter in the rest of Spain.[3]

Sign languages have been commonly repressed in Spain in educational contexts, but not in associations for Deaf adults. Because sign language is hidden in large schools, individual institutions have developed their own vernacular, or dialects. This has led to a considerable fragmentation, so deep and wide that deaf people can identify the school someone attends just by seeing that person sign.

Clearly, therefore, noticeable differences exist between LSC and LSE. But because until now there has been very little linguistic research on sign languages in Spain, the differences between LSC and LSE are not well cataloged. Indeed, we are not even sure whether we are justified in referring to them as two languages.

We do know that the evolutions of oral languages and sign languages are independent. However, we believe that the bilingual situation existing in Catalonia between oral languages (both spoken Catalán and spoken Spanish are the country's official languages) may influence decisions about sign languages. That is, a parallelism is being established that might be stated as follows: In Catalonia, Catalán is spoken, and this language is different from Spanish. Thus Catalonian sign language must also be different from the sign language used in the rest of Spain.

Research on Sign Language and the Deaf Community

In our country linguists have only recently become interested in sign language; until 1992 there were just three or four dictionaries compiled by deaf people from various parts of Spain (Pinedo 1981, 1989; Perelló and Frigola 1987). In 1992 the first general description of LSE was published by a linguist (Rodriguez 1992). So far, research has centered around conventional psycholinguistic fields (compilation of dictionaries, description

3. Although Spain has been organized into autonomous "communities" since it became democratic, the communities vary with regard to their legal and administrative authority. Catalonia, for instance, may determine its own educational system provided it follows the legal framework devised by the national government.

of sign language, acquisition and development of sign language by both deaf and hearing children with deaf parents, comparison of language acquisition by deaf and hearing children, dyad interaction between mothers and children, etc.).

At present there are several research teams connected with universities (Universidad de Barcelona, Madrid, Santiago de Compostela, and others). These teams include Deaf people and are linked to the corresponding associations in their area. Nevertheless, not a single university has a department or grant money available specifically for developing a curriculum that focuses on the language or culture of the Deaf community.

Moreover, sociological research is also scarce. The most consistent study was done through the Inter-Sign European project, which analyzed the educational, employment, and social situations of 367 people from eighteen to sixty-nine years of age, residing in Madrid (Diaz-Estébanez et al. 1996).

Official Recognition of LSE and LSC and the Right to Access to Social Information

In 1994 the Catalonian Parliament promoted the knowledge and use of LSC. In addition, the Spanish government is currently formulating an answer to a petition to establish and recognize LSE. This formal request was made in 1997 by the Social Policy and Employment Commission of the Spanish Congress.

The right of deaf people to have access to information by modern communications technology is not yet regulated. A few advances have been made, but much remains to be done. A few television channels occasionally have specific programs in sign language and some regular programs, particularly newscasts and movies, are captioned. However, the interpretation of oral language into sign language is implemented only when a deaf person is invited to a discussion or interview. Television channels that provide teletext include a section to report on the activities of Deaf associations.

To facilitate interpersonal communication between deaf and hearing people, in 1998 a system of phone intermediation was begun throughout Spain. At the same time in Barcelona—in compliance with a law promoting accessibility and elimination of barriers—municipal information services were provided with telephones that deaf people could use.

Associations of the Barcelona Deaf Community

Deaf associations play an important role as essential elements in the community life of Deaf people. Such associations are a forum for interaction, for organizing activities, and for using sign language; in a word, they are the source of Deaf culture. Kyle describes them as "the very heart of the village of deaf people" (1990, quoted by Diaz-Estébanez et al. 1996).

Associations have long been a tradition in Barcelona. In 1909 the first association of Deaf people, the "Sociedad de Ayuda Mutua," was founded. Today there are four. In 1979 the "Federación de Sordos de Catalunya" (FESOCA) was established, uniting Deaf associations from throughout Catalonia. In turn, FESOCA participates in the "Confederación Nacional de Sordos de España" (CNSE). In 1995 FESOCA began publishing a bimonthly journal called *InfoSord;* the organization also hosts a website and provides an e-mail information service.

More recently a number of entities have been formed whose members are Deaf people or people who belong to *solidarity communities* – which include both deaf people and hearing people who are involved in the deaf community and who share the same ideology (Skliar et al. 1995). These new groups include the Asociación de Intérpretes de Lenguas de Signos de Catalunya (Association of Interpreters of Sign Language of Catalonia), created in 1991; the Asociación de Comunicación Visual y Lengua de Signos de Catalunya (Association of Visual Communication and Sign Language of Catalonia), created in 1994; the Asociación de Profesores de Lengua de Signos Catalana (Association of Teachers of Catalán Sign Language) and the Asociación de Padres de Niños Sordos de Catalunya (Association of Parents of Deaf Children of Catalonia), both created in 1996; the Asociación de Investigación de Lengua de Signos Catalana (Association of Research of the Catalán Sign Language), created in 1997; and the Centro de Difusión Audiovisual Verde, Amarillo, y Azul (Center of Audiovisual Diffusion Green, Yellow and Blue) and the Escuela de Lengua de Signos Catalana (School of Catalán Sign Language), both legally registered in 1998.[4]

All of these associations are currently collaborating with an autonomous television network on a plan to incorporate LSC into a children's television program. Deaf children respond very favorably to finding their own language promoted through this important medium of communication.

4. Our thanks go to Esther de los Santos for generously providing the establishment dates of every association.

PRESENT-DAY EDUCATION OF DEAF CHILDREN IN BARCELONA

Integration

In the mid-seventies discussion focused on finding the most adequate educational context for deaf people: Was it a center exclusively for the deaf, or was it integration? Very well received in a number of European countries, the integrational approach reached Barcelona through the diffusion of a number of integrational experiences that took place in Italy.

In principle, the integration of deaf pupils into mainstream schools began in private educational entities, but in 1981 this was put forth as the official model by a public institution then called Centro Municipal Fonoaudiológico de Barcelona.

Since 1981 oralism and integration have been the two primary approaches that have guided the planning of educational opportunities for deaf youth in Barcelona.

Toward a Bilingual Model

However, in specialist journals of psychology of the mid-eighties, a number of articles on sign language — particularly American Sign Language — appeared. And in 1987 the first book was published that pointed out the value of sign language in the development and education of deaf children (Marchesi 1987). The book had a great impact on deaf education professionals, some of whom considered it anathema, whereas others visualized the possibility of introducing certain changes into their practice.

Indeed, some educators in Barcelona, in addition to using oral language, started introducing signs into their communications with deaf youth. Thus, for a time there was bimodal intervention — until the parents' association requested bilingual education for their children.[5] Because of both this request and the educators' strong belief in the benefit of LSC for development and training, the educational authorities of Catalonia introduced changes in the educational model for deaf youth.

5. At present this association manages a grant from the European Union in which more than 300 hearing relatives of deaf schoolchildren in Barcelona and nearby towns participate in LSC classes. It has also sponsored meetings on bilingual education, and it publishes and distributes to interested families a quarterly bulletin on bilingual teaching (APANSCE 1999).

During the 1997–1998 term, the school administration approved three different models of education for deaf children aged three to sixteen years, who were required to attend school. The administration also affirmed the right of families to choose the type of educational methodology they preferred for their children. Those models resulted from a combination of two linguistic models (bilingual and monolingual) on the one hand and from the type of placement of deaf pupils within an educational context (integration into either an ordinary school or a special center for the deaf) on the other. For the moment, these options are available only in Barcelona. Specifically, they are:

- *Oral model.* Deaf pupils are mainstreamed into ordinary schools.
- *Bilingual model* (LSC and Catalán). Students may choose either of two environments: a special school only for deaf pupils or a center of joint education with both deaf and hearing pupils.

Table 1 shows the number of deaf pupils educated in Barcelona from 1996 through 1999 in the oral and bilingual educational models.[6] The center columns correspond to the current periods of compulsory education (essentially, ages three through sixteen). The data suggest that the greatest number of deaf pupils was educated by the oral method in integrated ordinary schools. The data also show that from 1996 through 1999, the number of pupils participating in the bilingual model in joint education steadily increased.

The greatest challenge is to ensure that families with very young deaf children recognize the value of beginning their children's education in a bilingual model while the children are still quite young. It appears that these families regard the bilingual option as desirable for their children when the youngsters reach the age of six years and, later on, at twelve years. Unfortunately, this means a belated bilingualism with serious repercussions for the education and development of deaf children.

Institutions

At present the Barcelona center that pioneered deaf education in Spain has given place to two institutions. The first institution is the Centre de

6. We have no data on the educational development of deaf children and youth who attended under the bilingual model (LSC and Catalán) of a special school only for deaf pupils.

	Cycles of the Existing Educational System							
	1st Cycle Preschool Education (0–3 yrs.)		2nd Cycle Preschool Education (3–5 yrs.) & Primary (6–12 yrs.)		Secondary Education (12–16 yrs.)		Totals	
School Terms	oral	bilingual, joint education	oral	bilingual, joint education	oral	bilingual, joint education	oral	bilingual, joint education
1996– 1997	7	1	76	8	25	4	108	13
1997– 1998	6	0	82	19	32	7	120	26
1998– 1999	6	0	77	23	26	13	109	36

Recursos Educatius per a Deficients Auditius de Catalunya Pere Barnils, known as CREDAC Pere Barnils.[7] The second is the Centre d'Educació Infantil i Primària (Kindergarten and Primary Education Center), also known as CEIP Municipal Tres Pins.[8]

The CREDAC Pere Barnils provides itinerant speech therapists, who service the three educational models in Barcelona. Here, also, audiological and psychopedagogical diagnoses are made, families are oriented, educational material is produced, and so on. The CEIP Municipal Tres Pins is a mainstream school. It is where the bilingual model for joint education of deaf and hearing pupils was developed.

7. The CREDAC Pere Barnils is an institution run jointly by the Departament d'Ensenyament de la Generalitat de Catalunya and the Institut d'Educació de l'Ajuntament de Barcelona.

8. CEIP is the name given to public centers in Catalonia that provide the three educational levels of the second cycle of preschool and the six levels of primary education.

Since the 1984–1985 school year, young hearing children have shared the CEIP Municipal Tres Pins with deaf children under the oral modality. Through reflection, analysis, and evaluation of the types of educational attention developed since that time, educators have redefined the educational model for all pupils with serious deafness.

In 1992 the educational community, represented by the Consell Escolar,[9] approved the Projecte Educatiu de Centre,[10] which gave priority to the educational needs of deaf pupils (González de Ibarra and Molins 1998; Cedillo 1999). The two main features of the project are joint education and bilingual intervention — Catalán Sign language (LSC) and the Catalán language — for deaf pupils. The project supports maximum development of the deaf pupils' capacities for language, which are the concern of professionals from the CREDAC Pere Barnils.

In the 1994–1995 school year, for the first time, a small group of deaf three-year-olds embarked on bilingual schooling in a joint system for both hearing and deaf students.

Joint Education of Deaf and Hearing Pupils

Joint education groups deaf pupils together with hearing children in the same grade level. The school is a frame of normalized education providing deaf pupils with the means required for their personal, emotional, intellectual, linguistic, and social development.

Primary Goals of Joint Bilingual Education

The primary goals of joint bilingual education are:

- To establish respect and cooperation among a variety of pupils, with both hearing children and deaf children in the same classroom

9. The Consell Escolar is the governing body for primary schools, and is composed of a representative team of teachers, parents, service personnel, and city officials.

10. The Projecte Educatiu de Centre is a document that defines the educational program of each school and must be approved by the Consell Escolar.

- To ensure the access of deaf pupils to maximum information so that they can develop in all spheres and within a framework that guarantees plurality and normalization
- To potentiate maximum curricular development for every deaf child, with the referents of the standard curriculum and the dynamics of the classroom
- To foster the full participation of deaf pupils in all of the school's activities (festivals, pedagogical outings, workshops, etc.)
- To ensure that each child achieves a maximum level of competence in written and spoken language as appropriate
- To adjust and diversify the organization and functioning of deaf pupils through teachers' participation in training activities and consultation with a team of psychopedagogical advisors

Bilingual Education: LSC and the Catalán Language

Bilingual education assumes the compatibility of two different languages for joint teaching situations, in our case LSC and the Catalán language, both valued and used to different degrees by the educational community of the school. Bilingualism starts with the basic assumption that deaf children are natural users of a language that responds entirely to their capacities of understanding and expression: sign language. It allows them to acquire language in a normal manner from a chronological point of view. Therefore, we regard sign language as deaf pupils' first language (L1) of communication and learning.

The bilingual program also incorporates the learning of our community's language, that is, Catalán, both written and spoken. The written language appears as a second language (L2), and the children learn it by exploring and interacting with written texts. They also experience situations that permit them to share their knowledge of the written language and the real world with their classmates. This methodology is based on the psychogenetic theories of E. Ferreiro and A. Teberosky (1982) and the constructivist proposals widely developed in Spain by A. Teberosky. The teaching methodology adopted by the school for deaf children is oriented specifically toward this paradigm and aspires to meet the needs of our pupils (Bellés 1989, n.d.; Bellés and Molins 1999a, 1999b; Bellés, Cedillo, and Molins 1999). The deaf children's individual characteristics define the type of attention they receive in learning the spoken language.

The curriculum for the deaf pupils uses as reference the Projecte Curricular del Centre (PCC),[11] which aims for the highest degree of educational achievement and promotes attitudes of egalitarian treatment and respect for the rules of sociability, solidarity, and cooperation between deaf and hearing children.

Organization of the Educational Model

The most significant features that facilitate the development of the educational project are the groupings and the professionals. Deaf pupils in each grade are incorporated into groups of hearing pupils of the same age. The average numbers in such bilingual classes are four deaf and twenty-one hearing children.

The groups of deaf children function differently, according to the specific and curricular needs of the group members. Likewise, the distribution of time spent studying sign language and spoken Catalán is determined by the specific needs of the deaf pupils and the type of activity or the curricular area to be developed.

The professionals intervening with deaf children include the following:

- The classroom teacher, who has a basic knowledge of sign language. She is responsible for teaching the pupils and planning the activities jointly with the other professionals in the groupings.
- The teacher of the deaf, who is fluent in sign language. She works with deaf pupils in the classroom group and the specific group. As "coteacher," she interprets all discussion into sign language to ensure that all of the deaf students have complete access to all information generated in the classroom; she teaches sign language (using a vocabulary that is appropriate for the activity at hand, with special expressions and signs applicable spontaneously, etc.); she teaches the core curricular areas when working with deaf children in specific groups; when necessary, she anticipates and augments the material being taught in the ordinary classroom.
- The LSC teacher, who is a Deaf teacher and who teaches sign language. She works with the pupils on aspects of their identity as deaf people and on the culture of the Deaf community.

11. The Projecte Curricular de Centre is a document that defines the curriculum of each school and must be approved by the Consell Escolar.

- The speech therapist, who is responsible for the oral language instruction of deaf children. She works with students individually, in pairs, or in small groups, and stimulates the learning of talk and hearing through corporal and musical rhythms (verbotonal methodology) and through the use of audiovisuals.
- Deaf monitors of groups, who are responsible for nonacademic activities (noon leisure breaks, lunch breaks, and afternoon workshops).

The Pupils

In 1999, the school had 185 hearing and 23 deaf children distributed into six groups, to which deaf children who can function on different educational levels have access. At present the 12.4 percent of registered deaf pupils is distributed as follows:

- First course, second cycle of preschool education: one deaf child
- Second course, second cycle of preschool education: four deaf children
- Third course, second cycle of preschool education: three deaf children
- First course of primary education: three deaf children
- Second course of primary education: six deaf children
- Fourth course of primary education: one deaf child
- Fifth course of primary education: five deaf children

All the deaf pupils in the school have hearing parents. Only two of the pupils joined the school at three years of age with a prior knowledge of sign language. Others also joined the school when they were cognizant of LSC, but they were older. Most of them, however, had their first contact with LSC and other deaf people on beginning their schooling. Joining the school helps the deaf pupils to encounter an LSC atmosphere, and this allows them to discover "the world of names": their own names as well as names of their schoolmates, their educators, and common objects.

Once this awareness has been attained, the school's priority is to create and "christen" both deaf and hearing students with sign names. Indeed, the task of finding names for the twenty-five pupils is not at all easy! It is the deaf LSC teacher who promotes the creation of sign names and looks after the youngest deaf children joining the school.

The hearing pupils use some signs in their communication with their deaf schoolmates. In 1998 LSC classes for the hearing children were held, but only for that year. The fact that there is only one deaf teacher limits the school's ability to offer such classes, even though the families of the hearing children do want it. Indeed, a study in Italy confirms that having hearing children learn sign language influences a school's curriculum with reference to values (such as acquiring greater respect for deaf people and affording a greater possibility of interacting with them); it also affects the spatial and cognitive development of hearing children (Capirci, Cattani, Rossini, and Volterra 1997, 1998).

EVALUATION, NEEDS, AND CHALLENGES

Evaluation

Because in 1998–1999 the class of deaf pupils who initiated the bilingual joint education model was at only the second level of primary education, we were unable to conclusively appraise the project at the CEIP Municipal Tres Pins. However, research has begun that will evaluate the developing educational model and identify those aspects requiring future improvement. The investigation will examine various aspects of the model, such as the acquisition of LSC and learning of written Catalán; social interaction among the children during both formal teaching and spontaneous leisure activities; and the teaching method and the linguistic model presented by the LSC teachers. The latter aspect includes their activities in different educational contexts, defined as (a) the presence of the two languages, (b) the composition of the learning group, and (c) the curricular objectives and content and the attitudes of the teachers and the pupils' families.

To undertake such research, it was necessary to develop elaborate instruments for gathering data because no similar model of bilingual teaching currently exists in Spain. Data were gathered on the seventeen children who began their schooling under the school's present educational model and also on the school's teachers and parents.

However, the students' personal and educational experiences have been remarkable. For example, the development demonstrated by these pupils is highly satisfactory when compared with the work done by deaf children who were educated only in the oral language. Such pupils show a great interest in learning and participating, both when they are in the classroom with their hearing schoolmates and when they work in their group with other deaf pupils. Their levels of acquisition of LSC, of general curricular material, and written language are considerably higher than those found for deaf pupils in earlier years. There are even children who show a desire to speak orally. This is a surprising fact for other speech therapists who continue being oralist, but we feel that it is easily explained. When deaf children become able to communicate, acquire sign language, and thus develop both intellectually and emotionally (when they observe that their differences are now respected), they are also ready to learn another language and wish to do so.

Another very important fact that also contrasts with our previous experience is that the bilingually educated deaf children are very happy, sure of themselves, and emotionally more stable than those from earlier classes who were educated only orally.

Moreover, LSC is wholly accepted by the school's entire educational community. One of the purposes of this educational project is to achieve equality of opportunities between deaf and hearing pupils. To accomplish this, the different educational contexts offered by the school are being revised. For example, the school's literary and artistic festival (organized annually on the Sant Jordi holiday) now includes a prize for writing couplets and poetry in LSC (Molins et al. n.d.).

With regard to the continuity of the bilingual model in secondary education, the school administration agreed to continue the educational project of the CEIP Municipal Tres Pins. In the 1997–1998 school year, the Institut d'Educació Secundària Consell de Cent (Secondary Education Institute Consell de Cent, or IES) began functioning as a center for bilingual secondary teaching on joint education of both deaf and hearing adolescent pupils.

In a wider context, a sizeable number of the school's teachers have already shared their experiences with others through workshops, articles, interchanges, and so on. This exchange is having a remarkable impact on other professionals involved in the education of deaf children in Barcelona. Currently, it is no longer an "anathema" to discuss the merits of bilingualism even if there still are professionals who disagree with such education.

Needs

Despite the relative newness of bilingual education in Spain, two areas must be addressed. First, bilingual education requires a greater number of signing deaf teachers, but in the whole of Catalonia there are at present only four, and they are "strategically" distributed among different centers in order to promote more bilingual experiences. The way to provisionally solve this problem would be to incorporate deaf adults—without teacher qualifications—into activities that are not strictly formal. Likewise, it has been suggested that the Catalonian Deaf Federation, FESOCA, use the school's facilities for some of their activities.

Second, young deaf children need to begin bilingual education as early as possible. Many professionals in charge of the diagnosis of small deaf children and of the guidance of their families greatly resist the bilingual model. This means, as we have already seen, that these children must wait until a later stage of their academic development to enter bilingual education.

Challenges for the Future

Although substantial changes in the education of deaf pupils and in the programs led by the Deaf community have recently occurred in Barcelona, two areas deserve primary attention in the future. The bilingual educational model must be extended into programs that are currently exclusively oral. Regardless of what happens in other countries, in Barcelona we have been able to introduce—to deaf schoolchildren within the scholarship circuit and not from specific centers for the deaf—sign language as a language of teaching and of learning. It would be beneficial to extend—even if only gradually at first—the bilingual experience to a greater number of pupils. During the 1998–1999 school year, only 23.6 percent of the deaf school children in Barcelona from three to sixteen years of age were schooled in the bilingual model, whereas the remaining 74.63 percent received exclusively oral teaching.

We have recently witnessed the administrative recognition of bilingual education for parents so wishing for their deaf children, the creation of associations that support LSC through different channels, the professionalization of interpreters, an increase in the demand for sign language courses, and important methodological changes by adult deaf teachers. These facts suggest that the present situation is not going to reverse itself.

However, all these actions that we hope will spread the knowledge of sign language and promote the rights and the public presence of deaf people may come to a halt unless there is sufficient research that expands the theoretical and descriptive corpus of such languages and unless such research informs the teaching curriculum.

REFERENCES

APANSCE (coord.). 1999. *II Jornadas de educación bilingüe en el niño Sordo (II sessions of bilingual education for the deaf child)*. Barcelona: Ediciones Mayo.

Bellés, R. M. 1989. *Producción e interpretación de textos escritos por niños Sordos pequeños integrados en escuelas ordinarias* (Production and interpretation of texts written by deaf children integrated into ordinary schools). Madrid: CIDE del Ministerio de Educación.

―――. 1993. Los Sordos como paradigma de la diferencia: acerca del lenguaje de signos (The deaf as paradigm of the difference: About sign language). *Revista de Logopedia, Foniatría, y Audiología* XIII, 1:32–39.

―――. 1995a. Presentación: Modelos de atención educativa a los Sordos (Presentation: Models of educational attention to the deaf). In *Monográfico Modelos de atención educativa a niños Sordos,* comp./ed. R. M. Bellés. *Infancia y Aprendizaje* 69 (70): 5–18.

―――. 1995b. Qué dicen los Sordos adultos de la educación de los niños Sordos? Entrevista a R. Boldú, M. Calafell, P. Cedillo, and M. González de la Federación de Sordos de Catalunya (FESOCA) (What do deaf adults say about the education of deaf children: An interview with R. Boldú, M. Calafell, P. Cedillo, and M. González, of the Catalonian Federation of the Deaf). In *Monográfico modelos de atención educativa a niños Sordos,* comp./ed. R. M. Bellés. *Infancia y Aprendizaje* 69 (70): 61–74.

―――. n.d. La construcció interactiva de l'escriptura en nens i nenes Sords petits mitjançant la dactilologia (The interactive construction of writing by small deaf children by means of fingerspelling). In *Suports: Revista Catalana d'Educació Especial i Atenció a la Diversitat,* Universitat de Vic-Eumo editorial.

Bellés, R. M., P. Cedillo, and E. Molins. 1999. El signo personal y el nombre propio: Aportaciones a la enseñanza de la escritura desde la práctica educativa bilingüe (LSC y catalán) con niños y niñas Sordos pequeños (The sign-name and the proper name: Contributions to the teaching of writing from bilingual educational practices [LSC and Catalán] with small deaf children).

In *Enseñar o aprender a escribir y leer? II,* coords. F. Carvajal and J. Ramos Sevilla, 15. Publicaciones del MCEP, col. Colaboración Pedagógica.

Bellés, R. M., and E. Molins. 1999a. El trabajo de los periódicos con adolescentes Sordos (The work of newspapers with deaf adolescents). In *I Simposio Nacional Sobre la Lecto-escritura en las Personas Sordas,* comp. ASSC. Madrid: Fundación ONCE y CNSE.

————. 1999b. Aportaciones a la enseñanza del lenguaje escrito desde la práctica bilingüe (LSC y catalán) desarrollada en educación conjunta (Contributions to the teaching of written language from the bilingual practice [LSC and Catalán] developed in joint education). In *Lenguaje escrito y sordera: Enfoques teóricos y derivaciones prácticas,* ed. A. B. Domínguez and C. Velasco, 137–59. Salamanca, Spain: Publicaciones Universidad Pontificia de Salamanca, col. Bibliotheca Salmanticensis, estudios 216.

Bonet, J. P. [1620] 1992. *Reducción de las letras y arte para enseñar a hablar a los mudos (Reduction of letters and art for teaching the mute to talk).* Madrid: CEPE.

Capirci, O., A. Cattani, P. Rossini, and V. Volterra. 1997. La lingua dei segni come seconda lingua nella scuola elementare (Sign language as a second language in the elementary school). *Psicologia Clinica dello Sviluppo* 2:301–11.

————. 1998. Teaching sign language to hearing children as a possible factor in cognitive enhancement. *Journal of Deaf Studies and Deaf Education* (spring): 135–42.

Cedillo, P. 1999. CEIPM Tres Pins. In *II Jornadas de educación bilingüe en el niño Sordo* (II Sessions of bilingual education in the deaf child), coord. APANSCE. Barcelona: Ediciones Mayo.

Díaz-Estébanez, E., D. Salvador, M. J. Serna, A. M. Vázquez, J. C. Ferrer, J. M. Serna, and M. Valmaseda. 1996. *Las personas Sordas y su realidad social. Un estudio descriptivo* (The deaf and their social reality. A descriptive study). Madrid: Ministerio de Educación y Ciencia.

Ferreiro, E., and A. Teberosky. 1982. *Literacy before schooling.* Portsmouth, N.H.: Heinemann.

González de Ibarra, J., and E. Molins. 1998. CEIPM Tres Pins. In *Experiencias bilingües en la educación del niño Sordo (Bilingual experiences in the education of the deaf child),* coord. APANSCE. Barcelona: Ediciones Mayo.

Itard, J. [1801] 1982. *Victor de l'Aveyron.* Madrid: Alianza Editorial.

Lane, H. 1984. *El niño salvaje de l'Aveyron* (The primitive child of Aveyron). Madrid: Alianza Universidad.

Llombart, C. 1991. *De 1800 al CREDAC Pere Barnils: Biografía de dos segles d'atenció educativa a l'alumne Sord* (From 1800 to the CREDAC Pere Barnils: Biography of two centuries of educational attention to deaf pupils). Barcelona: Generalitat de Catalunya–Ajuntament de Barcelona.

Marchesi, A. 1987. *El desarrollo cognitivo y lingüístico de los niños Sordos* (The cognitive and linguistic development of deaf children). Madrid: Alianza Psicología.

Molins, E., P. Cedillo, P. Todolí, and R. M. Bellés. n.d. Los pareados en LSC (Couplets in LSC). Institute of Education of the City Hall of Barcelona. Manuscript.

Perelló, J., and J. Frigola. 1987. *Lenguaje de signos manuales* (Manual sign language). Barcelona: Ed. Científico–Médica.

Perelló, J., and F. Tortosa. 1978. *Sordomudez* (Deaf-muteness). Barcelona: Ed. Científico–Médica.

Pinedo, F. J. 1981. *Diccionario mímico español* (Spanish mimical dictionary). Valladolid: Federación Nacional de Sordos.

———. 1989. *Nuevo diccionario gestual español* (New Spanish gestural dictionary). Madrid: Fomento de empleo a minusválidos, S. L.

Rodríguez, M. A. 1992. *Lenguaje de signos* (Sign language). Madrid: CNSE y Fundación ONCE.

Skliar, C., M. I. Massone, and S. Veinberg. 1995. El acceso de los niños Sordos al bilingüismo y al biculturalismo (The access of deaf children to bilingualism and biculturalism). In *Monográfico Modelos de atención educativa a niños Sordos,* comp./ed. R. M. Bellés. *Infancia y Aprendizaje* 69 and 70: 85–100.

Woodward, J. C. 1972. Implications for sociolinguistic research among the deaf. *Sign Language Studies* 1:1–7.

World Federation of the Deaf, Scientific Commission on Sign Language. 1993. *Report on the status of sign language.* Finland: World Federation of the Deaf.

Part 4 **Language Policy and Planning**

Niños Milagrizados: Language Attitudes,

Deaf Education, and Miracle Cures in Mexico

Claire Ramsey and José Antonio Noriega

"When I woke up, my toe was *throbbing*. I couldn't stand on that foot, much less walk! And there were bite marks—not broken skin mind you, but actual teeth marks! Those marks were *real!* The *bite* was real!" Farrokh insisted.

"Of course it was real," the missionary said. "Something real bit you. What could it have been? . . . The point is, you were really bitten, weren't you?" the Jesuit asked him. "People get so confused about miracles. The miracle wasn't that something bit you. The miracle is that you believe! Your faith is the miracle. It hardly matters that it was something . . . common that triggered it." (Irving 1994)

In all but deaf cultural groups, the appearance of a deaf child is an extraordinary event that must be accounted for. Many "causes" of deafness emerge from cultural accounts that have at best shaky bases in science; even unknown causes wield cultural power, illuminating the mysteriousness of this condition to hearing people. In addition, the deaf child must be dealt with (treated or rehabilitated). All sociocultural groups offer possible solutions to the dilemma that a deaf child presents to the larger group. This information may not be widely distributed because few hearing people have ever met a deaf person. Specialists (physicians, teachers, and audiologists) handle the child's needs on behalf of the group. Accordingly, special knowledge of the practices undertaken to deal with a deaf child is held by only a few members of the group.

One set of common solutions for deafness aims for "unification" of deaf children with the rest of the world, from which they have been isolated. In nineteenth-century North America, deaf people were commonly defined as isolated beings who needed special treatment (training or education) that would "restore" them to society. This theme can still be detected in contemporary U.S. definitions and treatment of deaf children and accounts in part for the popularity of mainstreaming and of spoken languages rendered in signed form (e.g., Signing Exact English and Signed Spanish). A second set of solutions attempts to create equilibrium or order out of the "unnatural" (or "out-of-order") state that deafness brings upon a child; for example, it is common practice to exploit a child's residual hearing. Accordingly, maximizing the use of hearing via hearing aids or auditory training allows the deaf child to use her or his sense of hearing for the purpose nature intended. A child who has "learned to listen" is a child who is no longer out of order.

Not surprisingly, in Mexico themes of unification and of restoring or rediscovering the true nature of the world also appear in cultural responses to a deaf child. In this chapter we describe a set of popular "cures" used with deaf children in Mexico. The treatments take speech as the pathway for restoration or, in Mexican terms, "unification" of the deaf child with "real" people. The initial objective of a cure is to connect a hearing, speaking parent to a deaf child. Through this connection the child can be unified with others and become part of the "real world." A second objective is to take what is "out of order" and restore its order and its nature. Mexican parents refer to children who have been "cured" as *niños milagrizados,* or "miracle-ized children."

This chapter has two primary goals. First, recognizing that knowledge about other cultures and their responses to deafness is limited in the United States, we focus on rituals that are not widely known to North Americans, and that may seem peculiar or at best exotic. We offer descriptions of these Mexican rituals to advance our understanding of the ways other cultures interpret the meaning of deafness. (It is worth pointing out that the objectives of the Mexican cures are not unique. The desire for unification of the different ones with the group and the yearning to restore the true balance of nature to a world in disequilibrium also underlie educational, medical, and rehabilitative practices common in the United States.) Second, the rituals are indicators of beliefs and attitudes toward language and communication — powerful, serious issues in any sociopolitical context. This chapter highlights a straightforward and basic underlying issue in the study of language attitudes: that is, that attitudes about language and communication reveal cultural views about what is required for recognition as a "real" or "normal" person (and by extension, the characteristics that mark a person as *not* a "real" person). From our analysis we come closer to understanding the ways language attitudes underlie our definitions of group membership and of humanity.

This is not a novel topic. Sacks (1989) reports that he was initially drawn to deaf people because he was "haunted by descriptions of isolated deaf people who had failed to acquire any language whatever" (37), a kind of deaf person that culturally deaf people also recognize as disabled. He also recognizes the power of language to unify us, both as a species and in cultural groups when he asks, "What is necessary . . . for us to become complete human beings?" (37). Fasold (1984) reviews language attitude research and notes that language attitudes can be inferred from observing the responses people make to the language and communication features of their immediate social contexts. He also points out a line of logic commonly detected in studies of language attitudes. Although it is possible in the abstract to examine attitudes about various languages and modes of communication, what often occurs is that these attitudes extend beyond the language to the users of the language. Accordingly, examinations of language attitudes are simultaneously also studies of attitudes toward people, their group membership, and the characteristics that differentiate genuine group members from those who do not completely qualify as genuine members of the group. Finally, language attitude, language variation, and language choice research—which underlie measures of "solidarity" in sociolinguistic research—acknowledge the unifying function of language.

One might argue that the situation we are examining is not, on the surface at least, about choices between two languages or attitudes about two languages. Rather, for the parents in our research, the choice appears to be between speech and the unnatural lack of language and communication ability that they perceive in their deaf children's lack of speech. Tabouret-Keller (1997) reviews the complex metaphoric links between language and identity and suggests that because speech itself is a physiological act "with organic associations" to other life-supporting acts such as breathing and eating, speech and language are "easily confused with life itself" (317). Language is not only the bridge between individual and social identities, it is the "existential locus" (324) of human beings. Despite the starkness of the "choice," the values and attitudes underlying the desire for spoken language as a marker of identity are identical to those that underlie the more commonly described issues in the study of language in society (e.g., choices between "high" and "low" varieties of one language or between two languages with unequal status).

The social fact is that your language and the way you communicate is your best—perhaps your only—direct path to other "real" people. The parents in this study—in part because they are loving parents, in part because of the sociopolitical context of educational opportunity for deaf children in Mexico, and in part because of the culturally defined obligations of parents to children in Mexico—sincerely want the best for their deaf children. In essence, they want them to be unified with the other members of human society.

BACKGROUND

The practices described in this chapter will seem highly "unscientific" to North American readers, although in the Mexican context, "an intricate interlocking relationship between historical forces, socioeconomic structure, religion and health" (Finkler 1985, 11), the cures have a secure and meaningful cultural niche. First, the rituals reported to us rest upon cultural and religious recognition of the nature of miracles, in particular, an understanding of the time element involved with asking for and waiting for miracles to occur. Although the rituals carry a sense of promise, those who participate also know that miracles impose a condition of waiting for the hoped-for outcome. Symbolically, the miracles that modern Mexican parents of deaf children seek have their antecedents in the miracles of Christ in the distant past. Nonetheless, few of the parents expect that miracles of such surprising magnitude will occur in modern times. Conventionally, they believe that these miracles occurred only once—the original time. They know that the antecedent miracles of Christ do not assure us that miracles will occur today at our bidding. Rather, the Biblical miracles make it possible for them to hope that contemporary miracles can take place. Accordingly, asking for God's intercession in modern times means that parents understand that they will likely have to wait for the outcome to unfold—perhaps for a long time, perhaps forever.

Second, it is critical to emphasize that we are describing phenomena that are not isolated or random acts of fantasy but integral parts of the world of folk or popular medicine well known to Mexicans and to Mexican-Americans. They are embedded in the economic, political, and cultural realities of life in contemporary Mexico. In the medical anthropology literature, several types of healers are reported in Mesoamerican cultures (see Finkler 1985; Huber and Anderson 1996; Trotter and Chavira 1997). As with many social institutions in contemporary Mexico, folk medicine is a blend of pre-Conquest practices and beliefs and the well-elaborated

Hispano-Arabic medical system brought to Mexico by the Spanish after the Conquest in 1519.[1] One foundation of this system is that illness is caused by disequilibrium. Health is viewed as a condition of social, physical, and spiritual balance and harmony, and healers must readjust the imbalance. This principle is carried on in Mexican folk medicine. The second continuing tradition is that remedies can be found in nature, in both plants and animals. Again, the Mexican practice of *curanderismo* (roughly, curing) makes widespread use of remedies from nature.

Within diverse contemporary Mexican medical practice are healers who learn through experience and sometimes apprenticeship to treat "natural" conditions almost exclusively. *Parteras* (midwives), *hueseros* (bonesetters), and *sobadores* (therapeutic masseurs) use physical manipulation and heated oils and herbs in their specialties. Other healers, *curanderos* (curers) and spiritualists, have received a spiritual call or gift (often during a serious illness of their own) and use their gift to recognize supernatural causes for physical and psychological complaints. They employ traditional treatments (material objects with powers and herbal remedies as well as contacts with the spirit world and invocations for divine assistance) to undo the effects of sorcery and soul loss and to treat traditional Mexican cultural ailments, such as *bilis* (extreme unexpressed anger), *susto* (effects of a bad shock), or *empacho* (stomach ailments). The conventional explanation for healers' powers is that although God can heal directly, others can do so in his name, with the abilities God has passed on to them. Although physicians trained in the Western medical tradition represent the dominant treatment paradigm in Mexico, access to them is not equally distributed. In addition, in the Mexican context patients commonly visit both physicians and folk curers. Sometimes this course is recommended by the healers themselves. In other cases, after a physician's ministrations appear to have failed, patients consult a curandero. (In the Mexican folk medical tradition, many physical complaints can have either natural or supernatural causes. Because only a curandero can recognize a supernatural cause and treat it, if a physician's remedy proves ineffective, patients infer that the cause is supernatural and requires a curandero's attention.)

It is well worth remembering that religious rituals, faith healing, and other "miracle" cures are not exclusive to third-world or predominantly Catholic countries. In these contexts they may be more recognized or closer

1. The Spanish system was itself a blend of Greek and Roman Hippocratic medicine with Arabic medicine introduced by the Moors.

to the mainstream than they are in the primarily Protestant United States, where a less elaborated tradition of miracles exists. But descriptions of quackery, trips to charismatic healers, and requests for divine intervention as cures for deafness are widely available among deaf Americans.[2] (See also Lane et al. 1996, 16–17.)[3]

DEAF EDUCATION IN MEXICO'S SOCIOPOLITICAL AND ECONOMIC CONTEXT

Mexico's constitution guarantees equal rights for all. However, the notion that rights extend to people with disabilities is a new one in many areas of Mexican public life.[4] Only limited information is available to the public about deaf people and the condition of deafness, and the number and proportion of deaf people in the Mexican population is unknown (Noriega 1996). Indeed, even deaf people deny that there is one unified deaf community in Mexico. Rather, they report that there are many communities of deaf people and that there is no genuine national-level organization that unites them. (In Mexico City, for example, there are between nine and fifteen communities of deaf people, and all see themselves as distinct from the others.)

In deaf education pedagogy, Mexico is still an overwhelmingly oral country (Adamé 1996; Jackson-Maldonado 1993). Even an oral education is difficult to access, however, because education for deaf children is unevenly distributed over Mexico's states and social groups. There are approximately 100 private oral schools, or "clinics," in Mexico. These

2. A diagnostician at a large U.S. research hospital who has seen several hundred deaf children and their families in her career reports that U.S. parents seek a range of alternative treatments for deafness, including chiropractors, herbalists, and Christian healers who practice the "laying on of hands." Additionally, she reports parents who read the Bible or sit in prayer during their deaf child's audiological and educational evaluations and parents who, through prayer, seek atonement for their past sins that caused God to punish them with a deaf child (Malinda Eccarius, personal communication, January 15, 1999).

3. We are grateful to Barbara Gerner de Garcia for pointing out to us that American Irish-Catholics also request priests' intercession for their deaf children. In her account, parents do this "just in case" it might have an effect.

4. In some areas, such as Tijuana, access and accommodation for people with disabilities are more common than in the interior of the country.

schools are available to parents who can afford to pay for their children's education. In a few of these schools, "Signed Spanish" is used with older children after they fail to become *oralizados* (oralized). Government-supported services are also available in communication clinics. To our knowledge, there are no government-supported communication clinics that provide anything beyond speech and auditory training. Public opinion favors oralism, and Mexican national news magazines (counterparts of *Newsweek* or *Time*) continue to publish "news" articles by physicians and hearing-aid dealers that offer proof that signing deaf people cannot enjoy educational opportunity or economic success in Mexico. Underlying the power of oralism is the implicit belief among communication professionals in Mexico that most deaf children can benefit very little from education and that rehabilitation and medical intervention are their most urgent needs.[5] The arguments mirror those well known to deaf Americans about the requirement of oral abilities for living successfully in the "real" world.

The Constitution of Mexico mandates universal, free, obligatory, secular education. Mexico's system of public education is centralized, with one school board that governs education for the republic and one federal agency that oversees all education, the *Secretaria de Educación Publica* (SEP). In recent years the SEP has developed ambitious goals for educating deaf children in Mexico. Some proposed new programs are modeled on U.S.-like public school deaf education, and there is great enthusiasm for both total communication and for *grupos integrados* (deaf students integrated with hearing students) (e.g., Adamé 1996). However, Mexico is not a rich country. The reality falls far short of the plans. In a country where able-bodied children often have access to only a few years of free

5. Our experiences with an experimental Mexican Sign Language-based laboratory preschool are suggestive. Through the courtesy of the medical directors, the school was housed at one time in a large human communication clinic. White-coated clinic staff politely inquired about our young deaf "patients" and our therapeutic and testing procedures and quietly disapproved of our use of signing and the noise that the preschool classroom infused into the hushed clinical environment. The notions that the children were students and that we harbored expectations about their learning were difficult to explain in these circumstances. Moreover, as in other human communication clinics, the support for oral methods was very powerful; several families who decided to place their deaf children in the signing preschool class were denied future oral and auditory services for their children because of their perceived rebellion.

public education, special education is not a high priority. As has occurred in other countries and in some states in the United States, integrated education, a seemingly cost-effective and humanitarian approach, has replaced or even blocked development of education designed specifically to meet deaf students' needs.

As in the United States, the original school for deaf students was established as a signing school. In the mid-1800s, a French missionary teacher, F. Huet, was invited to Mexico from Brazil, where he had established a school. In 1866, then-President Benito Juarez established the National School for the Deaf (ENS) in Mexico City. Both hearing and deaf people taught at this school, and ENS held a clear position on instruction. The school was intended to serve as a school rather than an asylum of sheltered education or rehabilitation. Students acquired basic literacy and numeracy skills and learned a trade. Reportedly, the medium of instruction was Mexican Sign Language (LSM is a creole of indigenous sign languages already in use in Mexico and the French sign language imported by the French teacher).

Mid-twentieth-century developments in the organization of Mexican medical specialties indirectly contributed to the closure of ENS. In the United States the "medical/pathological" and "cultural" dichotomy in views of deaf people is well-known; historically, the medical view has dominated. In Mexico, the situation is even more extreme. In the 1970s, human communication achieved recognition as a medical specialty, on a par with pediatrics or cardiology. As a result, deaf children (and all people whose conditions result in perceived communication problems) are the legitimate territory of physicians. To a greater extent than in the United States, deafness is the intellectual and professional "property" of the medical world. When ENS was closed, a medical institution was established in its place; symbolically, teaching and learning were replaced by training and rehabilitating. It should never be surprising that hearing parents want their deaf children to speak, but the circumstances in Mexico make it very difficult for parents to even imagine, much less access, alternatives.

METHODS

The data reported here were gathered in two regions of Mexico using interviews embedded in two research traditions. Noriega, a Lacanian clinical psychologist, worked in Mexico City, where he used an extensive interview protocol with forty hearing families with deaf children. Ramsey, a sociolinguist with ethnographic training, worked in the state of Baja California, Mexico and used ethnographic interviews and participant observation to study a group of parents and children from the Tijuana/San Diego metropolitan area. All parents are hearing. Noriega's interviews were conducted in Spanish.

As in any group of participants in Mexican government-supported health and education programs, the parents differed on a range of background variables, including education and socioeconomic status. Moreover, this report describes the beliefs of a group of people and attempts to interpret those beliefs in a cultural context. Accordingly, neither research project used sampling techniques. Rather, we included all participants who came into contact with us. We encountered them because they had sought education and other assistance for their deaf children at one of the institutions we were studying.

RAMSEY'S STUDY

Three major questions organized Ramsey's study of the education of deaf children in the transnational Tijuana/San Diego region. The first two questions focused on classroom language and school settings and on the mix of languages in classrooms with Mexican-heritage deaf children. This work is reported in Ramsey (2000). The third question focused on parent and community perspectives about raising and educating deaf children. Descriptions of folk cures emerged during qualitative research on the third research question.

Ramsey's study was carried out using several qualitative methodologies, including participant observation in classrooms and at parent group meetings, individual interviews, and interview/discussion groups of parents and other family members. To collect and analyze data on Mexican and Mexican-American community perspectives about raising deaf children, Ramsey participated in scheduled parent group meetings at schools and conversed informally with mothers and other relatives of deaf children (grandmothers, aunts, uncles, and godmothers) who attended the meetings. The parent meetings were both videotaped and audiotaped and later transcribed by native speakers of Spanish and English.

Five parent meetings were held (two in the United States and three in Mexico), each lasting approximately two hours. Meetings in the United

States were held in English, Spanish, and American Sign Language (a deaf father participated in the U.S. group). The meetings in Mexico were held in Spanish.

Ramsey's study included a group of twenty-five to thirty informants (not all parents participated in all activities), and even in private face-to-face conversations she did not directly ask about alternative cures. Accordingly, the topic arose only when one of the parents raised it. During discussions, participants exhibited some reluctance to report participation in a religious cure or other alternative treatment, implicitly acknowledging that the cures are controversial even though they are well known. When a cure was mentioned, however, other discussion group members did not dispute its existence. Several people reported that they knew of someone who lived elsewhere who had sought a cure, or that a relative had arranged a visit to a priest, an herbalist, or a spiritualist, so they felt obligated to go along with it. Only one informant provided details about a visit to a curandero; she also reported that when she saw where the treatment was to take place and learned the price, she took her deaf child home.[6]

Cures were mentioned by Mexican and Mexican-heritage parents on both sides of the border; however, the parents who mentioned cures at the U.S. parent meetings were recent immigrants who maintained a large network of family ties in Mexico. These parents claimed that cures were unavailable in the United States. To participate in one of the cures, parents would have to seek assistance from someone in Mexico.

Data Analysis in Ramsey's Study

Meeting and discussion transcripts were reviewed by Ramsey and two Mexican-heritage research assistants, both of whom acquired Spanish as their mother tongue and are English–Spanish bilinguals in adulthood. As noted in Ramsey (2000), the corpus of data provided intriguing information about several dimensions of the education and raising of deaf children in Mexican and Mexican-heritage families.

---

6. In the traditional Mexican folk medicine system, patients reimburse curanderos for their services, but curanderos do not charge for their services, recognizing their skills as a *don,* or a gift from God.

The various dimensions were abstracted from transcripts using text-analysis techniques. When Noriega mentioned his data on cures, Ramsey searched her transcripts and notes for mention of cures. Although folk traditions were not originally part of this study, Ramsey's data on the topic converged with Noriega's.

NORIEGA'S STUDY

Noriega's study (reported more fully in Noriega 1998) was part of a clinical epidemiological investigation conducted at the Mexican Instituto Nacional de la Comunicación Humana (the National Institute of Human Communication, or INCH). The primary objective of the investigation was to examine the strategies followed by hearing families seeking services for their deaf children. As a medical institution, INCH was concerned about the high number of profound, prelinguistic deaf children with late diagnoses (after the age of four years) and about children who might have been identified as deaf early in their lives but who did not receive services immediately. The institute was also concerned about the high number of patients who began services and then failed to continue them. In this context, Noriega considered it relevant to document the actions and the fantasies of the parents during the entire process, from the moment when parents first noted (consciously or unconsciously) indications of deafness through the moment when they initiated formal treatment.

The study lasted eighteen months and included forty families selected according to the following criteria:

- one or more deaf children between the ages of 0 and 14 years
- children with profound, bilateral, prelinguistic, nongenetic deafness
- residents of Mexico City
- maternal access to prenatal services during pregnancy, birth of the deaf child in a hospital, and access to medical services up to the diagnosis of deafness[7]

7. We accepted families who had interruptions of medical services, as long as the interruption was less than six months and interruptions did not occur in consecutive years.

Families were excluded according to the following criteria:

- the deaf child was already receiving treatment
- the deaf child was formally or informally adopted, and the parents and teachers lacked information about the child's development, especially information about the child's hearing loss
- the deaf child had been separated from the parents for more than six months in consecutive years
- the child's deafness was part of a syndrome that compromised higher functions of the central nervous system

We accepted any type of family structure. Families were accepted regardless of the parents' level of schooling, their religious beliefs, their socioeconomic status, and their sociocultural environment. One family dropped out and did not complete the study. The sample of families included in this study is representative of the population that is seen by the diagnostic services office of INCH.

Each family participated in a series of interviews. On average, the interviews took 10 hours, divided into between four and seven sessions, lasting from 90 to 120 minutes. Interviews followed a 247-item protocol that explored the following variables: suspicion of deafness, confirmation of the suspicion, diagnosis, and consultation with a specialist. Within this broad framework, the following specific dimensions of parents' experiences were explored: use of time; type of medical attention received; indications of deafness observed by parents; adaptive and nonadaptive emotional indicators self-reported by parents and reported about their deaf children; development of patterns of family relationships; socialization of the deaf child and the family; information obtained about deafness; expectations with respect to the deaf child's and the family's development; and the child's access to formal education and rehabilitation. Most of the interview items were designed as open-ended or semi-open-ended questions, contextualized in everyday scenarios related to each dimension of study. Each question was explored as deeply as necessary to determine actions and responses that might occur in each context.

Traditional cures were talked about during discussions of the everyday scenarios. If parents did not spontaneously mention a cure, they were asked directly which cures they knew of. Discussions of cures included ways parents learn about them, whether they had participated in or witnessed any cures, the expected and real effects of the cure, and whether traditional cures helped or hindered formal professional treatment. Responses were recorded by hand on the interview guide during each session by a research assistant. Although at times the parents' responses appeared to be off topic, our analysis is that their explanations are not deviations from the topic but associations among topics.

Data Analysis in Noriega's Study

Because of the variety of data types generated by this study, qualitative and quantitative analyses were performed. When interviews were completed, all parent comments were entered in a text database. These entries were divided into those that required statistical analysis (i.e., yes-no responses, numerical responses) and those that required qualitative analysis (i.e., descriptions of actions and fantasies, and the context described by participants). The data on popular cures fell into the second category. Noriega analyzed this category using Barthes's (1957) semiologic system for the study of myths and Lacan's (1966) semiologic-psychoanalytic perspective on symbol use.

Despite our differing methodological and analytical approaches to research, we both collected a number of reports and anecdotes about Mexican parents who sought alternative cures or treatments for their children's deafness.[8] Of the cures we learned about during our research, we focus on three of the most commonly reported: *La Llave* (the Key), *La Golondrina* (the Swallow), and *El Perico* (the Parakeet).

CURES

These three popular cures are well known in Mexico.[9] The treatments reported here have several traits in common. All are centered on the voice rather than on the ears or on lack of hearing. All are rituals of incorporation. That is, each depends upon the use of a ritual object—a key or a

8. Fewer parents reported visits to herbalists, or "naturalistic" healers, although many reported looking to the church, other religious groups, and older family members for support in raising their deaf children.

9. Other treatments were mentioned only once and were not widely known. For example, a Mexican teacher mentioned that she had heard of "country" parents pouring hot lemon juice in a deaf child's ears as a cure. A Mexican mother reported that she had heard that injections of a liquid made of shark fetuses was available as a cure for deafness on the west coast of Mexico.

bird—in the hope that a desired property of the ritual object will be transferred to the child. Finally, each depends upon belief in, and the invocation of the power of, a ritual object, which serves as the medium through which the properties pass to the deaf child.

The Key

In the most basic form of this ritual, a priest or other intermediary inserts a key in the deaf child's mouth and turns it while praying aloud. Although it is possible to use any key, the most frequent version of the ritual requires the key to the *sagrario,* the cabinet where the wine, the host, and the implements for communion are stored. The ritual may be performed at any time, although the night of a full moon and the Saturday before Easter are meaningful dates for many informants. The ritual's most elaborated form requires that a priest conduct the cure on the night of a holy day, using the sagrario key. Most commonly, prayers are said during the ritual and the priest reads a passage describing one of Christ's miracles, generally the resurrection of Lazarus or the wedding in Canaan where Jesus turned the water into wine. This is a very well known cure that can be applied to deaf children or to any child who has perceived problems with language.

In this context, the role of the voice is fundamental. The metric for speaking with one's voice is absolute; the child's voice is either present or absent. None of the parents seriously proposed that their child was willfully remaining silent (although many reported this as a fantasy), and the meaning of the voice appears to be only loosely connected to the silence of the deaf child. Rather it points to God's "silence." If a child's voice is absent, it marks God's abandonment, withholding of love, or punishment of the parents for a past sin. If the child's voice is "recovered," it implies redemption, forgiveness, and consent to a renewed relationship with God. Accordingly, parents do not propose that speech has been generated by the child alone—the child has been a vehicle for God's punishment and, postritual, becomes a vehicle for forgiveness. As noted, belief in miracles acknowledges a necessary waiting period. The existence of a child's voice signifies to parents that their period of waiting and hoping is concluded.

The voice also suggests another theme in the meaning system of parents of deaf children: the elimination of differences between the parent and child. Other religious rites, such as baptism, also mark identity and create an emblem of belonging to a group, a race, or even a species.[10] In the same way, the miracle of the child's voice provides evidence of group membership. No parents ask that the priest revive their child's auditory nerves or that he repair the child's cochlea. They ask that their child speak, as a testament to identity. Because it is in the voice where the difference between parent and child is most evident, the miracle must operate on the voice, not on the ears.

Miracle cures endeavor to reestablish a person or object to its natural state. The key ritual presupposes that the deaf person is out of legal or natural order, with a characteristic that is not "natural" to people. One way that deafness disturbs the human condition is that it creates an enclosed space that has no exit. (If there were an exit, the child's voice would come out.) The use of a key in this ritual indicates a desire to open something that is closed. The deaf child is conceived of as an enclosed space that allows nothing to escape and, even more, entraps what is most valued. The key symbolically opens the deaf child's mouth so that the voice will be able to exit. We suggest that the reason the key is never used in the ears, but only in the mouth, is that the symbolic goal is create an exit, rather than an entry, in an enclosed space.

Very few parents expected a dramatic immediate effect from the ritual. In general, after the ceremony, they reported feeling depressed and tired but "hopeful." They also reported frequently checking their child to determine whether there had been any change or "progress." (In one case, parents claimed that the ritual worked.) We also observed that they were not waiting for anything in particular. They hoped that their deaf child would be able to speak to them, to tell them how she felt, or what she wanted, but at heart they did not hold a very precise idea of the effect of the cure. The parents were interested in communication with the child, but the content and function of that communication was vague in their minds. They fantasized about their child saying "something" but could not express exactly what they wanted the child to say.

The few clearly imagined conversations with the child referred to utterances whose value resides less in the information itself than in the interpersonal emotions conveyed. To say "Mommy," "I love you," or one's

10. Wars against infidels are based on the characteristic of sameness or identity. The same phenomenon operated against the Native Americans during the Conquest. Not until the rite of baptism marked them as "the same" as the Catholic conquerors were the original peoples of Mexico regarded as "also" having souls.

own name are testimonials that a human being resides within the child's body. To be preoccupied with the voice suggests that actually communicating is secondary to the fact that there is someone there to communicate with. In this analysis, they do not wish to open the enclosed space so that the valuable contents can be obtained. Rather, they do it so that the child himself will come into existence.

The Swallow

In this ritual, a swallow is placed in the deaf child's mouth and is held there until the bird's song is heard resonating inside the child's head. It is common to pray during the ritual and to ask for blessings on the bird. Some believe that the bird must sing three times before it is released, others only once.[11] In this ritual a parent serves as the intermediary, and either a parent or the child can hold the bird. In some versions the ritual concludes when the bird is set free. In others, the deaf child is expected to smother and kill the bird. The child's killing of the bird ensures that the transmission of the bird's sound-making ability goes from bird to child, without returning to the bird.

Most of our participants knew of this ritual although it is less common than the key ritual. Parents reported the death of the bird as a possible conclusion of the ritual; no one who had participated in the Swallow reported doing it. Parents mentioned some concrete obstacles to carrying the ritual to its morbid conclusion, reporting that intentionally killing a bird is simply cruelty and that asking a child to participate in such a horrifying act would merely create more suffering. Finally, parents reported that under the circumstances, it would have been almost impossible to explain to their child why it was necessary to kill the bird, much less the reasons why the child himself or herself must participate.

This is not a particularly religious ritual, and a priest is not necessary. Parents themselves can conduct the ritual. Naturally, those who participate are believers, and their prayers invoke God's blessings. In several ways, this ritual is different from the Key. The prayers do not make the swallow into a holy object. Rather, because the swallow already has the desired property (the ability to emit sounds from the mouth), the prayer only facilitates the transfer of these properties to the child. Parents who

11. Over time and in many cultures, three is a "magic" number. In addition, Hand (1980) reports that the swallow is a "magical" bird. In eastern European traditional medicine, the swallow is used to "cure" blindness.

employ the Swallow tend to be oriented toward simple truths of nature—that is, birds sing, people talk. Once the bird helps the child find her or his voice, the deaf child will speak because in nature, that is what people do. In fact, over time the prayers may have been included to reconcile an essentially pagan ceremony with Catholic beliefs, which hold that nature is not parallel with, but subordinate to, God. The use of prayer may help eliminate this contradiction.

The Parakeet

In this ritual, participants place a parakeet near a dish of water. As with the Swallow, parents may serve as the intermediaries. After the bird drinks from the water, the deaf child drinks the remaining water. This ritual can take place with or without prayers and varies in the frequency and the number of times the child drinks the parakeet's water. Some parents reported that once a day was indicated, whereas others believed the child must drink the water three times a day. Others reported a major variation of this ritual: Instead of having the child drink the parakeet's water, the bird's tongue is remove and mashed and then fed to the child. Although some informants were aware of this version of the ritual, no informant reported actually following the treatment to this sacrificial conclusion.[12]

The parakeet ritual was well known among informants and recognized for its impudence. In fact, the one father who reported using it jokingly told us, "It was cheaper than speech therapy." [13] Although transferring the parakeet's properties of "speech" to a deaf child via shared drinking water is certainly economical (especially if you already own a parakeet), the ritual's symbolic features merit discussion.

In this transformation ritual, the child ingests the parakeet's power of "speech" by drinking water. This is the fantasized outcome despite the fact that the "speech" of a parakeet is mimicry without content. The sounds that parakeets emit do not offer meaningful conversation, and parakeets are not conversational partners. What parakeets do offer is a kind of entertainment, where a person can hear her or his own "words" repeated and where the bird can only appear to be a conversant. As conversation,

12. The ingestion of the tongue marks this as a literal ritual of incorporation. Destroying the tongue prevents the "speech" from returning to its source, and, as with the Swallow, we also see the bird as a propitiatory victim.

13. *Sale más barato que la terapia de lenguaje.*

though, the bird's "speech" is doomed to failure because it is only a meaningless reproduction of human speech sounds. In addition, the parakeet's sounds, because they are meaningless, are by necessity decontextualized. Humans are in control, and the human interlocutor supplies everything that makes the sounds meaningful.

An admittedly more sinister analysis is that parakeets offer humans an opportunity to exercise omnipotence over another creature. It suggests training and careful manipulation of reality, where the audible sounds of language are taken for the whole—meaningful interaction between people. This is omnipotence taken to the extreme, somewhat like the delirious omnipotence of Henry Higgins in *Pygmalion,* who wanted to guarantee proper comportment and speech through domination of another. However, this disturbing sense of omnipotence may have deterred the majority of parents from submitting themselves and their children to the Parakeet ritual.

THE CURES: SIMILARITIES AND DIFFERENCES

The Swallow is a clear ritual of transmission; the bird's song in the child's head is the pathway by which the transformation from nonspeaker to speaker is accomplished. Belief in the ritual's power depends upon accepting that the bird's song is a marker of its essential nature. It also requires the conviction that it is possible to fit one being's properties (the bird's singing) to another (the nonspeaking child) since animals and humans are both instruments of nature. Metaphorically, the swallow and the deaf child are like two tuning forks. When one begins to vibrate, the other resonates at the same frequency. Accordingly, the swallow's song, which the child "hears from within," awakens in the child his or her essential ability to make sounds.

In the Key ritual, the child does not actively participate. In the Swallow, in contrast, the child plays an active role. This indicates a theme that was only hinted at in the Key. When the deaf child is considered an enclosed space, the closure is seen as voluntary, and an act of will is necessary to open it. Many parents who reported using the Key ritual at one time harbored the suspicion that their deaf child was intentionally withholding speech and that the lack of speech was voluntary.

The Key does not offer the gift of speech. It only opens the mouth. Although volition is suggested, nothing in the ritual suggests that child is unable to open it and produce sound. The ritual mandates that once the mouth is opened, the child find her voice and express what is in her own power to express. The Swallow works differently. It is a call to the deaf child to recognize her true nature as a "speaker" (with the bird's song as a prompt) and to reacquaint herself with it. In the Key ritual, the will to finally open the mouth comes from outside the child. In the Swallow, it comes from within, once the child recognizes that in nature birds sing and people speak.

Although the swallow is external to the child until it is placed in her mouth, what counts in the ritual is its function inside and the capacity of its song to awaken the child's true nature. The ritual is not valid when the bird sings outside the child's body, but only when it is physically inside the child. The child's participation—holding the bird and putting it into her own mouth—indicates that one true nature (here, of the mouth to speak) wants intuitively to be recognized by the other.

The bird's death prevents two kinds of cycles from continuing. First, the bird is killed to prevent the properties that have been transferred to the child, that is, its speaking voice, from returning to the bird. Reflecting Christian theology, one must die so that the other may live. In this case, the swallow must be silenced so that the deaf child might speak.

In addition, the child's participation (or potential participation) in the bird's death is a symbolic expression of blame for the damage that the condition of deafness does to nature. To bring the child's voice back, someone must pay, although this analysis seems to present a contradiction. Hypothetically, if the child's nature as "a speaker" is truly awakened through recognition of the bird's song, there is no need to kill the bird. Once the essence is awakened, it can be reawakened again and again, it can awaken others, and the original essence, the "voice" of the bird, does not need to be eliminated. What resolves this apparent contradiction is the overlay of a second belief system expressed in this ritual. Like many parents of deaf children in North America, our informants were very anchored in the search for answers and an explanation of why their child was deaf. Virtually all of them reported seeking blame somewhere, and, as with those who participated in the Key, most expressed the fantasy of having done some kind of unintentional damage to their child. Accordingly, operating along with the symbols of nature is the symbolic search for someone to blame for the deaf child and his failure to speak. In this set of symbols, the swallow is a propitiatory victim whose death retroactively undoes the parental damage that was done to the child. The bird is not merely harmed but eliminated altogether, and in this way the "chain" of damage is broken.

The Parakeet equates the child to a trainable but not-quite-human being. In general parents are reluctant to admit that their children are empty objects, despite the cures they seek and the strength of their need to assign blame. On the other hand, though, as in the other two rituals, the Parakeet suggests that to be identified as a genuine human being and a member of one's group, speech, acquired at any cost, is necessary. This marker of identity is so critical that its content, the feature that might supply much more evidence about group membership, is secondary. Although the child's silence is not linked to God's silence as it is in the Key, silence continues to denote the difference between the deaf child and real people. Discussions of these rituals with parents suggest that they cherish the idea that their child's condition—the inability to hear and speak—is a disguise that is temporarily hiding their "real" child, who *can* both hear and speak. Again, this cure is not about the ears or the sense of hearing. Rather it centers on the need to establish identity and to assure parents that there is indeed a "real" person inside the silent child's packaging.

In contrast to the other two rituals, the parakeet's metaphor is not about the bird but about the other participants—the parent who trains the bird to "speak" and the child who incorporates this ability. It is notable that the parakeet ritual was well known to the parents, that many playfully reported that they considered using it, and that most of them ultimately dismissed it, although perhaps not wholeheartedly. Some referred to it with an indulgence that bordered on affection. In this system of beliefs about language and communication, parents can refer to magic or to "rustic," naive believers (with a touch of compassion for their lack of education) without admitting that they share a belief in miracles or that they are ambivalent about the temptation to exercise their own omnipotence. A parent who participates in the Key can gently criticize the parent who obtains a parakeet in preparation for a ritual cure.

The Role of Humor

The three rituals differ in their appeals to humor. The Key is a very serious ritual and lacks all sense of humor. Its execution depends upon a Superior Being, and its meaning rests in part on the Christian tradition of the forgiveness of sins. It unambiguously expresses a set of beliefs that are not properly the subject of jokes. This frequently used ritual places participants in direct contact with a set of profoundly important symbols.

The Swallow, with its suggestion of preconquest paganism and its brutality, also lacks humor. The search for the true nature of things, the desire to restore harmony to a natural system in disequilibrium, and the wish to help the child recognize her or his role in nature through the bird's song are also solemn matters.

The Parakeet, in contrast, is full of humor. In Mexican popular culture, the parakeet is a humorous icon that appears in two forms. One icon is a parakeet disguised as a man. This anthropomorphized parakeet has the human gifts of intelligence and sexuality. He is astute, sly, deceitful, salacious, and erotic. The second parakeet icon is a caricature of stupidity, a living cartoon who learns a word or phrase and is then placed in a situation where he must repeat his words in a shifting context. His "speech" generates error, misunderstanding, and double entendre. Although parents may not consciously recognize the connection between the ritual and popular culture, the ritual can play a liberating role. It allows the expression of an unconscious or semiconscious fantasy—the wish to employ training and the simple force of will to change the deaf child into a being acceptable to society and in balance with nature—in a tolerable way.

Parents, however, cannot explicitly refer to any of these jokes, although the ritual employs their elements. Placing a deaf child in a parakeetlike role unavoidably suggests the disturbing metaphor of the trained pet. This, of course, is also a potential analysis of speech therapy and oral methods of education. It is a costly practice to render a child "nearly normal" on the outside but empty on the inside. Like the parakeet, these children can make speechlike sounds. Unfortunately, they frequently have nothing to talk about.

Using Barthes's schema of the myth (Barthes 1957), we examine both folk cures and medical-rehabilitative cures in more detail in Noriega and Ramsey (1998). In a Barthesian analysis, the social use of myths gives them different weights and functions. For example, a person who decides to seek one of these rituals can still criticize another parent who chooses one of the others. A parent could even employ all three of the cures without feeling contradictory. The relationship between the rituals makes them almost interchangeable. (The same man who snickers at the traditional Maya-Quiché origin myth that Gucumatz created man out of corn can believe with great conviction that God created man from clay.) In addition, as we note in the next section, understanding the common underlying structure allows us to look for continuity between popular curing rituals and those that come to us from the discourse of science.

CONCLUSION

In this chapter we have located supernatural popular "cures" for deafness in both the contemporary Mexican context and in the theoretical context of language attitudes and language and identity. We argue that the widespread use of alternative folk treatments represents nothing more and nothing less than parents acting within their cultural traditions, which themselves are embedded in the reality of educational and economic opportunity in Mexico.

To North American readers, it may seem that we have overlooked the most obvious explanation for the parents' behavior, that they are slowly moving through the "stages of grieving." In this account, of course, employing supernatural cures might indicate either "denial" or "bargaining." In other texts, however, we both argue that the discourse of grieving, so common among North American special educators, is not comprehensible to most Mexican parents and psychologists. When Ramsey mentioned grieving as a possible response to a deaf child in a group of Mexican and Mexican-American parents, one of the mothers asked, in all seriousness, "Grieving for a *living* child?" Another commented, "We don't talk about it that way." When she asked Mexican psychologists about grieving, several were incredulous that this set of ideas had such popular explanatory power among North Americans.[14]

Accordingly, we analyze the folk alternative medical tradition and the place of treatments such as the Key, the Swallow, and the Parakeet using categories that are meaningful in the Mexican context—that the natural and supernatural (including religious) worlds coexist and that people should acknowledge this fact, that speech is a marker of a "real" human being, that speech indicates unity with the social group, and that the way to live in the world is in harmony with nature. The cures we describe all

---

14. We cannot emphasize enough that grieving as an account of the reported data is simply not explanatory. See Noriega (1998) and Ramsey (2000) for discussions of the misapplication of "grieving" to Mexican families.

provide symbolic pathways to these ends. In the general Mexican socio-political context, it would be absurd if most parents did not recognize that they and their deaf child live in a precarious situation of constrained opportunity. With little information about what it means to be a deaf Mexican, parents are even more likely to expect that their child will survive only if she or he has speech and can act like a hearing person.

Furthermore, we find that the three cures and their use also provide examples of behavior from which we can infer attitudes toward language at their deepest level: Speech can represent life, members of groups use language to mark both solidarity and the boundaries of the group, and admission to the group depends to some extent upon language or communication behavior that demonstrates convergence rather than divergence.

It is important here to briefly discuss the interaction of the "miraculous" and the "real," or the discourse of popular cures and the discourse of science. Recall that we met our informants in nonsupernatural contexts. All were seeking medical, rehabilitative, or educational services for their deaf children. (In Ramsey's group of twenty families and extended families, all had enrolled their children in schools that were experimenting with signing. In Noriega's group, all were seeking public "human communication" services; of that group, approximately 25 percent were either using signs or exploring that possibility.) The point is that these parents live in the same world that their Mexican neighbors do. We suggest that North Americans also inhabit a corner of that world.

After the key, the swallow, or the parakeet treatments, an interesting thing happens. Parents undertake the rituals, they wait (as those who seek miracles must do), and during that time the child begins a rehabilitation program or simply matures and develops. Parents begin to note progress in their child. Alternatively, progress of some kind is confirmed by a medical professional. It is never possible for parents to know for sure whether the improvements were caused by the ritual, by the child's development, or by the professional intervention. On some occasions, parents recognize that the changes were indeed brought about by rehabilitation. These parents also commonly say that the rehabilitation was "helped along" by the power of the ritual. Even parents who had abandoned the belief that the ritual had an effect retained the possibility of resorting to a similar folk ritual in the future. Parents even reported willingness to conduct the same ritual again if they believed that it had failed the first time because of their own lack of faith or because they had the ritual performed in the wrong church or by the wrong priest. Even though the majority are destined to face the reality that they were deceived by the ritual, it is difficult for parents to stop waiting for an effect.

Again we emphasize that belief in these rituals does not depend on a particular mood of grief or a particularly fantastical frame of mind. Parents do not see the rituals as either trade-offs or purchases (I organize the ritual, and in exchange I get a hearing child). Rather, the issue is the nature of people and of the world; the belief in rituals provides consistency to the world, and even to deny the belief does not make it go away. The fact that some parents leave behind one kind of myth and take on another indicates only that they are working within the same structure—a system of believing and hoping that forces consistency on the world, a place where the nature of people is to talk and where language and communication mark sameness and group membership.

Like most North American readers, we would be very surprised if the rituals we describe had immediate or even delayed successful outcomes. Still, our final point is this: Like the Mexican parents who seek supernatural treatments for their deaf children, most hearing North American parents of deaf children must also wait for the outcomes of the miracles they are promised by professionals. Nothing happens immediately in North American deaf education, despite the wealth of the nation, the training of our teachers, and the miniaturization of our technology. In our tradition, it is unusual to place faith in miracles. Rather, we maintain great faith in special education methods, medical interventions, and sophisticated hearing aids. Nevertheless, "magical thinking" is common in North American deaf education, where optimism about pedagogy often overwhelms the need for carefully analyzed empirical findings about outcomes.

Attitudes on both sides of the border reveal the extent to which waiting and hoping are built into the structure of conventional educational and rehabilitative practices used with deaf children. Whether we look at Mexican popular rituals or North American educational rituals, we must acknowledge that we have all participated in creating *niños milagrizados* – "miracle-ized" children—out of deaf students.

REFERENCES

Adamé, E. 1996. El Sordo y la lengua (The Deaf person and language). *Psicologia Iberoamericana* 4:57–60.
Barthes, R. 1957. *Mythologies.* New York: The Noonday Press.

Fasold, R. 1984. *The sociolinguistics of society.* New York: Basil Blackwell.

Finkler, K. 1985. *Spiritualist healers in Mexico: Successes and failures of alternative therapeutics.* New York: Praeger.

Hand, W. 1980. *Magical medicine: The folkloric component of medicine in the folk belief, custom, and ritual of the peoples of Europe and America.* Berkeley: University of California Press.

Huber, B., and R. Anderson. 1996. Bonesetters and curers in a Mexican community: Conceptual models, status, and gender. *Medical Anthropology* 17:23–38.

Irving, J. 1994. *A son of the circus.* New York: Ballantine Books.

Jackson-Maldonado, D. 1993. Mexico and the United States: A cross-cultural perspective on the education of deaf children. In *Multicultural issues in deafness,* 1st ed., ed. K. Christensen and G. Delgado, 91–112. White Plains, N.Y.: Longman.

Lacan, J. 1966. *Escritos 1 y 2.* Mexico City: Siglo XXI.

Lane, H., R. Hoffmeister, and B. Bahan. 1996. *A journey into the DEAF-WORLD.* San Diego, Calif.: DawnSignPress.

Noriega, J. A. 1996. Consideraciones preliminares para la terapia psicoanalítica con sujectos sordos (Preliminary considerations of psychoanalytic therapy with deaf patients). *Psicologia Iberoamericana* 4:61–67.

——. 1998. *Tacticas seguidas por familias oyentes para acceder a la atención especializada del niño sordo (Tactics used by hearing families in accessing special services for their deaf child).* Master's thesis, Mexico City. Ciudad Universitaria: Universidad Nacional Autónoma de Mexico, Graduate School, Department of Psychology.

Noriega, J. A., and C. Ramsey. 1998. *Sordera, mitos en serie: Curas populares y médico-rehabilitatorias (Deafness in a succession of myths: Popular and medical-rehabilitative cures).* Manuscript. Mexico City: Grupo Tessera.

Ramsey, C. 2000. On the border: Cultures, families, and schooling in a transnational region. In *Deaf plus: A multicultural perspective,* 2d. ed., ed. K. Christensen and G. Delgado. San Diego: DawnSignPress.

Sacks, O. 1989. *Seeing voices.* Berkeley: University of California Press.

Tabouret-Keller, A. 1997. Language and identity. In *The handbook of sociolinguistics,* ed. F. Coulmas, 315–26. Oxford: Blackwell Publishers.

Trotter, R., and J. A. Chavira. 1997. *Curanderismo—Mexican-American folk healing.* Athens, Ga.: University of Georgia Press.

Sign Languages and the Minority Language

Policy of the European Union

Verena Krausneker

The political demands and requests — formulated in unequivocal terms — by the Deaf community (and their interest groups) in the 1990s served as the impetus for this chapter. The key issue within these demands has been the request for linguistic rights, which one might even call linguistic *human* rights.

From a linguistic point of view, the world's sign languages are minority languages "surrounded" by phonetic languages. Although every country has a Deaf community that uses a national sign language, sign languages are nearly legally recognized in the European Union in only Denmark, Finland, Greece, Portugal, and Sweden (and in thirteen other countries worldwide, according to the World Federation of the Deaf [1998]). In many other countries, because of missing language rights, schooling is still done in a mode that deaf children cannot access, the general level of education is low, and access to higher education is often not provided by the states. Participation in public life, the media, politics, and so on is therefore rather difficult. It is not that deaf people cannot participate because they have an auditory problem; rather, it is because the majority are unfamiliar with the language that deaf people use and interpreters are rarely provided. In the field of social and political work, deafness-related issues are generally dealt with in the confined area of "disabilities," which ignores the important linguistic question of the status and rights of sign languages.

Skutnabb-Kangas and Phillipson extended the notion of human rights to the realm of languages and developed the strong concept of linguistic human rights. They observed: "Often individuals and groups are treated unjustly and suppressed by means of language. People who are deprived of Linguistic Human Rights may thereby be prevented from enjoying other human rights, including fair political representation, a fair trial, access to education, access to information and freedom of speech, and maintenance of their cultural heritage" (1995, 2). This concept is a crucial one in the perception and handling of the question of linguistic minorities. Some of these linguistic human rights are not available to the majority of the world's deaf people.

In this chapter I analyze the minority language policies of the European Union in general and try to localize the position of sign languages in this context. The question we are concerned with is this: Representatives of minority languages have fought hard for certain rights that have now been granted to all European minority language speakers—but not to the users of sign languages. Why? Why does one hesitate to acknowledge that sign languages are also minority languages and that they are also a part of the "rich cultural European heritage," which is so often quoted as being worthy of protection? And why is there a total absence of sign languages in all European Union minority language statistics, networks, studies, guidelines, reports, and service facilities? [1]

THE INSTITUTIONS OF THE EUROPEAN UNION: A SCHEMATIC OVERVIEW

The European Union differs from all previous national and international models. It is founded on treaties among sovereign nations, rather than a constitution that binds individual states (as is the case in the United States). Another unique aspect of this structure is that EU institutions have the power to enact laws that are directly binding on all citizens of EU member nations.

The Union has been described as a supranational entity. The member states have relinquished part of their national sovereignty (although only for those policies that cannot be handled effectively at lower levels of government) to the EU institutions. The Union is inherently evolutionary; that is, it was designed to allow for the gradual development of European unification.

The European Union is governed by five institutions: the European Parliament, the European Council (also called the Council of Ministers),

1. I use the spelling "EU-rope" and "EU-ropean" to differentiate between the political European Union and geographical Europe respectively. I consider it important to clarify that there is still much more to Europe than the fifteen member states of the EU.

the European Commission, the Court of Justice, and the Court of Auditors.[2] The European Council holds at least two summit meetings a year to provide overall political direction. Their major responsibilities are as follows:

- The Council of Ministers is the legislative body of the Union; that is, it passes legally relevant acts in collaboration with the Commission and the Parliament.
- As the executive body, the European Commission pursues community policies and launches initiatives to promote the Union. The Commission has the sole *right of initiative* to submit draft statutes that can be passed by the Council in cooperation with Parliament. The twenty commissioners are each responsible for at least one policy area. Although they are nominated by national governments, they are appointed by Parliament and act in the Union's interest (independently of the national governments that nominated them).[3]
- The European Parliament comprises 626 delegates from the fifteen member countries. The members of Parliament are elected for five years by citizens of the European Union and are supranational; that is, they form political rather than national groups. The Parliament cannot enact laws as typical national parliaments can, although it does have budgetary power and some involvement in the legislative process, depending on the procedure in question.
- The European Council is the highest decision-making body of the European Union. It is composed of the heads of state and government and the Commission president, who meet at least twice a year to provide political direction and overall strategy. The European Council sets the Union's political course in the form of decisions of general principle or work assignments to the council or the commission.
- The Court of Auditors examines the legality of receipts and expenditures and is responsible for managing the Union's budget.
- The Court of Justice is the Union's "Supreme Court." The Court's fifteen judges ensure that the treaties are interpreted and applied correctly by other EU institutions and by the member states. The Court's judgements are binding on European Union institutions,

2. Also see the following website: http://www.europa.eu.int.
3. Fritzler et al. 1997, 39.

member states, national courts, companies, and private citizens and overrule decisions by national courts.

This chapter focuses on the Council of Ministers, the Commission, Parliament, and the European Council.

LANGUAGE POLICY OF THE EUROPEAN UNION

Majority Languages

Since the Treaties of Rome were concluded in 1957, the European Union and its institutions have striven to promote the language rights of member countries. When the Union was established, only four languages were deemed official languages. Additions were made as new countries were admitted to the European Union. Currently, the European Union has eleven official languages (Danish, German, English, French, Finnish, Greek, Dutch, Italian, Portuguese, Swedish, and Spanish; a twelfth language, Irish, has had a special status since 1972). All citizens of the European Union are theoretically entitled to communicate with the institutions in their mother tongue; that is, if it is one of the official languages. Politicians can work in their own languages. In practice these language rights are restricted to the speakers of the twelve languages just listed.

EU citizens and politicians are quite aware of the exceptional quality and importance of this regulation, and many take pride in it. It can be said that the political significance of multilingualism has been recognized and is considered a serious factor, particularly in connection with the important goal of achieving a "single Europe."

Minority Languages

The numerous other languages (e.g., Catalan, Welsh, and Yiddish) spoken in the EU are accorded minority status. Various official reports on the topic place the number of minority languages in the EU at between 40 and 48. According to the estimates, the number of speakers of minority or regional languages in the EU member countries ranges between 40 and 50 million.[4] In relation to the existing 370 million EU citizens—a considerable share—approximately 12 percent use a minority language.

4. Forrest 1998, 27; *European dialogue,* 1; and European Bureau for Lesser Used Languages, *Unity in diversity,* 2.

These counts do not, however, take the sign languages of EU-rope into consideration. Neither can the users of sign languages be found in the statistics. Determining the exact number of signers is no easy undertaking, but if we use the rule of thumb method of calculating, which estimates one deaf person per thousand of the population, this amounts to almost 400,000 people in the EU who are ignored in the minority language statistics.

Legal Matters

There is no legal basis for minority language policies in the EU; there is no compelling legal framework for a budget line; and the EU has no right to launch activities that might have political or legislative consequences in member countries because the field of minority languages comes under the principle of subsidiarity. Directorate General 22 of the European Commission is responsible for minority languages and has the following formulation on its homepage: "Taking into account the responsibilities of the Member States themselves and in full respect of the principle of subsidiarity, any activity having political or statutory impact is ruled out." [5] Nevertheless, there are activities in the field of minority languages.

DIRECTORATE GENERAL 22: EDUCATION, TRAINING, AND YOUTH

The European Commission is made up of individual directorates general. These, in turn, have a pyramid-like structure and comprise directorates and departments. Directorate A, department 4 of Directorate General 22 is in charge of language skills, open and distance learning, and adult education. A subdivision of this department comprising four people is responsible for regional and minority languages.[6] However, this department does not consider itself responsible for sign languages. Richard Howitt is a British Member of Parliament who actively promotes sign languages and the Deaf community. Regarding the EU's sign language policy, he commented, "I do know now that there is the problem that it is stuck in DG 5 [employment, labor relations, and social affairs], where it is seen as

5. *Community action in favour of regional or minority languages and cultures.* Homepage of the DG 22 (May 11, 1999).

6. Commission official. Personal interview, August 1998.

a social policy issue, a welfare issue, a charity issue and that many Deaf people would disagree with that pigeonhole stereotyping of their issue, their needs and their interests." [7]

As Jäger noted: "Concerning oneself with sign language beyond the paradigm of pedagogy for the handicapped is still a highly controversial issue" (1997, 411 [my translation]). This is reflected in the way authorities and states, including the EU, treat sign languages.

BUDGET LINE FOR MINORITY LANGUAGES [8]

A key issue in the EU's minority language policy is the budget line for minority languages. Created in 1983, it is managed by the European Commission. In the first year, the budget amounted to a modest 100,000 European currency units (Ecu), increasing constantly until it reached 1.1 million Ecu in 1991. Since 1993 it has fluctuated between 3.5 and 4 million Ecu. [9]

At the highest level of funding, each country's budget is approximately U.S. $260,000. To gain a better idea of the dimension of 4 million Ecu, consider this quote from a commission report: "Despite the increase, the overall sum is still very modest — from a statistical viewpoint virtually nil in relation to the overall budget of the European Union." [10]

The directorate general that manages this budget states that "the languages intending to benefit from this action are the autochthonous languages traditionally spoken by a part of the population of Member States of the European Union, or of EEA countries. This definition does not include migrants' languages or artificially created languages." [11] The fact that only spoken languages are meant does not clearly emerge from this definition. In an interview, however, the official responsible for regional and minority languages stressed "traditionally oral languages," [12] thus justifying the long-standing rejection of financial support for sign languages.

7. Directorate General 5 is responsible for the "integration of the handicapped."

8. Called B3-1006 (formerly B3-106, formerly 636, formerly 630, formerly 636).

9. One Ecu is equivalent to approximately U.S. $1.00.

10. KOM (94) 602 final, 11.

11. *Community action in favour of regional or minority languages and cultures*, May 11, 1999. Homepage 22, directorate A, department 4. [Available online: http://europa.eu.int/en/comm/dg22/dg22.html].

12. Telephone interview with Profili, March 27, 1998.

Aside from this concise piece of information, I was able to find neither an objective reason nor proof of the permissibility of such procedure.

EUROPEAN BUREAU FOR LESSER USED LANGUAGES

Established in 1982, the European Bureau for Lesser Used Languages is financed 90 percent by the Commission, according to information officer Christian Demeuré Vallée.[13] The bureau generally aims to provide legal and political support with the procurement of resources for projects to promote lesser used languages, to produce and distribute information material to interest groups, and to set up structures to support native languages. The bureau's very existence is an elementary and important signal. Yet as far as I know, it has so far taken no measures or actions whatsoever for sign languages.

MERCATOR

Mercator is an Internet-based network created in 1987 "to promote the interests of the minority/regional languages and cultures within the European Union."[14] It provides the general public with a comprehensive database on the topic of minority languages in the European Union. Sign languages are not mentioned anywhere in the database. My attempts to clarify the reason that this comprehensive overview of minority languages excludes the sign languages of EU-rope (and who I should contact to ensure their inclusion) amounted to nothing more than an animated exchange of e-mails with a representative. Despite my repeated inquiries, the representative would not tell me who is actually in charge of what. The replies I did receive merely explained that "their [sign languages'] characteristics do not match with the languages included in Mercator. The languages included in our network are those which have not been created artificially, in the sense that they have a long historical background.[15] The representative did not react to my objection that sign languages were not artificially created and actually had a long history, nor

13. Personal communication, January 28, 1998.
14. See the following website: http://www.troc.es/mercator/index.htm.
15. Castellanos of CIEMEN, e-mail of March 24, 1998.

did she respond when I cited a resolution of the European Parliament on Sign Languages.

EUROPEAN PARLIAMENT (EP)

The role the Parliament plays in the field of minority language policies is not to be underestimated. Parliament often acts as a mouthpiece for groups with urgent concerns and initiates new budget lines. It acts in various ways with varying degrees of success. For example, it passes resolutions that amount to mere expressions of opinion. Although they are not law, they are still taken seriously and typically result in money for research, teaching, and so on. Such resolutions are often the result of thorough research and can be quite innovative. This was the case with one resolution that was decisive for the passing of a Charter of the Council of Europe[16] and another that paved the way for the creation and extension of a budget line dedicated to minority languages. Interestingly, none of the Parliament's resolutions on minority languages mentioned sign languages. Even the resolution of 1994 (entitled "On the linguistic and cultural minorities of the European Community"), which cites all the resolutions and motions ever passed with anything to do with the subject, makes no reference to the Resolution on Sign Languages of 1988 (discussed below; see appendix A).

INTERGROUP OF LESSER USED LANGUAGES

There are fifty-four nonpartisan intergroups in the European Parliament formed by delegates from various political factions that go about achieving extremely diverse goals with varying degrees of dedication.[17] Established in 1983, the Intergroup of Lesser Used Languages has played a major role in submitting minority language concerns to the European Parliament and supporting them in this forum. Richard Howitt had the following to say on the approach of the Intergroup: "One of the things we

16. In legal and institutional terms, the Council of Europe has nothing whatsoever to do with the EU. Nevertheless, it is the largest, international organization in Europe. The Council of Europe focuses on topics such as democracy, human rights, and culture. To date it has passed more than 150 conventions that become legally effective in the countries that ratify them.

17. Status as of January 28, 1998, according to the Direction chargée des relations avec les groupes politiques, Cabinet du Secrétaire Général.

have been struggling with in the EP [European Parliament] is that other people that are involved in the minority languages lobbying, from the hearing world, the Welsh, the Catalan-speakers, have not really recognized sign languages as minority languages with equal status as theirs. So we haven't been able to get together and get a common argument with them" [18] (1998).

Documents of the Council of Europe

The Council of Europe is the oldest European organization (est. 1949) and comprises forty member countries. It is independent of the EU, and that is why its activities do not compete with those of the community. The Council focuses on topics such as democracy, human rights, and culture. To date it has passed more than 150 conventions that become legally binding in the countries that ratify them.

Because its argument for the exclusion of sign languages is very similar to that of the EU and because two fundamental and comprehensive papers (the "European Convention for the Protection of National Minorities" and the "European Charter for Regional and Minority Languages of the Council of Europe") took effect recently, it is important to briefly discuss the Council of Europe's treatment of the topic of sign languages.

Both of these papers are extremely comprehensive, and neither mentions a minority language by name, let alone a sign language. In my endeavors to interview contact people, EBLUL's information officer suggested I contact administrator Fernando Albanese. Mr. Albanese is Director of Environment and Local Authorities in the Secretariat General of the Council of Europe. Albanese wrote me a letter on sign language that stated:

Article 1 (a) of the Charter gives the following definition:

a) "Regional or minority languages" means languages that are:
   i) traditionally used within a given territory of a State by nationals of that State who form a group numerically smaller than the rest of the State's population; and
   ii) different from the official language(s) of that State; it does not include either dialects of the official language(s) of the State or the languages of migrants.

18. Albanese. Personal communication, February 4, 1998.

Personally, I think that, in the case of the Sign Languages, some of the essential elements required by such a definition are missing:

—the historical character of the regional or minority languages, since the Sign Languages are connected with a handicap and not with the membership to a group that is ethnically, religiously, or linguistically different from the majority of the population of a state;

—the concentration on a given territory, that is a restricted geographical area in a State; the users of the Sign Languages are widespread on the whole territory of a State;

—the difference in respect of the official language(s) of a State.

If I understand it correctly, Sign Languages are a means of communication within any language. Therefore I do not think on the basis of the information in my possession that the Charter applies to Sign Languages. In any case, such a problem was never raised during the negotiations of the Charter.[19]

Mr. Albanese's three arguments as to why sign languages do not fit in with the Council of Europe's paper have something in common: They are all based on erroneous information and erroneous interpretations. The criterion of "historical character" seems to be sufficiently fulfilled in the case of sign languages. Furthermore, the argument that we are talking about a language that is connected with a handicap and not with a group that differs from the majority is questionable. The definition given by Deaf people themselves should be taken into consideration and respected in this context: "Deaf people view themselves as a cultural and linguistic minority. Cultural because they are part of the Deaf community and a minority because they live in the majority society of hearing people" (European Union of the Deaf 1997, 11).

It is true that Deaf people are distributed all over the country and do not live in a defined geographical area. However, the same applies to speakers of Romany or Yiddish, for example, which have already been recognized as minority languages by the EU. (In contrast to Albanese's argument, one might maintain that such a wide distribution of Deaf people is better than ghettoization.) Albanese's third argument is so imprecise that it allows no serious analysis.

19. Personal communication, April 2, 1998.

The first papers of the European Parliament on the topic of sign languages are the motions for resolutions of 1985.[20] They are important because they prompted the parliamentary Committee on Youth, Culture, Education, Information, and Sport to decide that a report on sign languages should be drawn up. Appointed rapporteur in 1986, Delegate Lemass compiled an extensive and precise report that was concluded after one and a half years (after a public hearing of representatives of the World Federation of the Deaf and a discussion of the draft report). The committee unanimously adopted the draft motion for a resolution in February 1988.

Shortly afterward, the "Report on Sign Languages for the Deaf" was submitted, and the motion for a resolution was added to the EP's agenda in June 1988 to be put to a vote. (The resolution can be found in appendix A.)

The *Negotiations of the European Parliament* (1988) precisely record all the statements and happenings in the plenum and paint a picture of the mood of the meeting: A group of Deaf people are in the visitors' galleries, and they are warmly welcomed by the president. An interpreter is at their disposal. Furthermore, the rapporteur uses sign language to begin her speech. All factions agree almost euphorically with the report; even the member of the commission reacts positively. One speaker turns out to be "someone who has had to come to terms with the problem of being hard of hearing for the most part of his life,"[21] and he too fully supports the motion to recognize sign languages. The resolution is voted on after eight speeches. The motion carries, and delegate Lemass closes the session with these words: "This was an important day for the Deaf in our society."

Both the report and the wording of the resolution clearly show that the rapporteur had taken her duties seriously and carried out very thorough research. It was evident that she herself had asked the people concerned about their needs, wishes, and ideas. She had also integrated their responses into her report. It is no coincidence that the first item of the res-

20. I am talking of a motion (Doc. B2-767/85) tabled by delegates Kuijpers and Vandemeulebroucke, who both took an active part in the field of minority languages that is, for example, reflected in the so-called Kuijpers resolution (1987) and in the great number of questions submitted by these two delegates on the topic of minority languages. The second motion is Doc. B2-1192/85.

21. *Negotiations of the European Parliament,* June 17, 1988, 334.

olution calls upon the commission to make proposals to the council concerning official recognition of the sign language used in each member state and also calls upon the member states themselves "to abolish any remaining obstacles to the use of sign language." All other items also reflect the most urgent concerns known today (e.g., interpretation, the media, teaching sign languages, dictionaries, and institutional and funding aspects).

Lemass's report explains that Deaf people did not approve the content of the very motions for resolutions that triggered the report: The demand for the standardization of sign language is clearly rejected by those who would be affected.[22] The next key issue is discussed in paragraph 1.1: "The preferred or only method of communication of the profoundly deaf is usually sign language." The hearing–pedagogic standpoint, whose main concern is the oral assimilation of this deaf linguistic minority to the hearing majority, is concretely dealt with in paragraph 1.2. The Deaf people's own opinion on oralism (oral methods of teaching) is clearly formulated: "The deaf have often been and in places still are denied the right to use sign language." It is stated that oral education has tried to turn them into "pale shadows of hearing people." Integration as advocated by the deaf community depends instead on equal status and mutual respect for signed and spoken languages.

It is also important to mention that the report stated that there are half a million profoundly deaf people in the European Community and that "the deaf are on a par numerically with many domestic linguistic minorities." This fact is significant. Although it does not argue for a definition of "minority" that relies solely on numbers, it makes an important point: *Users of European sign languages are more numerous than speakers of some European minority languages.*

The Lemass report and the resolution could have been pioneering for the European Union and its member states and could still be so for the oncoming processes that are so urgently required. Although a minority-language status for sign languages was "identified as being needed ten years ago by the European Parliament," says Howitt, "in these ten years there have been very few really known major legal changes."[23]

22. The report is therefore very progressive, for an inquiry (by MEP Mezzaroma) was submitted to the Commission in 1997 with regard to the standardization of European Sign Languages.

23. Interview on February 4, 1998.

The report and the resolution have therefore lost none of their relevance to the current situation in many member states of the EU, for the demand for recognition of sign languages is still topical and valid. The passing of a second resolution on sign languages by the European Parliament in November 1998, ten years after the first one, also points to the necessity of change.

Exemplary Documentation of Activities

To document actual measures taken with regard to sign languages and their users, I have collected all the parliamentary questions of members of the European Parliament (MEPs) that have anything to do with sign language or deaf communities: Fifteen parliamentary questions were submitted between 1986 and 1998, twelve to the Commission and three to the Council.[24] I give here an example of the typical discourse such parliamentary questions usually generate:

In 1991 a question was submitted asking for information concerning any action the council was taking regarding the resolution on sign languages. The Council answered that it "has taken careful note of the resolution" and pledges that it will "study with due care and attention at the appropriate time any proposal that the Commission might submit to it, though no proposal has yet been put forward on this matter."[25]

In 1992 the Commission was asked when it planned to submit proposals to the Council in line with the resolution. Their answer showed that the Commission had gathered information and was not as blank on the subject as it was just a while before. Some of its (largely basic) knowledge, which was already displayed in the 1988 report, was passed on instead of a concrete answer. Furthermore, the Commission said that it had "encouraged cooperation with the appropriate European nongovernmental organisations." Also, the commission again pointed out that the World Federation of the Deaf (WFD) was "opposed to harmonization of Sign Languages" or to the creation of a new sign language. The Commission stated that in cooperation with the European Regional Secretariat of the World Federation of the Deaf, it was promoting "the creation of local and regional national initiatives. In addition to organizing meetings, exchanges, and seminars, the Commission provides funding for sign lan-

24. Only the questions that are quoted in this chapter are listed in the references.
25. See question no. 29 by Lomas.

guage interpreters at meetings and is contributing to the publication of a multilingual dictionary of sign language together with a databank." Furthermore, the "training of sign language interpreters has been accepted as a priority under the Horizon initiative for the handicapped and less-privileged."[26]

These answers give an idea of the quality and style of all fifteen answers. All in all, it looks as though some very important and positive activities were developed—if they were really implemented.

Between 1996 and 1997 there were three questions that represent an important development: A special budget was made available for measures in conjunction with deafness. Due to an MEP's initiative, a motion was incorporated in a program to be used "for measures in conjunction with sign language for deaf people." Finally, the Parliament allocated an additional 500,000 Ecu to the program. Subsequently, the Commission, which manages the money, asked the European Union of the Deaf (EUD) to elaborate projects for 1996–1997. In 1996 the EUD decided to use the Parliament's 1988 resolution as the basis for developing the project. In July 1996, the EUD Sign Languages Project 1996–1997 started.

The large-scale project consisted of five parts: (1) a scientific survey of the situation and status of sign languages in the fifteen member states as well as Norway, Liechtenstein, and Iceland; (2) the establishment of national committees, among other things for the support of the survey just mentioned; (3) an information and sensitization program on sign languages; (4) a large-scale final conference in Brussels aimed at presenting the decision makers "with concrete proposals which will serve as the basis for the introduction of further measures with regard to sign languages and their status in the EU;"[27] and (5) a one-day introduction course to sign languages and Deaf culture for hearing people who work in the EU in Brussels.

In 1998 MEP Graenitz submitted yet another question to the Commission. As I was able to collaborate with her on the phrasing of this question and was familiar with all the previous answers to inquiries on this subject, we succeeded in phrasing the question in such a way as to ensure a concrete answer. However, the answer referred to the sign languages project, repeated some information contained in the survey, and emphasized the Commission's support of the EUD. "However," the response

26. See question no. 104 by Lomas.
27. EuroSign Fact Sheet, vol. 1, issue 1, 4.

stated, "the Commission presently does not plan to present any specific proposals to the Council." This one sentence sums up the reason for the inactivity of the entire EU.

CONCLUSION

It is possible to summarize the situation as follows: Silence and inactivity exist not only at the topmost level of linguistic policy and legislation but also at all levels below. Sign languages are apparently not considered minority languages in the EU, especially not by the Commission, which represents the executive body of the European Union. The Commission does seem to have been active in the field of promotion — but little was done in the spirit of the key concern, that is, the recognition of sign languages. There was no change at EU level with regard to the foremost demand of the resolution: recognition of the language and the establishment of the pertinent language rights.

Deaf citizens continue to be regarded as the exclusive concern of those responsible for disabled people, despite their requests, which have been clearly stated for years. Moreover, the official opinion and practice are incorrect from a linguistic point of view and clearly do not reflect the scientific findings of the past few decades that have proven that sign languages are languages in their own right. In the majority of the countries, none of the demands put forth in the 1988 resolution by the European Parliament have been fulfilled. That may be the reason that, in November 1998, the Parliament passed yet another resolution on sign languages.

The following synopsis summarizes the current legal situation of sign languages at both the supranational EU-ropean level and in the individual countries.

- Denmark: Official recognition of sign language was conferred in 1994. Bilingual education with sign language as the primary means of communication for deaf students is stipulated by law (Branson and Miller 1997, 93).
- Finland: Engman, a participant of the conference "Full Citizenship through Sign Languages," reported that Finnish Sign Language was already recognized in a number of laws and statutes prior to the mid-1990s — with extremely positive effects. ("The national teaching plan for the comprehensive school makes provision for Sign Languages as a mother tongue and the language of

instruction" and much more.) Bilingual education with sign language as the primary means of communication of instruction is thus mandated by law.[28] In August 1995 a revision of the constitution was effected. Since then Finnish Sign Language has been legally recognized as a minority language. Decisive action has already been taken (e.g., "Sign language has been added to the Law on the Research Institute for the Languages of Finland and the Finnish Sign Language Board has been established to advise on the usage of Sign Language"). The Ministry of Justice has a working group that determines which measures are necessary to ensure that the speakers of Finnish Sign Language will achieve a secure and equal position beside other linguistic and cultural minorities. A lot of practical work has yet to be done, but the legal basis for linguistic equality has been fully established.[29]

- Greece: In March 2000, the Greek Parliament voted for a new law on special education that includes a provision for "Greek Sign Language as the language of deaf and hard of hearing students" (Law 2817, cited in the German Association of the Deaf 2000).
- Portugal: Portuguese Sign Language has been recognized in the national constitution (World Federation of the Deaf 1998).
- Sweden: Sweden officially recognized sign language as a language in 1981. Bilingual education with sign language as the primary means of communication for deaf students is mandated by law.

The Centre for Deaf Studies at the University of Bristol developed the survey "Sign on Europe" (Kyle and Allsop 1997), which presents a systematic overview of the present status of Europe's national sign languages and their users. The first survey of its kind, the study investigated which individuals and organizations in the member countries believe that their national sign language was legally recognized. Unfortunately, however, it did not investigate whether those languages actually were recognized.

Worldwide, sign languages are legally recognized in twenty countries: Belarus, Canada, Colombia, Czech Republic, Denmark, Finland, France, Greece, Lithuania, Norway, Portugal, Slovak Republic, Sweden, Switzerland, South Africa, Thailand, Uganda, Ukraine, Uruguay, and the United States (German Association of the Deaf 2000; WFD 1998). Of these twenty countries, only seven are members of the EU.

28. See Branson and Miller 1997, 93.
29. See EUD 1997.

REFERENCES

Branson, J., and D. Miller. 1997. National sign languages and language policies. In *Encyclopedia of language and education,* vol. 1, ed. R. Wodak and D. Corson, 89–98. Netherlands: Kluwer Academic Publishers.

European Bureau for Lesser Used Languages. n.d. *Unity in diversity.* n.p.

European Commission. May 11, 1999. *Community action in favour of regional or minority languages and cultures.* http://www.europa.eu.int/en/comm/dg22/mercator/connact.html.

European Parliament. 1988. *Report of the committee on youth, culture, education, information, and sport on sign languages for the deaf.* A2–302/87, February 19.

———. 1988. Resolution on sign languages for the deaf. *Official Journal of the European Communities,* no. C187: 236–38, June 18.

European Union of the Deaf. 1997. *The guide: A European guide to the Deaf community.* Brussels.

Forrest, Alan. 1998. The politics of language in the European Union. Paper.

Fritzler, M., C. Poske, and S. Vieser. 1997. *Stichwort EU.* München: Heyne.

German Association of the Deaf. 2000. Gebärdensprache im Grundgesetz und öffentlich anerkannt. Kiel, Germany: German Association of the Deaf. Photocopied.

Howitt, R. 1998. Personal interview in the European Parliament, February 4. Brussels.

Jäger, L. 1997. Linguistik als transdisziplinäres Projekt: Das Beispiel Gebärdensprache. *Das Zeichen* 41:402–11. Hamburg: Signum.

Kyle, J., and L. Allsop. 1997. *Sign on Europe: A study of Deaf people and sign language in the European Union.* Bristol, England: University of Bristol.

Skutnabb-Kangas, T., and R. Phillipson, eds. 1995. *Linguistic human rights: Overcoming linguistic discrimination.* Berlin, New York: Mouton de Gruyter.

Wesemann, J. 1997. Deaf people as visible citizens. Deaf Nations Symposium. Manuscript.

World Federation of the Deaf. 1998. Personal communication.

Part 5 Language in Education

Educational Policy and

Signed Language Interpretation

Earl Fleetwood

Signed language interpreting in educational settings has seen more than twenty-five years of concerted effort.[1] As a result of laws intended to provide deaf children a greater variety of educational opportunities (e.g., PL 94–142, PL 101–476), signed language interpreters have enjoyed increased employment opportunities in educational settings. Educational interpreting is evidently motivated by a real need, the education of deaf children. At the same time, the educational opportunity theme has become increasingly synonymous with placing deaf children in mainstream educational settings. Given the outcomes of most mainstream placements, this trend appears to disregard the intent of a "least restrictive environment" provision of the law (Commission on Education of the Deaf 1988).[2]

Whereas circumstances surrounding the advent of educational signed language interpreting are well documented, goals and processes defining the practice are not. Since its inception, educational interpreting has taken on a "try everything" attitude resulting in a practice that is highly unstable with regard to the nature and scope of its responsibilities and, consequently, the outcomes it yields. A variety of contrived signing systems, an acquiescent and vacillating role, and inconsistency with regard to

1. "Interpretation refers to the process of changing messages produced in one language immediately into another language" (Frishberg 1990, 19). Signed language interpreting is distinct from spoken language interpreting in that the former involves a natural sign language. In signed language interpreting, messages are transposed between a signed and a spoken language or between two signed languages. The term *educational settings* refers to classrooms found at the kindergarten-through-senior high school level (K–12) in which hearing children are the mainstream population.

2. The Education for All Handicapped Children Act (PL 94–142) regards placement that provides the "least restrictive environment" as the appropriate educational placement for students with disabilities.

aims and processes have come to define the practice of educational signed language interpreting. Furthermore, efforts to codify educational interpreting are founded in descriptive rather than prescriptive processes. Such efforts serve to denote and promulgate a practice without its propriety ever having been demonstrated.

Patrie (1993) raises serious questions about the effectiveness of educational interpreting, concluding that it is important to "step back and see in which settings and for what ages an interpreted message is effective (and in which settings it is not). To date we have no empirical basis from which to operate in making these decisions" (30). Moreover, Patrie states, "we may have been pouring millions of dollars into a practice which, in fact, may have no theoretically defensible basis" (31).

This chapter explores the notion that the current state of educational signed language interpreting is a product of the cyclically reinforcing process of resting educational interpreting job descriptions on descriptive data (and vice versa). It examines the nature of educational interpreting policy as well as responsibilities expected of practicing educational signed language interpreters.

LITERATURE REVIEW

As one outcome of changes in public law (e.g., Section 504 of the Rehabilitation Act of 1973; PL 94–142 [the Education for All Handicapped Children Act]), the early 1970s saw an increase in the number of deaf/hard of hearing students placed in public mainstream schools. One result of this demographic change was an increase in the demand for signed language interpreters to work in elementary, secondary, and postsecondary educational settings. Research on educational signed language interpreting began as well.

Sociohistorical Background: Adult versus Child Consumers

Signed language interpreting as a profession was born in deference to the service requests of deaf adults who utilize a signed language to communicate. The beginnings as well as the history of signed language interpreting do not presume that mainstream integration of deaf people into hearing society is a functional goal (Frishberg 1990). Instead, signed language interpreting has developed as a profession in response to requests of deaf adults to have access to, rather than integrate with, the mainstream.

The nature of this genesis is significant, as the *Report of the National Task Force on Educational Interpreting* begins: "Interpreting for deaf students in our nation's schools is a relatively recent development, extending back only about thirty years. It is both a product of, and an enabling factor in, the mainstreaming movement for deaf students" (Stuckless, Avery, and Hurwitz 1989, 1). The report identifies mainstreaming as a goal to which educational interpreting efforts should defer. Clearly, interpreting for deaf adults is driven by an implicitly different end than is interpreting for deaf children in mainstream educational settings. This becomes evident when the evolution of educational interpreting is examined.

The beginnings of educational signed language interpreting are rooted in the wake of the mainstreaming movement that followed the passage of several laws, including PL 94–142 and its 1990 amendment, which changed the law's name to the Individuals with Disabilities Education Act (Seal 1998). The beginnings of signed language interpreting for deaf adults has a much longer history (Frishberg 1990, 10). When mainstream education of deaf children became a part of the services rendered by the profession of signed language interpreting, practitioners answering the call were those whose experience and/or training was toward serving non-mainstream-oriented deaf adult consumers (Frishberg 1990, 102–105).

After numerous years of pairing deaf adult-focused interpreters (access-oriented) with deaf children in mainstream classrooms (integration-oriented),[3] the need was seen for providing interpreters avenues to address the apparent mismatch. Toward this end, the established access-oriented approach was altered to provide for the goals of the integration-oriented group (Frishberg 1990). No agreement was or has been reached regarding the nature and scope of these changes.

In response to this need, a variety of revised signed language interpreter models and directives has emerged. For example, the Code of Ethics of the Registry of Interpreters for the Deaf (RID), "principles of ethical behavior" established before the educational mainstream population was

3. The terms *access-oriented* and *integration-oriented* denote the perspective of deaf consumers regarding their relationship with the mainstream group. Access-oriented consumers attend interpreted events for reasons that are a function of the events and without the goal of establishing a mainstream group identity. Integration-oriented consumers are motivated by both goals.

a consideration, has been modified for use in educational settings in some states, including Florida and North Carolina. School systems and individual schools in these states have invariably established job descriptions founded in these modifications. Others have written job descriptions in deference to more idiosyncratic understandings and endeavors. However, altering the RID Code of Ethics and establishing job descriptions without agreeing to or even understanding the outcomes supported by such changes means that signed language interpreting for deaf children in mainstream classrooms is neither consistently defined nor systematically approached.

This lack of consistency and systematicity affects services provided by the gamut of educational signed language interpreters, from those who are experienced access-oriented interpreters to those who have no training or experience whatsoever. Regardless of the interpreter's background, the realization of any particular outcome is elusive because the pursuit of any particular goal is an illusion.

Sociolinguistic Background: "Interpreting" without Language

The unbounded nature of educational interpreting supports practices that directly counter the enabling posture described in the task force report discussed earlier. This flexibility allows an interpreter to function without using a language and to take on roles already occupied by others. Although the former of these is not the focus of this chapter, the enormity of its impact serves as a backdrop for the latter and thereby warrants further elaboration.

The process of interpreting assumes the employment of two languages, a *target language* and a *source language* (Frishberg 1990). Mainstream educational institutions in the United States present curricula in spoken English. Thus, spoken English serves as the source language for the educational signed language interpreter. Significant debate has arisen with regard to the target language in interpreted educational settings. Whether overtly motivated or existing simply by default, issues regarding the linguistic integrity of the interpreter's target rendering are central both to the practice of educational interpreting and to outcomes for students mainstreamed into public school classrooms (Gutierrez 1998).

In light of these issues, it is significant that research regarding signed language use native to the United States has led to distinctions among the various forms noted. Beginning with William Stokoe's (1960) work, one form in particular—American Sign Language (ASL)—has been identified as a language to the exclusion of the others. Among the typically excluded languages are contrived signing systems designed to teach English to deaf children. The shortcoming of these contrived systems is that they neither model nor teach English (Supalla 1991). Instead, they take the vocabulary of one language (ASL) and place it in the order of another language (English) while adjusting or inventing parts that do not readily adapt to this prescribed mold (Johnson, Liddell, and Erting 1989). This reordering, adjusting, and inventing process is the same as if German were put into English word order in an attempt to teach English to German-speaking children. The result would be the representation of neither English nor German but, rather, of inconsistent and sometimes conflicting aspects of each. Recognizing that similarly contrived systems do not teach English to deaf children should require no great leap of faith.

Deaf children are not acquiring English when they are exposed to either another language (e.g., ASL) or a contrived system (e.g., Signing Exact English), neither of which accounts for the linguistic structures of English. In point of fact, "the validity of the underlying assumption that any system of signs (either natural or invented) is capable of representing speech in a way which will allow it to serve as a model for the natural acquisition of a spoken language has never been demonstrated" (Johnson, Liddell, and Erting 1989, 8).

To many educational signed language interpreters, this point of fact is a point of oversight. Consequently, they strive to better their interpreting/ transliterating (signing) attempts, unaware that the nature of language, rather than of effort, serves as the obstacle to successfully using sign language to convey to (or teach) deaf children the language and curriculum of the hearing mainstream. Without access to the language of the classroom, neither curricular nor social access can occur (Johnson, Liddell, and Erting 1989; Ramsey 1997). Moreover, the practice of allowing the educational interpreter to sign without using language works directly against the deaf/hard of hearing child's opportunity to ever internalize any particular language (Johnson, Liddell, and Erting 1989, 9).

Implications of Related Literature

With regard to utilizing interpreting services, the issue of linguistic exposure and accessibility has implications for deaf children in educational settings that are distinct from those that affect deaf adults in noneducational settings. For example, a deaf adult who is interested in having access to an event such as a theater performance might not be interested in also having access to the language of that event. In this case, the deaf adult is considered successful if he or she simply has the opportunity to enjoy the show. However, children attend school in order to, among other things, learn vocabulary, study grammar, and—through a variety of supposedly incidental and accessible opportunities—acquire and use the language of the school environment. Students' progress and success are measured through academic testing and social experience germane to that setting. Unlike a deaf adult attending an interpreted theater performance, deaf children in hearing mainstream classrooms are also faced with the reality that their success demands competence in, and therefore consistent access and exposure to, the language of the event—the language of the classroom.

Winston (1992) conducted an ethnographic examination of the mainstream educational setting in terms of the demands placed on both the educational interpreter and the deaf student. She (1994) addressed "the myth that interpreting is a simple substitute for direct communication and teaching and the myth that an interpreted education is an 'included' education" (55). Winston discussed the concomitants of the interpreting process with regard to their effect upon the inclusion (or exclusion) of deaf children in classrooms with hearing children. Comparing the experiences of deaf and hearing children in educational settings, she found that the "difference is not merely a superficial [one], it is a difference of both quality and quantity" (62). As Winston (1992, 1994) pointed out, linguistic accessibility in public school classrooms is impeded because of the presumption that students will listen to instructions while engaged in a visual activity, which is not appropriate for deaf and hard of hearing students watching an interpreter. This example points out that language and educational practices are inextricably intertwined.

La Bue's (1998) findings underscore the nature of the deaf student's struggle to be educated through a signed language interpreter. She found that a deaf student in a mainstream classroom with hearing students (1) has limited access to instructional goals, (2) "receive[s] bits and pieces of content through context, and through an interpretation of the discourse" (233), and (3) "become[s] more socially distanced from the rest of the class" (225). These points support Ramsey's (1997) conclusion that the question of accessibility and integration for deaf students has to do not only with the language of the classroom but also with the sociocultural and academic aspects of the classroom itself.

In educational settings both issues of accessibility and integration are related to expectations of interpreter behavior. Several studies based on surveys of expectations about educational interpreters have been conducted in recent years.

Survey Research Regarding Educational
Signed Language Interpreters

Review of the literature finds some research on educational interpreters conducted in the form of surveys (Rittenhouse, Rahn, and Morreau 1989; Mertens 1990; Hayes 1992; Jones 1993; Taylor and Elliot 1994; Seal 1998). This approach involves the use of studies in which the responses of various groups, including parents, teachers, interpreters, and administrators, are solicited via a questionnaire. Responses are tallied and analyzed, and conclusions are drawn and cited as evidence of an existing need for educational interpreters.

Rittenhouse, Rahn, and Morreau (1989) undertook a two-part study. Part one of the study focused on the availability of educational signed language interpreters versus the demand for their services. The study finds that in the one state examined, supervisors of programs for mainstreamed deaf students reported that 56 percent of mainstream interpreting requests are filled. The supervisors find this to be "slightly less than adequate."

The second part of their study is particularly relevant to the current research question. Twenty-four teachers of the deaf, eighteen college-aged deaf individuals, and twenty-seven interpreters were surveyed to elicit their views regarding thirty-eight characteristics and skills the study deemed relevant to educational interpreting. Rittenhouse, Rahn, and Morreau find agreement among these groups with regard to the necessity of "manual dexterity; hand coordination; general mental abilities; knowledge of lighting, elevation, seating, and visual background; knowledge of content area to be interpreted; ability to interpret another's remarks; ability to reverse translate; and ability to interpret in a specific setting" (60).

Disagreement occurred about a variety of items as well. Their study notes that in order to "more accurately assess the adequacy of the supply of interpreters in public school settings," other questions must be explored, including "What other responsibilities does the interpreter fulfill for the school district or cooperative or region?" (62). The study does not attempt to elicit the views of the surveyed groups with regard to the goals pursued by educational interpreting. It also does not propose a goal to serve as a reference point for the data collected.

Mertens (1990) utilized participant observations, semistructured interviews, document review, and questionnaires to "explore the quality of the educational experience of deaf adolescents when they communicate with a hearing teacher through an interpreter and to determine the implications of that experience for the students' classroom behavior" (49). Mertens finds that hearing mainstream classroom teachers are not adequately knowledgeable about the ideal learning environment for a deaf student and that classroom disciplinary procedures "interfered with the staff's ability to interact with the students" (49).

Mertens also finds dissatisfaction among deaf students with regard to the interpreter's role, especially when interpreters took on disciplinary tasks. Mertens suggests that teacher and interpreter agree on the role of the educational interpreter early in the school year to avoid conflict later. "If the interpreter noticed that the students were not paying attention, for example, she or he could point that out to the teacher" (52).[4] Thus, the study proposes conflict resolution where conflicts are defined by individual perspectives. Although real opinions are reflected in the data collected, and although educational interpreters are one aspect of the study, Merten's suggestions prescribe educational interpreter behavior as a product of a variety of perspectives rather than of a single and explicitly defined goal. If that goal is to yield deaf "products" of mainstream education who perform on a par with their hearing peers, then the educational interpreter role must be driven by such outcomes—rather than by a collection of opinions and perspectives.

Hayes (1992) studied educational interpreting through a series of interviews and a questionnaire. The study focused on "the roles and responsibilities of educational interpreters and the problems/concerns they encounter in and outside the classroom" (7). Hayes's research yielded job titles, specific work settings, and forms of communication used by the educational interpreter. Hayes also elicited information from the educational interpreters surveyed regarding their educational background and prepa-

---

4. This suggestion regarding the educational interpreter's responsibility in addressing lack of attentiveness by deaf students harbors conflicts of its own. This will be discussed later.

ration as well as their recommendations for modifying the curriculum of interpreter preparation programs. More to the point of this chapter, Hayes questioned educational interpreters about their role and responsibilities. Hayes finds that "they tutored students (81.2 percent), assisted students with homework (75 percent), developed signs for technical vocabulary (75 percent), served as liaison (72 percent) between regular and special education teachers, and worked with regular education students (56.2 percent). In addition, 50 percent were responsible for grading papers, duplicating materials, making bulletin boards, disciplining students—tasks much like those of a teacher's aide" (12).

Hayes concludes that educational interpreters, students, administrators, and teachers do not understand the role of the educational interpreter and that educational interpreters want more information about their roles and responsibilities. "School districts need to work together to develop adequate job descriptions. Educational interpreters cannot be expected to provide adequate services without a well-defined job description" (19). In light of the current study, the application of Hayes's findings is noteworthy. Hayes uses descriptive data to formulate prescriptive suggestions, without having defined the outcomes that those suggestions are to support.

Jones (1993) received responses to a fifty-seven-item questionnaire from 217 educational signed language interpreters. Jones's demographic examination revealed that in Kansas, Missouri, and Nebraska, an educational signed language interpreter was likely to be a "white female, 31–40 years of age, with 2–3 years of experience, having earned a vocational certificate but not interpreter certification. She transliterates in her job, is earning $9.01–$11.00 per hour in a full-time job and may be working in a rural or urban setting. She has expressed the need for continued skill upgrading opportunities, but those opportunities are not readily available" (Jones 1993, 94). Jones also finds that within the population surveyed, educational signed language interpreters perform a variety of duties in addition to interpreting and use an English-based sign code when working. Jones also finds no significant correlation between the use of a particular signing system and injuries related to the process of interpreting.

Taylor and Elliott (1994) surveyed the opinions of seventy-one individuals toward determining the competence educational interpreters are perceived to need in three areas: skill, knowledge, and attitude. Individuals from three groups were surveyed, including members of the Alabama Registry of Interpreters for the Deaf, students enrolled in a one-year educational interpreter preparation program, and teachers who used the services of an educational interpreter in their classrooms. Although Taylor and Elliot did not find agreement among the groups on all items surveyed, they did find agreement among the groups with regard to the importance of "proficiency in English, interpreting into ASL and into English, sensitivity to students' needs (including their need for independence), rapport with deaf people, and appropriate behavior" (188).

Taylor and Elliott subsequently recommend that "developers of preparation programs for educational interpreters may well consider the items for which there was significant agreement among the groups as a solid starting point for a curriculum" (188). Their recommendation implies that "significant agreement" rather than deaf student outcomes should serve as the foundation for determining an appropriate educational interpreter role. Moreover, because "significant agreement" does not define an educational goal for mainstreamed deaf students, it does nothing to qualify the pursuit of mainstreaming as a prudent and purposeful educational policy.

Seal (1998) surveyed forty-nine educational interpreters with regard to five study questions. The answers to these questions provide data regarding (1) the cognitive, linguistic, and chronological age/stage at which deaf students become aware that they are receiving an interpreted message; (2) the relationship between the age at which a deaf student begins to use interpreting services and how that deaf student functions as a consumer of interpreting services; (3) the relationship between an interpreter's skill level and a deaf student's learning in the classroom; (4) whether and at what age deaf students benefit from utilizing one or multiple interpreters; and (5) personal and professional attributes considered "most critical for interpreters."

Seal (1998) looks for relationships between the success of a deaf student who uses interpreting services and certain attributes of both the student and the interpreter that might affect that success. However, the data collected were based on personal opinions about what factors constitute success without a clearly articulated definition of the concept.

Previous survey-based research on educational signed language interpreting has resulted in at least two suggestions: (1) there must be agreement among teachers, interpreters, and student interpreters regarding the interpreter's role, and (2) educational interpreters need well-defined job descriptions. Such conclusions overlook the reality that role agreement and detailed job responsibilities are not inherently goal driven. Such con-

clusions also overlook the reality that even well-defined goals are sometimes inherently unattainable.

To explicate educational signed language interpreter goals as well as
implications regarding the convergence or divergence of those goals with
reality, the current study elicited expectations of coordinators of interpreters working in public schools and interpreter job descriptions from
school systems throughout the United States.

A LACK OF INTENDED OUTCOMES FOR EDUCATIONAL
SIGNED LANGUAGE INTERPRETING

Survey research has described educational signed language interpreter
practices or solicited a variety of perspectives in an attempt to identify desired educational interpreter skills and knowledge. However, the propriety of documented practices and the relevance of particular skills and
knowledge have not been examined and grounded in terms of explicitly
identified goals for educational interpreting. It is, therefore, not surprising that educational signed language interpreter job descriptions seem to
aim for and lead to no consistent outcome.

This study began with the underlying assumption that a target must be
identified for success or failure to be measurable. This posture was taken
with the hope that the study would not contribute to the cyclically reinforcing process of resting educational interpreter job descriptions on
descriptive data (and vice versa). This study solicited the views of coordinators of educational signed language interpreters to determine whether
these coordinators did the following:

- Worked under the assumption that equity between hearing and
  deaf student outcomes is a goal;
- Believed that it is possible to construct an educational interpreter
  job description that can lead to equity between hearing and deaf
  student outcomes;
- Noted a link between the educational interpreter job description
  under which they work and deaf student outcomes

Implicit in this study were the following questions:

- What outcomes is educational signed language interpreting sup-
  posed to support?

- Is it possible for educational signed language interpreting to support those outcomes?
- Is educational signed language interpreting currently supporting those outcomes?

Methodology

Two avenues of investigation were pursued. First, ten U.S. school systems were asked to provide job descriptions under which educational interpreters are asked to work. These job descriptions were examined for consistency with the recommendations of the National Task Force on Educational Interpreting. The descriptions were also analyzed with regard to their potential impact on both the educational interpreter role and, ultimately, deaf student outcomes. Second, sixteen coordinators of educational signed language interpreters across the United States were mailed a list of five questions.[5] Coordinators were given the written direction "Please check the box that is most appropriate." Each question was followed by the answer choices "yes," "no," and "cannot judge." The coordinators' responses can be seen in table 1.

The questions were designed to elicit the coordinators' views regarding the relationship between educational interpreting practices (as defined by educational interpreter job descriptions) and deaf student outcomes. Ultimately, the questions provide a backdrop for determining whether the coordinators perceive the seeming connection between educational interpreting practices, educational policy in the form of job descriptions, and deaf student outcomes. The study did not document qualifications of these coordinators.

Results: What Job Descriptions Reveal

Half of the ten school systems answered the requests for educational interpreter job descriptions: one from Virginia, one from Massachusetts, one from Maryland, and two from California. The five job descriptions each included at least one of the following duties: "Interpreter/Aide," "Interpreter/Tutor," "Mainstream Interpreter for the Hearing Impaired," "Edu-

5. Eleven coordinators responded. One respondent did not complete the back of the double-sided questionnaire. This incomplete set of responses was set aside, leaving complete data from ten respondents.

TABLE 1. *Survey Results*

| | Responses | | |
| | Yes | No | Cannot Judge |
Questions			
Do you think that mainstream education supports the same outcomes for deaf/ hard of hearing students as it does for hearing students?	30% (n = 10)	60% (n = 10)	10% (n = 10)
Do you think that the job description for educational sign language interpreters in your school effectively leads to deaf/hard of hearing student outcomes that are on a par with hearing student outcomes?	30% (n = 10)	70% (n = 10)	0% (n = 10)
(Only answer #3 if your answer to #2 is "no.") Do you think that an educational interpreter job description can be formulated that would effectively lead to deaf/ hard of hearing student outcomes that are on a par with hearing student outcomes?	28.5% (n = 7)	28.5% (n = 7)	43% (n = 7)
Do you think that an educational interpreter job description should support the same outcomes for deaf/hard of hearing students that are experienced by their hearing student peers?	80% (n = 10)	10% (n = 10)	10% (n = 10)
Do you think that the job description for educational sign language interpreters in your school provides a clear boundary between the job expectations for educational sign language interpreters and the job expectations of others who work in the educational setting?	30% (n = 10)	70% (n = 10)	0% (n = 10)

cational Interpreter/Transliterator," and "Educational Interpreter." All job descriptions included: "facilitate communication," "provide interpreting," or "interpret" as relevant duties. Four of the job descriptions listed tutoring as a job-related responsibility or option, and one includes the additional responsibility of serving as a "classroom aide, interacting with all children in the classroom" (Amherst-Pelham Public Schools 1992). One job description listed "interpret[ing] for tutoring sessions conducted by the regular education teachers," separating tutoring and interpreting responsibilities among school personnel (Hampton City Public Schools 1991).

As a job-related expectation, three job descriptions listed "confidentiality." These descriptions included statements such as "Will maintain confidentiality at all times in all circumstances," then immediately countered with statements such as "Will report to the appropriate school personnel any information that may be potentially detrimental to the HI/D student's health and personal welfare," as well as "any illegal or suspected illegal acts occurring during class sessions and involving any student(s)."

Two of the job descriptions included a statement of purpose—for example, that the interpreter's primary function is to "act as the facilitator of communication between the students and the mainstream teacher" and noting that the interpreter is "an extension of the HI/D student(s) and his/her relationship with other parties. At the same time, the Interpreter acts as a liaison between other parties and the HI/D student(s)" (Hampton City Public Schools 1991).[6] Although both commonality and variability were found among the job descriptions scrutinized, it is noteworthy that none referred to the purpose of educational interpreting roles and responsibilities with regard to deaf student placement or desired deaf student outcomes.

IMPLICATIONS OF JOB DESCRIPTIONS

Because findings of the National Task Force on Educational Interpreting, work of the RID/CED (Council on Education of the Deaf) Ad Hoc Committee on Educational Interpreting Standards, development of the Professional Development Endorsement System (PDES), and findings of the aforementioned survey-based research appear to mark major points in the evolution of the educational interpreter role, it is noteworthy that the methodology driving each of these devices rests in descriptive processes. For example, the task force report is the product of a discussion of job descriptions, working conditions, and pay rates; the RID/CED Committee's work is the offspring of the task force's findings; the survey-based research represents a tally of opinions; and the PDES is an educational construct aimed at preparing educational interpreters to support an unspecified goal. Any job conducted in the absence of a specified goal leaves such discussions, opinions, and constructs undirected and, consequently, purposeless.

6. HI/D refers to "hearing impaired/deaf."

Patrie (1993) notes that "In practice, school systems in the United States are permitted to establish their own parameters for the job of *educational interpreter*. . . . Their goals may be to address the complex set of issues which surround the placement of deaf children in public education" (24–25). In other words, existing job descriptions are not founded on absolute or even explicit attention to desired deaf student outcomes. Because none of the aforementioned approaches begin with an explicit definition of the goals regarding the student outcomes they aim to support, perhaps they defer to the same ambiguous ends. Can any job description be deemed appropriate or effective if, in effect, it aspires to ambiguity? The causes and outcomes of such shortcomings warrant examination.

THE COMPROMISED JOB DESCRIPTION

An examination of comments found in prominent writings on the subject of educational signed language interpreting helps to identify the nature and scope of flexibility found in the educational interpreter role.

The job description should be developed by local school administrators to meet local needs and specifications. (Stuckless, Avery, and Hurwitz 1989, 5)

The role of the interpreter varies with grade level and type of task delegated. (National Information Center on Deafness 1991, 10)

Educational interpreters must be aware of, and adhere to, policies and procedures established by the district for its employees. (Stuckless, Avery, and Hurwitz 1989, 10)

An interpreter in a public school may be expected to report any instances of cheating and may therefore be expected to report to a school authority a hearing student who asks (via the interpreter) to copy a deaf student's work. This same dilemma would most likely not arise in a postsecondary setting. (Frishberg 1990, 106)

To assist with other duties as determined appropriate by the educational team and/or supervisor. (Seal 1998, 23)

These statements are nearly consistent with regard to the vagueness and mutability they bring to the development of the educational interpreter's role and function. The first statement (Stuckless, Avery, and Hurwitz 1989, 5) is particularly permissive, allowing interpreter duties and responsibilities to be generated in deference to a wide variety of potential external motivations. Resulting practices not only fall under the purview of responsibilities of other members of the educational team, often they run directly counter to the function of interpreting. As a result, the educational puzzle remains undefined. The last statement by Seal (1998) is not only permissive in terms of who defines "appropriate," it appears within a document that defines no particular student outcome from which to judge the effectiveness of the responsibilities that it lists. "Appropriate" duties cannot be meaningfully decided and designated if those duties are not directed toward a clearly articulated goal. As a result, the educational puzzle remains unsolvable.

A MELANGE OF DIVERGENT DUTIES

Duties appearing within the numerous educational interpreter job descriptions and codes of ethics analyzed in this study are particularly revealing with regard to the manner in which they codify conflict.

> Depending on the student's age, grade level, and experience, interpreters may need to remind them about homework, assist hearing students in accepting . . . hearing-impaired children, function as liaisons between the program for the hearing-impaired students and the regular teachers, tutor hearing-impaired students and possibly hearing students in the class. (Orange County Board of Education 1990)

> [Interpreter/tutor shall] assist in the implementation of the educational plans for hearing impaired students by: a) providing interpreting services in class, b) providing tutoring services within the class, c) serve as a classroom aide interacting with all children in the classroom. (Amherst-Pelham Public Schools 1992)

> Under the direction of the subject area teacher and as dictated by the individualized education program, the interpreter/transliterator may tutor hearing-impaired students and assist them to better comprehend the presented material. For nonacademic issues, the interpreter/transliterator should direct students to the appropriate professional. (North Carolina Department of Public Instruction 1991)

> At the elementary level, interpreters may assist any student within the classroom as directed by the teacher, provided the interpreter is always readily available to the hearing-impaired student(s) if needed, and pro-

vided this is the expressed desire of the classroom teacher. (Montgomery County Public Schools 1991)

Assist teacher in maintaining discipline and monitoring [the class-] room. . . . (Fresno Unified School District 1993)

The duties of reminding, assisting, authorizing, and enforcing are not traditionally associated with the role of interpreter. In fact, such behavior is generally considered counter to the purpose for which interpreting exists.

Often, disparate job expectations are inherent in job titles associated with the educational interpreter. For example, the job title "Interpreter/ Aide" reveals a foundation for fundamental conflict. Should interpreters be required to intentionally effect change in the environment to which they provide access? This seems analogous to requiring that one both create news and publish it. However, it should not be surprising that such conflict exists with regard to educational interpreter job titles. The sample job description appearing in the task force report lists "provide tutoring and/or notetaking services for hearing-impaired students when necessary and when interpreting is not needed" (Stuckless, Avery, and Hurwitz, 1989, 31). The report concurrently claims that "interpreting is both a product of and an enabling factor in the mainstreaming movement" (Stuckless, Avery, and Hurwitz 1989, 1).

Because tutoring by an interpreter is not an attribute of the mainstreaming process for hearing students and because tutoring inherently defines a power relationship different from that implicit in the traditional access-oriented interpreter role, how does placing the deaf/hard of hearing student in the wake of such a singularly affective situation enable a process that is inherently defined in terms of plurality? This is not to say that resolving such conflict will result in a realization of the "enabling" aims identified in the task force report; debate over the viability of an interpreted education hinges on other considerations as well. Rather, it underscores the point that educational interpreting policy fails at its foundation: the ability to frame its behavior in terms of its aims.

The collected data are revealing. Of the ten coordinators whose responses were analyzed, 60 percent answered "no," 30 percent answered "yes," and 10 percent answered "cannot judge" to the question, "Do you think that mainstream education supports the same outcomes for deaf/ hard of hearing students as it does for hearing students?" This question is not specifically about educational interpreting. However, in terms of the function of the environment of which educational signed language interpreting is a part, it defines the view of the coordinators with regard to deaf student outcomes. Still, the significance of the responses rests on answers to other questions as well.

An overwhelming 80 percent of respondents believe that outcomes for deaf students in mainstream settings should be equal to those of the hearing students found there. This appears to distinguish mainstreaming from mainstream placement as a goal for deaf students. This is an important distinction as the *mainstream* simply serves to identify the location of the deaf students' placement, whereas *mainstreaming* identifies a relationship with that setting and its affective processes. Outcomes of this relationship can be judged in terms of academic, intellectual, social, and emotional attributes. This suggests that if deaf and hearing student outcomes are to be equal, deaf students must be exposed to the same affective environment as their hearing peers. The current study does not answer the question of whether this is possible. However, responses to one question in the study suggest that the answer is, at least, controversial.

Of the five questions asked, the one receiving the most divided answers focused on potential with regard to the educational interpreter job description. Specifically, the question asked, "Do you think that an educational signed language interpreter job description can be formulated that would lead to deaf/hard of hearing student outcomes that are on a par with hearing student outcomes?" (Responses were solicited only from those coordinators who felt that their current educational interpreter job description was ineffective—a full 70 percent of the respondents.) Answers were divided with 28.5 percent responding "yes," 28.5 percent responding "no," and 42.8 percent responding "cannot judge." In light of the fact that 80 percent of respondents believed that equity of deaf and hearing student outcomes is a goal, it is significant that less than 30 percent of the respondents believed that an educational interpreter job description could be formulated that would lead to such an end. In other words, although 80 percent of respondents identified equity of outcomes as a goal, less than 30 percent believed that educational signed language interpreting can support it as a possibility.

The study also notes that 65 percent of respondents do not believe that the educational interpreter job description in their school "effectively leads to deaf/hard of hearing student outcomes that are on a par with hearing student outcomes." This is significant, as 80 percent of the respondents indicate that the educational interpreter job description should provide for such equity.

A full 70 percent of respondents indicate that the educational interpreter job description in their school does not provide for a "clear boundary between the job expectations of the educational interpreter and job expectations of others who work in the educational setting." Although the impact of this upon deaf student outcomes is not clear, it suggests that job descriptions for educational interpreters do not identify all of their responsibilities as being unique among educational staff members. In other words, educational signed language interpreter job descriptions require that educational interpreters assume some responsibilities also assigned to other members of the educational staff. In effect, at least some of the responsibilities found in educational interpreter job descriptions affect relationships between a deaf student and other members of the educational staff. One question raised by this finding is whether equity of outcomes among deaf and hearing students is a possibility if educational interpreter job descriptions differentiate student–staff relationships along deaf–hearing lines.

CONCLUSION

Examination of previous educational interpreting research, educational interpreter job descriptions, and the current research finds that today's educational signed language interpreting practices rest on decisions that are formulated without an explicitly established point of reference. In other words, educational signed language interpreting is a product of policy and practices that are implemented without an explicit understanding of the outcomes they are to support. Without such a point of reference, the relevance of any particular role, responsibility, or skill cannot be measured.

The need for clearly established viable standards and goals for educational signed language interpreters is undeniable. As with any profession, the establishment of functional standards is an essential precondition to ensuring, or at least scrutinizing, the existence of an effective, efficient, and, ultimately, purposeful service. Just as the direction of a profession depends upon the identification of clearly defined goals, the meaningful pursuit of these goals depends upon a rationally formulated and clearly articulated policy. Deaf student outcomes must drive such policy. Without a clear understanding of what a profession intends to support, the profession's accomplishments cannot be measured, the profession's value cannot be assessed, and the profession cannot be held accountable. Moreover, it is, at least, questionable whether a practice that defers to these shortcomings can be accurately labeled a profession.

Toward assessing the value of the practice of signed language interpreting in educational settings, the following sequential evaluative steps are recommended:

1. *Identify the purpose for which the job exists in light of the aims of its primary consumers.* The practice of educational interpreting exists as a result of the goals of its consumers. If that existence is to be meaningful, all that defines the practice must defer to those goals. Therefore, before a purposeful educational interpreter role or job description can be formulated, before a relevant skill and knowledge base can be identified, and before a meaningful and valid testing mechanism can be constructed, the goals of educational interpreting's primary consumers must be explicitly identified. Research that will provide an accurate and decisive identification of these goals must be undertaken.

2. *Define standards of practice that serve to bound the job in terms of its responsibilities.* A profession is defined not only in terms of its attention to explicitly identified obligatory behaviors but also by its ability to recognize the significance of exclusive behaviors. In other words, defining that which lies outside the domain of a profession's obligations is as important to defining the profession as that which lies within. Educational signed language interpreting must bound itself as a practice in deference to its unique obligations. Research must be undertaken that will lead to definitive identification of educational interpreting behaviors considered supportive of, and detrimental to, the aims of educational interpreting.

3. *Identify that corpus of knowledge and skills that provides for the effective and efficient pursuit of the standards of practice defining the profession.* Once the goals of educational interpreting have been explicitly identified, and following delineation of functional standards supporting those goals, the identification of requisite knowledge and skills is in order. To be meaningful, this body of

knowledge and skills must provide for realization of identified functional standards. Research in this area must focus on determining not only what body of knowledge and skills is required of the job but also whether it exists and can be learned. Ultimately, such research will determine the viability of educational signed language interpreting.

4. *Develop programs and materials that teach the identified corpus of knowledge and skills.* If research determines that knowledge and skills requisite of educational interpreting exist and can be learned, and once this has driven the delineation of qualifications for instructors and educational programs, the establishment of a meaningful course of study can be pursued.

5. *Develop a formal testing mechanism.* In deference to the job's identified purpose, standards of practice, and the corpus of relevant knowledge and skills, a meaningful mechanism can be formulated toward evaluating the competence of practitioners.

Signed language interpreting in educational settings is a relatively young phenomenon. At this point in its evolution, it seems that this practice is defined more by the opinions it collects than the goals it pursues. Job descriptions vary widely with regard to the expectations they define and the flexibility they allow. The field of educational signed language interpreting must clearly identify the outcomes it strives to support as well as the functional role that will achieve these ends. Only then can an educational interpreting policy be constructed. Only then can such a policy be meaningful. Only then can educational interpreting conclusively sustain or discount questions of viability.

REFERENCES

Amherst-Pelham Public Schools. 1992. *Interpreter/tutor job description.* Amherst, Mass.: Amherst-Pelham Public Schools.

Commission on Education of the Deaf. 1988. *Toward equity. Report to the President and the Congress of the United States.* Washington, D.C.: U.S. Government Printing Office.

Education for All Handicapped Children Act. PL 94–142, November 29, 1975.

Fresno Unified School District. 1993. Educational interpreter: Definition, examples of duties, employment standards. Fresno, Calif.: Fresno Unified School District.

Frishberg, N. 1990. *Interpreting: An introduction.* Silver Spring, Md.: RID Publications.

Gutierrez, P. S. 1998. The relationship of educational policy to language and cognition in deaf children. In *Pinky extension and eye gaze: Language use in Deaf communities,* ed. C. Lucas, 103–34. Washington, D.C.: Gallaudet University Press.

Hampton City Public Schools. 1991. *Guidelines for educational interpreters/ transliterators in the mainstream.* Hampton, Va.: Hampton City Public Schools.

Hayes, L. 1992. Educational interpreters for deaf students: Their responsibilities, problems, and concerns. *Journal of Interpretation* 5 (1): 5–24. Silver Spring, Md.: RID Publications.

Individuals with Disabilities Education Act (IDEA). PL 101–476, October 20, 1990. Amended July 17, 1997. 20 U.S. Code, Section 33.

Johnson, R. E., S. K. Liddell, and C. J. Erting. 1989. *Unlocking the curriculum.* Washington, D.C.: Gallaudet Research Institute, Occasional Paper 89–93.

Jones, B. 1993. Responsibilities of educational interpreters in K–12 public schools in Kansas, Missouri, and Nebraska. Ph.D. diss., University of Kansas.

La Bue, M. A. 1998. Interpreted education: A study of deaf students' access to the content and form of literacy instruction in a mainstreamed high school English class. Ph.D. diss., Harvard University.

Mertens, D. 1990. Teachers working with interpreters: The deaf student's educational experience. *American Annals of the Deaf* 136:48–52.

Montgomery County Public Schools. 1991. *Interpreter guidelines.* Rockville, Md.: Montgomery County Public Schools.

National Information Center on Deafness. 1991. *Mainstreaming Deaf and hard of hearing students: Questions and answers, research, readings, and resources.* Washington, D.C.: National Information Center on Deafness, Gallaudet University.

North Carolina Department of Public Instruction. 1991. *N.C. Educational Interpreter Code of Ethics.* Raleigh, N.C.: North Carolina Department of Public Instruction.

Orange County Board of Education. 1990. *Guidelines for mainstream interpreters for the hearing impaired.* Costa Mesa, Calif.: Orange County Board of Education.

Patrie, C. 1993. A confluence of diverse relationships: Interpreter education and educational interpreting. In *A confluence of diverse relationships: Proceedings of the Thirteenth National Convention of the Registry of Interpreters for the Deaf,* ed. Clay Nettles, 3–18. Silver Spring, Md.: Registry of Interpreters for the Deaf.

Ramsey, C. 1997. *Deaf children in public schools: Placement, context, and consequences.* Washington, D.C.: Gallaudet University Press.

Rehabilitation Act of 1973. Amended March 22, 1988. 29 U.S. Code, Section 794.

Rittenhouse, R., C. Rahn, and L. Morreau. 1989. Educational interpreter services for hearing-impaired students: Provider and consumer disagreements. *Journal of the American Deafness and Rehabilitation Association* 22:57–63.

Seal, B. C. 1998. *Best practices in educational interpreting.* Boston: Allyn and Bacon.

Stokoe, W. 1960. Sign language structure: An outline of the visual communication systems of the American deaf. In *Studies in linguistics: Occasional papers* 8. Buffalo, N.Y.: University of Buffalo.

Stuckless, E., J. Avery, and T. Hurwitz. 1989. *Educational interpreting for deaf students: Report of the National Task Force on Educational Interpreting.* Rochester, N.Y.: Rochester Institute of Technology.

Supalla, S. 1991. Manually coded English: The modality question in signed language development. In *Theoretical issues in sign language research,* vol. 2, ed. P. Siple, and S. Fischer, 85–109. Chicago: University of Chicago Press.

Taylor, C., and R. Elliot. 1994. Identifying areas of competence needed by educational interpreters. *Sign Language Studies* 83:179–90.

Winston, E. 1992. Mainstream interpreting: An analysis of the task. In *The challenge of the 90s: New standards in interpreter education,* ed. L. Swabey, 51–67. Proceedings of the 8th National Convention of the Conference of Interpreter Trainers, Pomona, Calif.

———. 1994. An interpreted education: Inclusion or exclusion. In *Implications and complications for Deaf students of the full inclusion movement,* ed. C. Johnson and O. Cohen, 55–62. Washington, D.C.: Gallaudet Research Institute, Occasional Paper 94–102.

Part 6 Discourse Analysis

Tactile Swedish Sign Language:

Turn Taking in Signed Conversations

of People Who Are Deaf and Blind

Johanna Mesch

In visual signing the eyebrows are used as articulators (raised or squinted brows signal interrogative sentences), and the eyes function as turn-taking regulators (Bergman 1984; Vogt-Svendsen 1990; Coerts 1992). Although many people who are deaf and blind use sign language, a deaf-blind addressee cannot receive such nonmanual signals. When I started working on my doctoral thesis, with special focus on conversations of people who are deaf and blind, I became interested in the way that deaf-blind people communicate by touching each other's hands, and particularly in how they regulated turn taking during their conversations (Mesch 1990, 1994, 1998).

Some similarities and differences exist between tactile sign language and visual sign language. One reason for the similarity is that tactile Swedish Sign Language is based on Swedish Sign Language (SSL). Many deaf-blind people are born deaf and experience deteriorating vision as they get older.[1] These native users of sign language continue to use SSL when their vision deteriorates, but do so using the tactile mode.

The author would like to thank Anna-Lena Nilsson for translating the chapter. All illustrations are courtesy of the author.

1. One common cause of deaf-blindness is Usher syndrome, a hereditary disease that affects approximately 5 percent of all profoundly deaf people in Sweden (Nordiska nämnden för handikappfrågor 1993; Kimberling and Möller 1995; Hyvärinen 1995; FSDB 1995). People with Type I are born with a profound hearing loss, retinitis pigmentosa, and balance problems. People with Type II are born with a moderate to severe hearing loss, retinitis pigmentosa, and no balance problems.

TABLE 1. *Informants and Their Backgrounds*

Partici- pant	Deaf– Blind Status	Age at Time of Study	Age at Onset of Deafness	Blindness Etiology	Primary Language	Primary Mode of Receiving Communication
1a	deaf	26	birth	——	SSL	visual
1b	deaf-blind	54	birth	USH I	SSL	tactile
2a	deaf	55	3–4 years	——	SSL	visual
2b	deaf-blind	59	birth	Physical assault at age 56	SSL	tactile
3a	deaf-blind	——	——	——	——	——
3b	deaf-blind	55	2 years	USH I	SSL	tactile
4a	deaf-blind	55	birth	USH I	SSL	visual
4b	deaf-blind	59	birth	USH I	SSL	visual and tactile
5a	deaf-blind	39	birth	USH I	SSL	visual and tactile
5b	deaf-blind	47	gradual onset	USH II	Spoken Swedish and SSL	auditory and tactile
6a	deaf-blind	62	birth	USH I	FSL	tactile
6b	deaf-blind	71	birth	USH I	FSL	tactile

Note: In this chart, informants 3a and 1b are the same person. USH I denotes Usher syndrome Type I, USH II denotes Usher syndrome Type II.

This chapter describes how deaf-blind people regulate turn taking when using tactile sign language. The material for this study consisted of six videotaped dyads recorded between 1989 and 1995. The participants were either born deaf or became deaf at an early age; sign language is their native language. All consider themselves culturally Deaf. Eight of the nine deaf-blind people in the study have Usher syndrome, either Type I or Type II. One of the participants became blind from another disease (see table 1).

Five of the dyads used tactile SSL and one dyad used tactile Finnish Sign Language (FSL).[2] Two of the dyads included one deaf person and one deaf-blind person; three included two deaf-blind people, and one dyad included two Finnish deaf-blind people. These people were all asked to converse freely in sign language. A total of three hours of videotaped conver-

2. These languages are not identical, but the turn-taking rules appear to be basically the same for the two languages.

sations resulted. Parts of this material have been transcribed (168 utterances that function as questions, with their context).

Deaf-blind signers use their hands in two different conversation positions. In the *monologue position* both the signer's hands are held under the hands of the addressee, whereas in the *dialogue position* both participants hold their hands in identical ways: the right hand under the other person's left hand and the left hand on top of the other person's right hand. The two positions affect the structure of one- and two-handed signs and the way that lexical as well as nonlexical signals (e.g., different kinds of tapping; cf. Collins and Petronio 1998 on tactile American Sign Language [ASL]), are used in the two positions.

Analysis shows that differences in the vertical and the horizontal planes are used to regulate turn taking. Using four different conversational levels, a signer can signal turn change by, for example, lowering her hands from the turn level to the turn-change level at the end of her turn. The horizontal plane is divided into three different turn zones (areas between two participants). The turn holder (the person who has the turn) uses her own turn zone close to the body and finishes the turn by moving the hands to either the joint zone (midway between the interlocutors) or into the addressee's zone.

MONOLOGUE POSITION AND DIALOGUE POSITION

In the monologue position both the signer's hands are held under the addressee's hands. The basic principle for using the monologue position is that interlocutor A articulates a sign by touching both hands under interlocutor B's hands. When A is nearing a turn transition, B has to move his hands from the addressee's position on top of A's hands and position them under A's hands (see figure 1).

The dialogue position is the most frequently used conversation position between two deaf-blind people. In this position the signer's right hand is held under the addressee's hand, and the left hand is held on top of the addressee's hand (see figure 2).

In the dialogue position A and B have their hands in different positions, touching each other. A has her right hand under B's left hand and her left hand on top of B's right hand. B's hands are held correspondingly: the right hand under A's left hand and the left hand on top of A's right hand.

FIGURE 1. *Monologue position. To the right, A makes the sign* HAFT *(perfect marker). B reads the sign with his hands on the back of A's hands.*

This positioning means that A and B do not have to change their hand positions during turn transitions. Both the dialogue and the monologue position require an equal amount of cooperation from the participants in the conversation (i.e., the signer verifies that the addressee understands, and the addressee uses back-channeling signals during the conversation).

In conversations with deaf-blind people, the position most suitable for the situation at hand is chosen. The monologue position is often used in interpreting situations and in conversations between deaf-blind people

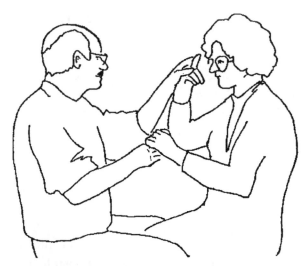

FIGURE 2. *Dialogue position. To the right, A signs* FEL *("wrong") with her right hand, which is under B's left hand. A's left hand is on top on the back of B's hand.*

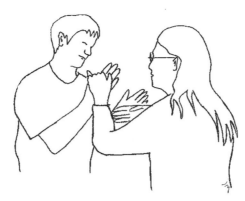

FIGURE 3. STÄMMA *("that's right") in the monologue position. Location: left flat hand, directed rightward, palm turned upward. Handshape: right flat hand, directed forward, palm turned leftward. Movement: repeated contact with the other flat hand.*

when the signer holds a long turn and the addressee is receiving the whole time. It is also used when the signer is left-handed, in which case his left hand will be placed on top of the addressee's hand in the dialogue position. A left-handed person will therefore sign in the monologue position with his active left hand under the addressee's hand. I found that the dialogue position was more frequently used by all informants. Only one of the study participants was left-handed.

Parts of the Manual Sign Structure

Whether the signer's hands are held in the monologue or the dialogue position also affects parts of the manual sign structure (see Bergman 1979 for the structure of one- and two-handed signs; Svenskt teckenspråkslexikon 1997). The addressee's hands may constitute obstacles for the signer's articulation of signs. Examples of signs from my study illustrate their structure in visual signing and their articulation in the monologue and the dialogue positions. For *single-articulator* signs (one-handed), the difference between the two positions is not great. For double-articulator signs, however, the signer's left hand in the dialogue position has to be modified because the addressee's hand is held under the signer's palm. For single-articulator signs and with the other hand as the manual place of articulation, contact in the dialogue position can vary (e.g., STÄMMA ["that's right"]). See figures 3, 4, 5, and 6.

FIGURE 4. STÄMMA *("that's right") in the dialogue position with contact on B's right palm.*

Comparison of the Monologue and the Dialogue Positions

The only signs that differ from the monologue to the dialogue position are those in which the back of the hand is the place of articulation. Contact then is made on the back of the addressee's hand (compare figure 7 to figures 8 and 9).

CONVERSATIONAL LEVELS

Deaf-blind people regulate turn taking by moving their hands in both the vertical and the horizontal planes (see figures 10, 11, 12, and 13). The former is divided into different conversational levels:

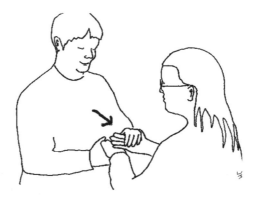

FIGURE 5. *B to the right, making the sign* STÄMMA *("that's right") on the back of her own hand.*

FIGURE 6. *STÄMMA ("that's right") in the dialogue position with contact made on the forearm.*

- *the rest level* (marked in the following transcription with ⇑ when the hands move up from the rest level, that is, initializing, and with ⇓ when they move back to the rest level)
- *the turn level* (marked by a ↑)
- *the hesitation level* (marked by a ⊥ at the beginning and a ⊤ at the end)
- *the turn-change level* (marked by a ↓)

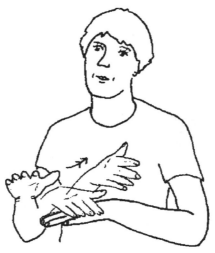

FIGURE 7. *KATT ("cat") in visual sign language. Single articulator and manual place of articulation. Location: left flat hand, directed to the right, palm turned down. Handshape: right flat hand, directed forward, palm turned down. Movement: moves inward a couple of times in contact with the upper side of the left hand.*

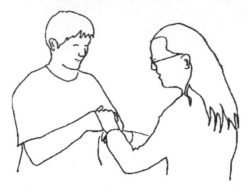

FIGURE 8. *KATT ("cat") in tactile sign language, in the monologue position.*
Location: the addressee's right flat hand, directed forward, palm turned down.
Handshape: right flat hand, directed to the left, palm turned down. Movement:
moves inward a couple of times in contact with the upper side of the addres-
see's hand.

In this study, deaf-blind participants regulate turn changes by lowering their hands to the turn-change level and by slowing down their signing at the end of their turn. Quick transitions that are made without lowering the hands are marked with an equal sign (=), without overlapping. Example 1 illustrates how deaf-blind people regulate turn taking by moving their hands in the vertical plane.

FIGURE 9. *KATT ("cat") in tactile sign language, in the dialogue position. Location:*
left: flat hand, directed forward, palm turned down. Handshape: right flat hand,
directed to the left, palm turned down. Movement: moves inward a couple of
times in contact with the upper side of the left hand.

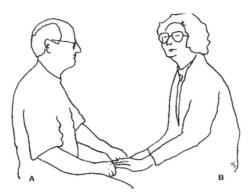

FIGURE 10. *Both A's and B's hands at rest level (marked by* ⇊*)* .

EXAMPLE 1. Finnish Sign Language in a Deaf-Blind Dyad
(English Gloss and Translation)

6b ↑ poly-CLIMB-UP BLOW HARD BLOW INDEX-c poly-CLIMB-UP STAND-dur poly-
CLIMB-UP STONE PATH poly-WALK-UP-MOUNTAINTOP ↓

6a ↑ STRONG INDEX-adr WITH IMPOSSIBLE INDEX-c ↓ (b:YES-tap) ⇊   (1.0)

6a ⇈ WANT MORE WALK INDEX-adr =

6b ↑ NOT-KNOW ((neg)) INDEX-c ↓ (.) ↓ INDEX-c STAY-HOME ⇊

6a ⇈ Y-E-S ⇊

6b I climbed up and it was blowing hard. I rested for a while and then continued to climb the path till I reached the top of the mountain.

6a That was strong of you! Impossible for me. (b: Yes)   (1.0)

6a Do you want to go there again?

6b I don't know. I think I'll stay home.

6a Yes.

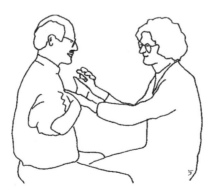

FIGURE 11. *A to the left holds the turn, the hands are at the turn level (marked by* ⇈ *when the hands move up from the rest level, or marked by* ↑ *when the hands move up from turn change level).*

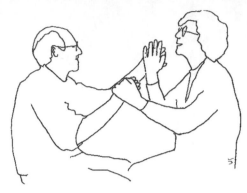

FIGURE 12. *B to the right now holds the turn and thinks for a while; the hands are at the hesitation level (marked by* ⊥ *at the beginning and* ⊤ *at the end).*

TURN ZONES

The horizontal plane is divided into three different turn zones: A's own turn zone (figure 11), the *joint* zone (figure 14), and B's own turn zone (figure 15). The signing space in front of the signer is used by both of the signers (i.e., they have a common signing space). B is made aware of A finishing a turn by, for example, A moving her hands to the joint zone (figure 16).

BACK CHANNELING

Back channeling refers to the addressee's use of various signals that tell the signer to continue and that signal understanding and assent during the

FIGURE 13. *A leaves the turn to B by lowering the hands to the turn-change level (marked by* ↓*).*

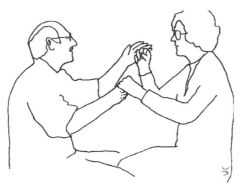

FIGURE 14. *The joint zone at the turn-change level.*

signer's turn (Duncan 1973; Linell and Gustavsson 1987; Norrby 1996). In tactile SSL these signals are divided into different kinds of nonlinguistic tactile tap signals: tap, YES-tap and thumb tap (figures 17 and 18; Mesch 1998). Two others are waving and thumb-press (used to mean "what"). The most frequent lexical back channeling is the fingerspelled sign J-A ("yes"), seen in figure 19. The signs JASSÅ ("is that so") and ALDRIG ("never") are also used.

In the monologue position, the addressee makes nonlexical back channeling by lightly touching the back of both the signer's hands. But if the addressee wants to give lexical back channeling, he must move his right hand to the position under the signer's left hand. In the dialogue position, nonlexical back channeling is usually given by the addressee by pressing or tapping with the thumb on the signer's left hand (example 2). In this position it is easier to give lexical back channeling without having to change the hand positions.

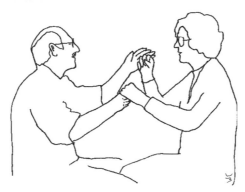

FIGURE 15. *B's (to the right) own turn zone.*

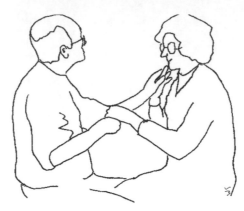

FIGURE 16. *B to the right signs* BRA *("good") with a single articulator in her own turn zone, and B's left hand is held in the joint zone.*

EXAMPLE 2. SSL in a Deaf-Blind Dyad
(English Gloss and translation)

5b ((body tilted forward)) WHAT-fl SAY-fl WAIT ((body tilted back)) UNDERSTAND
NOT INDEX-C REPEAT SLOW WORK GOOD → (a: thumb tap) SIGN EASY (a:
thumb tap)

5b What did you say? "Wait" is what I say when I don't understand and ask for
repetition. That works well. (5a: yes) It is easier with sign language. (5a: yes)

SUPPORT TURNS

Cooperation between addressee and signer is indicated by the use of
support turns. Questions consist not just of yes/no questions, alternative
questions, and wh-questions but also support questions. These questions
have an information-seeking function and are executed by the signer. Support questions are like yes/no questions and wh-questions. Their function

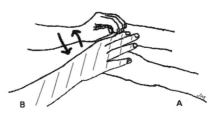

FIGURE 17. *Tap. B to the left is tapping with the flat hand on the top of A's hand
in the monologue position.*

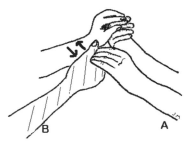

FIGURE 18. YES-*tap. The thumb and two fingers make contact repeatedly on A's hand.*

is to request feedback and clarification and can be executed by either conversational partner, the signer or the receiver.

In addition to support questions, the signer also uses other signs or signals requesting feedback. Delay in the sign is executed at the beginning of the utterance and repetition of the sign checks whether the receiver is following along, knows the sign, and so on. The receiver can request clarification by using nonlinguistic signals such as waving and thumb pressure (Mesch 1998).

The signer poses questions with a request for back channeling, often at the end of an utterance (e.g., UNDERSTAND INDEX-adr [example 3]), or with topic marking using an extended hold of the first sign, or with sign repetition. The addressee in turn asks for clarification or repetition of a sign or an utterance with the help of back channeling signals (e.g., waving or thumb press) or lexical back channeling (e.g., HOW MANY SAY INDEX-adr) as in example 4.

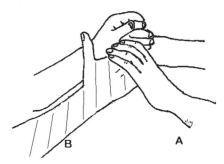

FIGURE 19. *B to the left fingerspells* J-A *("yes"); it is made with the flat hand where the index finger and the long finger touch the thumb.*

EXAMPLE 3. SSL in a Deaf-Blind Dyad
(English Gloss and Translation)

3b BUT INDEX-HERE STOCKHOLM ONE TICKET V-A-L-I-D THREE M-I-L-E I-F IN-
DEX-C GO TO A-R-L-A-N-D-A MUST TAKE TWO TICKET MEAN FOUR MILE MUST
TAKE TWO TICKET (.) YES ((nod)) (.) → UNDERSTAND INDEX-adr

3a UNDERSTAND

3b But here in Stockholm one ticket is only valid for three miles. If I go to Ar-
landa I have to use two tickets. That means if it is four miles you have to use
two tickets. Do you understand?

3a I understand.

EXAMPLE 4. SSL in a Deaf-Blind Dyad
(English Gloss and Translation)

5a REPEAT poly-WALK-fl PAY NEG "NEVER-MIND" × 2 INDEX-C REPEAT GOOD × 2
poly-GO-BY-LIFT TOTAL FIVE SIX TIME UP-AND-DOWN →

5b HOW-MANY HOW-MANY SAY INDEX-adr HOW-MANY TIME

5a FIVE OR SIX TIME UP-AND-DOWN FREE BUT NOT POSS-C HUSBAND PAY

5a I went for free with the ski-lift five or six times up.

5b How many how many did you say, how many times?

5a Five or six times for free, but my husband had to pay.

The occurrence of misunderstandings is lessened by using the dialogue position even though this position makes it more difficult to receive the information from the left hand, which is held on the right hand of the other person. But the advantage of the dialogue position is that it makes it possible to receive various kinds of back channeling in support turns.

CONCLUSION

I have shown how deaf-blind people use their hands in two different conversation positions when signing—the monologue position and the dialogue position—and how these positions affect the structure of one- and two-handed signs. People who are deaf and blind also regulate turn taking by using turn levels and turn zones, as shown in the examples. Both lexical and nonlexical back channeling—which signal continuation, understanding, or agreement—are also done in the tactile mode.

Support turns show an intense cooperation between the deaf-blind interlocutors, so that both may be involved in the dialogue and avoid major misunderstandings. Interestingly, the structure of the signs used in the dialogue is quite flexible and depends on the hand position in the monologue and dialogue positions.

I hope that this work will provide new perspectives to sign language researchers and interpreter trainers. Future research needs include sign language issues such as conversation analysis; we might also find it interesting to compare tactile SSL with other sign languages in tactile form.

REFERENCES

Bergman, B. 1979. *Signed Swedish*. Stockholm: Educational Research, National Swedish Board of Education.

———. 1984. Nonmanual components of signed language: Some sentence types in Swedish Sign Language. In *Recent research on European sign languages*, ed. F. Loncke, P. Boyes-Braem, and Y. Lebrun, 49–59. Lisse: Swets and Zeitlinger B.V.

Coerts, J. A. 1992. *Nonmanual grammatical markers: An analysis of interrogatives, negations, and topicalisations in Sign Language of the Netherlands.* Ph.D. diss., Amsterdam University.

Collins, S., and K. Petronio. 1998. What happens in tactile ASL? In *Pinky extension and eye gaze: Language use in Deaf communities*, ed. Ceil Lucas, 18–37. Washington, D.C.: Gallaudet University Press.

Duncan, S. 1973. Toward a grammar for dyadic conversation. *Semiotica* 9: 29–46.

Föreningen Sveriges Dövblinda (FSDB). 1995. *Våga se lite längre . . . Rehabilitering av dövblinda i ett livslångt perspektiv.* L. Hammarstedt. Slutrapport: FSDB's rehabiliterings-projekt.

Hammarstedt, L., ed. 1995. Våga se lite längre: Rehabilitering av dövblinda i ett livslångt perspektiv. Rehabilitation Final Project, Föreningen Sveriges Dövblinda (The Swedish Association of the Deaf-Blind).

Hedberg, T., ed. 1997. *Svenskt teckenspråkslexikon* (Swedish Sign Language Dictionary). Leksand, Sweden: Sveriges Dövas Riksförbund.

Hyvärinen, L. 1995. Nytt och gammalt om ögon och syn i Ushers syndrom. *Nyhedsbrevet* 2. Dronninglund: Nordisk Uddannelsescenter for Døvblindepersonale.

Kimberling, W. J., and C. Möller. 1995. Clinical and molecular genetics of Usher syndrome. *Journal of the American Academy of Audiology* 6 (1): 63–72.

Linell, P., and L. Gustavsson. 1987. Initial och respons. Om dialogens dynamik, dominans och koherens. *Studies in Communication* 15. Linköping: Linköpings Universitet, Tema Kommunikation.

Mesch, J. 1990. Dövblindas teckenspråk (Sign language of the deaf-blind). Manuscript, Stockholm University, Department of Linguistics, Sign Language Department.

——. 1994. Dövblindas teckenspråk. *Forskning om Teckenspråk XVIII.* Stockholm University, Department of Linguistics.

——. 1996. Dövblindas taktila teckenspråk. In *Rapport fra Nordisk Konference om Døvblindhed, København,* August 28–September 1, 1996, 25–28. Dronninglund: Nordisk Uddannelsescenter for Døvblindepersonale.

——. 1998. Teckenspråk i taktil form: Turtagning och frågor i dövblindas samtal på teckenspråk (Tactile Swedish Sign Language: Turn-taking and questions in conversations of deaf-blind people in sign language). Ph.D. diss., Stockholm University, Department of Linguistics.

Nordiska Nämnden för Handikappfrågor (The Nordic Committe on Disability). 1993. *Dövblindas livsvillkor i Norden inför år 2000* (Conditions of life of the deaf-blind in the Nordic countries facing year 2000). Report No. 8/93. Vällingby: Nordiska Nämnden för Handikappfrågor.

Norrby, C. 1996. *Samtalsanalys. Så gör vi när vi pratar med varandra.* Lund: Studentlitteratur.

Vogt-Svendsen, M. 1990. Eye gaze in Norwegian Sign Language interrogatives. In *SLR 1987: Papers from the Fourth International Symposium on Sign Language Research,* ed. W. H. Edmondson and F. Karlsson, 153–62. Hamburg: Signum Press.

Transcription Conventions

Example	Use
<u>Underline</u>	Indicates the line where the example in question is found.
SIGN	A signed word
S-I-G-N	A fingerspelled word
SIGN-f	Locus marker indicating directions and positions relative to the signer
-f =	front of signer
-c =	center, near or in contact with the signer's body
-l =	left
-fl =	front-left
-fr =	front-right
-r =	right
Poly-SIGN	Indicates a polymorphous (modified) or polysynthetic sign
INDEX-adr	Place-deictic reference to the addressee
-dur	Delay measured in tenths of a second, the last sign is held in the air
(.)	Micropause (under 0.3 seconds long)
(1.0)	Pause (measured in tenths of a second)
(5b: YES)	Feedback from the other signer
((neg))	Negation, nonmanual comment, etc.
=	Quick turn change without a pause after every utterance (called launching, a kind of relay between participants)
⇑	Indicates initialization with A (the signer) raising her hands to the turn level to take the turn
⇓	Indicates resting position with A lowering her hands to her knees or waist to complete the turn
↑	Indicates turn level with A raising her hands up from the turn change level
↓	Indicates the turn change level with A's hands being lowered to the turn change level (the hands are relaxed or A can hold her hands in the air a moment)
⊥	Indicates the beginning of the hesitation level
⊤	Indicates the end of the hesitation level

Semiotic Aspects of Argentine

Sign Language: Analysis

of a Videotaped "Interview"

María Ignacia Massone and Rosana Famularo

An examination of the semiotic aspects of a language involves asking questions such as: What is a text? What are the characteristics of an interview? What semiotic value does television have, especially when we analyze an interview with a Deaf signer? Although all of these questions deserve our attention, we explain each concept briefly in this chapter.[1] We intend to clarify some of the functions of these different aspects in order to understand their interrelationships in the corpus analyzed.

First, it is important to explain that all the communicative interactions among Deaf people in Argentina are conversational. Sign languages have an oral tradition, that is to say, they are transmitted from generation to generation in face-to-face communication. Several types of linguistic contact situations exist among Deaf people or among Deaf and hearing people (Massone and Menéndez 1997). Such interactions constitute oral exchanges as a series of events whose whole conforms to a text that it produces in a given context.

According to van Dijk (1978), an interaction is also an action that affects, alters, or maintains the relationships that participants establish in face-to-face communication. Van Dijk also implies that such relationships include those between the elements of a text as well as those that are created by the exchange between the participants. Discourse is thus conceived as the product of an interactive process based on a number of agreements that are sometimes spontaneous and at other times in need of the intervention of transaction procedures or negotiations. The participants in all

The authors wish to thank Gilda Bona for her careful reading and comments.

verbal exchanges should agree on the formal rules that govern the particular verbal game that they are playing.

We thus define *discourse* as human communication, whether it is written, oral, graphic, etc. But no matter how the discourse originates, ultimately, text is what the analyst must work with. Comprising a series of statements, a text is the product of discursive action, characterized by its relationships and resulting from cohesive features and from illocutionary and perlocutionary forces. Therefore, a text can be analyzed by conceptualizing the discursive rules that produce it. This perception of discourse implies the recognition of a dynamic structure that surpasses it even though it is manifested in and by the text. In many instances the text is a linguistic materialization of such rules of discourse. Although different in nature, a visual image may also be analyzed as text when it possesses these prescribed properties.

An interview is an essentially conversational situation with a formal hierarchy that defines the relationship between the participants. The interviewer conducts the discursive event, and the interviewee occupies a subordinate position. According to Labov (1983), the speech of the interviewee is formal because it is public, directed, and controlled in response to the presence of an outside observer. On the other hand, as every linguistic interchange may be compared to a marketplace in which valuable linguistic "goods" are exchanged, the interview may be seen as a linguistic "marketplace" in which the sociological relationships of the participants, the potential audience, and the video filming and editing teams are considered.

Television designs a global assembly that conveys reflection because it has been edited. What is seen is the final product of the complex process of editing. This process presupposes not only the physical act of editing, but also interpretation by the editors. The images that television produces must guarantee, on the other hand, the reality of what they show because they are seen by an audience, even though their "reality" must also be interpreted by the audience.

An implication process exists with regard to the audience, which participates in the ongoing presentation of images and texts. Researchers have shown that the theatrical nature of television thus implies social and communicative relationships mediated by images. There always exists equivalence in images and never similarity with the history of the world as it is always interpreted by the editors, directors, and so on. That is to say, television or any filmed product is a semiotic realization that conveys plural meanings due to the complex processes of interpretation on the part of the multiple participants. According to Baudrillard, "journalists and publicists are manipulators of myth: they stage an object or event as fiction" (1990, 93). Baudrillard maintained that, in the media,

> the discourse of the world tries to be detached. . . . [The media] prescribe through the systematic succession of messages an equivalence between story and news item, between event and spectacle, between news and advertising at the level of the sign . . . disarticulating the real into successive and equivalent signs. (1990, 88)

In this chapter we analyze a signed "text"—that is, a videotaped interview. Our objective is to determine discursive practices that regulate the ritual of a journalistic interview in Argentine Sign Language (LSA). The interview ("text") lends itself to several different types of analyses ("readings"). As linguists we could analyze certain discursive and textual properties. However, because the interview is captured on videotape, we examined it as though we were an audience that recognized the rules of television discourse in video format.

METHODOLOGY

We analyzed a signed interview in LSA that was videotaped in the hope of relating the experiences of a Deaf woman, Emilia Machado. The interviewee chairs the Argentine Deaf Confederation and is an important figure in the Argentine Deaf community. The seven-minute videotape is called "White Noise" (Schujman 1998). Although we refer to the interviewer as one person, we recognize that the videotaping was a collaborative effort. The videotape is interpreted as a final product within the framework of discourse analysis and semiotic interpretation. To ensure accuracy, we have transcribed and glossed the signed interventions both separately and together.

RESULTS

A description of the visual sequences and signed interventions will help illustrate our analysis of the data. The first visual sequence is that of a person seen from behind, casually walking along a sidewalk and totally immersed in her own silence, completely unconscious of or disregarding the ambient noises: the roar of a passing train, the cars on the streets, and several people walking their dogs nearby. The camera focuses on these elements, emphasizing the source of the noises. Unaware of these sounds, the person walking down the sidewalk seems to have a destination in mind.

Immediately after this opening scene, the title "White Noise" appears superimposed on the image of the woman and is followed by a "curtain" of white noise that blots out the picture. The first signed intervention appears. The interviewer informs the audience that the person they have seen is Deaf. The camera is positioned below the woman and at a diagonal angle (and remains in this position) in order to emphasize the perspective of her face and of the hands signing.

Next we see the woman sitting in a corner of her living room, signing. The only movement in the scene comes from her hands. As a counterpart to the first scene, the interviewee explains to the interviewer that she has no problems communicating with different people in different places — whether at the supermarket or the doctor's office. Her signing evokes in the audience a mental image of this Deaf person going from one social hearing place to another and communicating efficiently and naturally with different people and by different means — talking, writing, gesturing. Thus the static camera opposes the progressive image evoked by the signing. The interviewer is showing the audience that in spite of her apparent lack of awareness of the noises around her earlier and her seeming defenselessness, a Deaf person may accomplish daily communication efficiently and develop normally in life.

The curtain of white noise descends once again, and through it the audience gradually discerns the ticking of a clock and the dripping of a faucet. The next signed intervention shows the interviewee introducing herself in the same place as before and from the same angle. She states her name and the facts that she was born profoundly deaf and is married. Deaf people in the Argentine Deaf community always introduce themselves to an unknown Deaf or hearing person by identifying their deaf/hearing status (Massone 1999). Although the fact that she is married may seem superficial to an audience in a developed country, it is not considered insignificant in Argentina. Deaf people there continue to be perceived as handicapped (rather than from the perspective of the socio-anthropological model of deafness), and are thus considered unable to lead a normal and productive life. The interviewee overtly states this information with the clear intention of showing her absolutely normal condition to the interviewer and to the audience.

The next visual sequence is a long shot in slow motion as the camera enters the building of the Argentine Deaf Confederation. There the interviewee and other Deaf instructors are teaching Argentine Sign Language and Deaf culture to hearing students. The audience sees several close-ups of their hands signing. The black-and-white image evokes in the audience an awareness of the seriousness of this academic work and the weighty responsibility the teachers shoulder in helping students mainstream with hearing people. Here the interviewer presents the interviewee squarely in her own world. In previous signed interventions, the audience learned about her development in life from her answers; now she is shown in action.

The next image presents her once more in domestic surroundings. The interviewee explains the resources she uses, such as a fax machine. Through her own account of activities, she comes across as resourceful and competent. Her signing is interrupted by a close-up of her face, while her hands sign that she knows that the fax machine is receiving when her cat walks around her legs and on the machine. The noise and the image of her cat in motion again interrupts her signing. The camera finally focuses on her signed utterances.

Next, the interviewee is shown preparing tea in her kitchen. Each action is interrupted with a close-up in slow motion without the noises usually generated by such activity, such as the striking of matches, the hissing of gas coming out of the burner, and the stirring of the spoon in the cup. These silent close-ups reveal to the audience that although she does not hear those noises, she manages without difficulty.

The curtain of white noise returns once more, followed by a shot of the woman signing again in her living room. She is explaining how she knows when her daughter has returned home. Her signing is interrupted by a close-up in slow motion of her face; she continues signing, and, as the camera pans to her hands, she finishes signing. The following image shows the curtains ruffled by the stream of air produced when the door is opened as her daughter arrives home. In this final signing intervention, the image of the interviewee's hands is multiplied on the walls. The videotape ends with the curtain of white noise, followed by the title of the videotape and a close-up of a silhouette of the interviewee's face.

DISCUSSION

The signed "text" and the images in the "interview" are internally coherent. As analysts we observed a series of internal rules and relationships among these different aspects, and we made the videotape into a discursive production. First we analyzed the title of the videotaped interview — "White Noise"—which permits various interpretations. For instance, the word *white* connotes absence, in this case, deafness, meaning absence of sound. Also, the camera denotes gray rain at the beginning of the videotape, referencing the visual image of white noise and connoting fissure in the lack of sound. The connotations of the title are reinforced by the images. The camera shows different elements of life that produce noise: trains, vehicles, and dogs; however, the interviewee is seen walking naturally, quite detached from these elements. Because these aspects appear at the beginning of the videotape, the interviewer shows the audience — through written text and visual image—specific aspects of the world of Deaf people, the core of their condition.

Once this situation is presented, the interviewee explains her lack of communication problems, and this is the idea that is developed throughout the interview. The interviewer's purpose is achieved: to show the audience that, despite the nonexistence of sound, this Deaf woman manages quite normally and happily and experiences few conflicts, which she resolves when they arise.

The deaf woman's discourse evidences different existential facts about deafness, conflicts whose resolutions are given. The interviewee alludes, for example, to problems that are generated in intercultural communicative interactions among Deaf and hearing people and her ability to solve them by various means. Sound is conspicuous by its absence throughout the videotape; the emphasis is on the resourcefulness of Deaf people in finding solutions to everyday difficulties. Deaf people constitute a culture that uses visual and tactile behaviors to get on in life, behaviors that are sometimes unperceived by the hearing mainstream. Text and image throughout the videotape give voice not only to a Deaf woman's testimony but also to the Deaf culture that helps its members manage a normal daily life.

The videotaped interview constitutes a discourse because it has been coproduced as a collaborative work between interviewer and interviewee. Because a sign language interpreter was not visible in the film and because a Deaf person would not sign LSA to a hearing or Deaf person who had no knowledge of it, we thus assume that the interviewer knew LSA. The audience may be mixed—Deaf and hearing or simply hearing—as the signed interventions are captioned.

Because the interviewer is physically absent, the camera becomes his eyes. So why do we consider this discourse to be an interview? In the first place, at the end of each of her interventions, the interviewee places her body and hands in a relaxed position and crosses her legs; in this way she gives kinetic clues for turn taking because she appears to be waiting for the next question. Having her hands in a resting position indicates a suspension, a pause in the discourse during which the signer coordinates the previous text with the one to follow. When she takes her turn, her muscles tense slightly.

In addition, the interviewee on several occasions addresses a second person: PRO-1 SAY PRO-2 and uses the temporal marker IN-THE-PAST to indicate the end of her answer. She also addresses a second person when she uses the sign TO-WAIT in order to guarantee an uninterrupted period of discourse in which the narrative holds the attention of the other participant (a preface to narrative). She intends to narrate and thus must achieve a suspension of the normal turn-taking mechanism of the interview.

Furthermore, each intervention of the interviewee alludes to a specific topic, which implies that she is responding to questions (e.g., whether she has communication problems, what her name is, what function her cat fulfills in her domestic life, and how she knows that her daughter has returned home).

Finally, the camera interrupts the interviewee's signed "text" to show aspects of her daily life by means of alternating shots. That is, when the interviewee relinquishes her turn through the nonmanual features previously described, the interviewer is transformed into both the camera and the image.

After the first signed intervention, the interviewer begins to violate the classic parameters of an objective interview that has a purpose (his purpose is a positive social representation of Deafness through the presentation of images). He is physically present through the "eye" of his camera. Through the different images that depict the life of the interviewee, the interviewer demonstrates, on the one hand, his nonneutrality and his emotive interpretation of her testimony. He is thus presenting a model. We, the audience, know who the interviewee is, and we knew beforehand that she is a model because of her take-charge demeanor and her practically complete assimilation to mainstream society.

He exhibits a clear and unequivocal bias. Perhaps because he is aware of his predisposition, he prefers to physically disappear and give way to the images so that they may (1) reinforce the positive representation given by his interviewee and (2) add other aspects that help to portray the Deaf model that he is presenting to his audience.

The interviewer presents numerous hints to the audience that indicate that he is clearly moved by his interviewee, by her way of communicating, and by the diverse aspects of the Deaf culture. These hints include the close-ups in slow motion of the interviewee's hands signing, the amplification of this form of communication through the shadows on the walls, certain visual images (for example, the movement of the wind in the curtain) subordinated to the signed interventions that emphasize what the interviewee is explaining, and the constant perception of a Deaf person in total harmony with the different situations she encounters in the street, at home, at school. These devices point out the absence of dissonance between interviewer and interviewee.

Although there are two participants in this "interview" and despite the absence of conflict (rather, just the opposite), we did not consider analyzing this videotape as a conversation because all semiotic behavior implies a relationship of power. The camera (i.e., the interviewer) is dominant because the filming is the material support that begins and ends the interview, thus imposing its interpretation of the content as well as the purpose in presenting the interviewee as a Deaf model.

Clearly the filmmaker empathizes with the interviewee. In other words, the conversational territories that each participant manages, given their own competence, defers to the final materialization of the interview: that is, the image on video. The interviewer does not allow the interviewee to walk through his or her own territory—the organization of successive images that create the final video—thus the camera and the final editing issues assume the dominant role.

The interviewee is the one filmed and presented through the eye of the camera. This is another reason that this videotape is an interview and not a conversation, as it shows the proper hierarchy of all interviews in spite of an interviewer's bias. On the other hand, the interviewee makes use of a formal register because she knows that her discourse is public. The formal register is evidenced in the corporal inflexibility (the eye gaze toward the other participant and the use of a larger signing space). Massone (1999) describes three types of interpersonal social distances — public, private, and intimate. The use of the interviewee's formal register is another argument in favor of the existence of an interview and not of a conversation.

Given this peaceful negotiation, the result is a satisfactory commitment and success on the part of the interviewee. The communicative exchange is not for naught because the purpose remains clear to the audience. The semiotic value of television is presented in this reinforcement of the clarity of the purpose; the image guarantees the reality of what is seen. With this idea of reinforcing reality, the interviewer prefers to present the image instead of presenting himself in order to personally convince the audience of his purpose.

This interview is a succession of turn shifts. It is presented as a dual construction that is elaborated by both participants because both have the same purpose: to present a positive representation of Deafness. Neither tries to impose on the other a specific discursive organization.

Moreover, the interview is presented as a hierarchic organization constituted by variable-range units — transactions or successive communicative interventions of both participants — in which the interviewer allows the camera to reinforce and confirm his own vision of the interviewee. Through sign language and image, both participants show the same perception; a mutual self-confirmation appears to offer to their audience that same perception. It is as though we — as both interviewee and interviewer — see Deaf people. Between them is an implicit negotiation in order to offer their audience the same social representation of Deaf people.

In addition, we must take into account the fact that the visual medium shows only successful cases. Only rarely are marginal people interviewed and then only to explore marginality or to perpetuate the social representations of the dominant class. Deaf people have been most often represented socially as marginal, handicapped people who need society's assistance.

The interviewer could have followed the hierarchy of the classic interview and its merely referential function (i.e., objective, informative, purely denotative, and unique). In such a case, the location of both participants in an interview must defer, thus showing its hierarchic structure with the interviewer in the dominant position. However, in this videotape there is only a difference in the use of the filming techniques and the edited, final images.

Furthermore, because journalists represent their audience, the interviewer could have shown the negative social image that society has of Deaf people as a rule. The articles or interviews serve to validate, represent, and constitute public opinion; they purport to preserve the values of the dominant social groups. In Argentina the Deaf presence in written or audiovisual means of social communication practically does not exist. When the Deaf presence appears in the media, negative attitudes are expressed, and the audience is thus predisposed to view Deaf people as handicapped or needy. The media emphasize and reproduce a negative image of minorities, thus encouraging intolerance, prejudice, and discrimination against Deaf people.

According to van Dijk (1997), by means of discursive communication, the dominant majority promotes a mindset that it is essential to legitimate and sustain its dominant position. Prejudicial attitudes are not expressed solely in discriminatory actions but are communicated to other members of groups within the widest spectrum of ethnic ideological consensus; thus, their efficiency is based on persuasive normalization. We thus recognize that in order to permit the access of minority groups to the multicultural world of this new postmodern era, it is vital that the media present different cultural visions of minority groups in order to not only eradicate prejudice but also to endorse a new ethnic ideological consensus.

Therefore, the interviewer altered his filming technique as he began to empathize with the interviewee. With the "eye" of the camera in the foreground, the film performed an expressive function. Through close-ups, half-shots, and the dramatic capture of the shadows of the hands, this function assumes the foremost position in the video. The image may thus be interpreted as evoking distinct aspects of the interviewee's daily life as well as different expressive tonalities, such as (1) the image of the interviewee as teacher intended to elicit interjections of astonishment on the part of the audience, (2) the inclusion of elements that produce noise, (3) scenes of the interviewee living a normal daily and academic life, and (4) the shadows on the wall that seem to multiply the actual number of hands.

In the context of Kerbrat-Orecchioni's (1986) enunciation theory, we might consider the images as lexical units proper of subjective discourse with which the addresser explicitly agrees or recognizes himself as the evaluative source of information or, at other times, is simply enlightened regarding the cultural characteristics of Deaf people. In other words, the image employs the Deaf testimony to refer to different aspects of daily life related to deafness. The presentation of different aspects through signed text and images draws a portrait of a Deaf model and her successful interaction with hearing people. This expressive device aspires to influence the audience and also to become as emotionally involved as the interviewer.

The video image as sign thus not only portrays the interviewee's daily routine but also connotes a life lived naturally, without major conflicts, plus additional cultural aspects of the life of Deaf people. The videotaped interview may thus be considered as a discourse in which denotation plays an important role, with a series of articulated connotations that give a semantic richness and an aesthetic value to the message. A dialectic game exists between what is said (content level) and how it is said (expression level).

Due to the characteristics of the interview analyzed throughout this chapter, such work is in accordance with the Informative Creative school of journalism (Bernal and Chillon 1985). The productions of this school are descriptive or narrative-explanatory texts that use stylistic figures of text and image. The signing text in LSA is narrative because it reports experiences of the interviewee's daily life. However, the interviewee not only tells the audience about the things she does but also explains why and how: why she does not have communication problems, how the cat helps her to access auditory cues, how she realizes her daughter has arrived.

For his part, the interviewer also explains—through the images—how the Deaf model carries out activities just like any other individual. The explanatory discourse on one hand implies argumentation and, on the other, is used when a cognitive obstacle exists; then it gives rise to a phase in which the problem has a solution and restores the symmetry between participants due to the fact that the addresser generally knows what the addressee ignores. This type of discourse is defined as *metafunctional* because its objective is the functionality of interaction (Hante 1988; Leclaire-Hante 1988).

Taking these characteristics of explanatory discourse into account, we imagine that both participants know that the addressee is plural—an audience. And considering that the audience has a negative view of Deaf people, we use this type of discourse to analyze and synthesize the concepts of Deaf people that interviewer and interviewee share, with the ultimate goal of informing and persuading the audience. The presence of the audience is felt throughout the videotape.

In brief, our analysis presents the signed interview as a metatext with a metamessage that frames Deaf people as equal to hearing people in many respects and yet different from, but not inferior to, others. In Goffman's terms (1974), the filmed interview shows a symmetrical alignment between Deaf and hearing people.

The hierarchical structure of interviews seems to falter as the interviewee sends a metamessage of superiority because she is the one who has superior knowledge about Deaf people and their culture. Although, as we have shown, the interview cannot cast off its inherent structural characteristics, the interviewee (who has more information on a particular subject than either the audience or the interviewer) is framed as higher up in the hierarchy by virtue of greater knowledge and competence (Tannen 1990).

The metamessage is in accordance with the semiotic value of television or any filmed production. Even though the interview we have analyzed does not represent the "spectacle of the event" (Ramonet 1998, 19), the semiotic value of filmed information is nevertheless present through the pathos shown by the interviewer and the audience: "If the emotion that you feel is true, the information is true," and "it is enough to see in order to understand" (Ramonet 1998, 13).

We could hypothesize that if a positive social representation of the Deaf experience could be transmitted through the mass media, as happened with the "Diana effect," an "emotional globalization" would occur that would greatly benefit Deaf people (Ramonet 1998, 13).

REFERENCES

Baudrillard, J. 1990. *The revenge of the crystal.* London: Pluto Press.

Bernal, S., and L. A. Chillon. 1985. *Periodismo informativo de creacion* (Informative creative school of journalism). Barcelona: Ediciones Mitre.

Goffman, E. 1974. *Frame analysis.* New York: Harper and Row.

Hante, J. F. 1988. Point de vue sur l'explicatif (Point of view about explanation). *Pratiques* 7:3–9.

Kerbrat-Orecchioni, C. 1986. *L'enonciation. De la subjectivité dans le langage* (Enunciation: About subjectivity in language). Paris: Librairie Armand Colin.

Labov, W. 1983. *Modelos sociolingüísticos* (Sociolinguistic patterns). Madrid: Cátedra.

Leclaire-Hante, A. 1988. Elémentaire, mon cher Watson. Explicatif et narratif dans le roman policier (Elementary, my dear Watson. Explication and narrative in the detective novel). *Pratiques* 7:11–22.

Massone, M. I. 1999. La conversación en Lengua de Señas Argentina (Conversation in Argentine Sign Language). Manuscript.

Massone, M. I., and S. M. Menéndez. 1997. An interactional approach to the analysis of Argentine Sign Language. *Cadernos de Estudos Linguisticos* 33:75–82.

Ramonet, I. 1998. *La tiranía de la comunicación* (The tyranny of communication). Spain: Temas de debate.

Shujman, D. 1998. "White Noise." Capital Federal, Argentina: Argentine Deaf Confederation.

Tannen, D. 1990. *You just don't understand: Women and men in conversation.* New York: William Morrow.

Van Dijk, T. 1978. *La ciencia del texto* (The science of text). Spain: Paidós Comunicación.

———. 1997. *Racismo y análisis crítico de los medios* (Racism and critical analysis of media). Buenos Aires: Paidós.

Part 7 Language Attitudes

The Development of Sociolinguistic Meanings:

The Worldview of a Deaf Child

within His Home Environment

Laura A. Blackburn

Henry Camillo is one of the 92 percent of deaf children raised by hearing family members—his parents are hearing, as well as his five siblings and all of his extended family members (e.g., aunts, uncles, cousins, and grandparents).[1] Researchers have raised scientific questions and conducted lively discussions regarding the choices of communication modality that hearing family members make for their deaf child (Schwartz 1996; Stewart and Luetke-Stahlman 1998). Henry's life experiences are at the core of these debates because he uses American Sign Language (ASL) as his primary language of communication, whereas all of his family members use spoken English.

This chapter presents Henry's unique worldview, as well as detailed descriptions of his interactions with his immediate and extended family members during a ten-month period. The stories represent a sliver of the discoveries that are detailed in my dissertation research (Blackburn 1999).[2]

1. All names in this document are pseudonyms. Sara and Mark Camillo are the hearing parents of Daniel (6-year-old, hearing), Henry (4-year-old, deaf), Madeline (2-year-old, hearing), Mary (1-year-old, hearing), Luke (1-year-old, hearing), and John (1-year-old, hearing).

2. This work stems from a larger, ethnographic project conducted at Gallaudet University entitled "Language, Literacy, and Cultural Development in Bilingual Homes and Classrooms." The project involved, in part, my gathering in-depth information about the Camillo family through participant observation (Spradley 1979) and ethnographic interviews (Spradley 1980). These qualitative data collection methods are ethnographic methods of studying and describing cultural phenomena. From May 1996 to July 1997 I was "in the field" documenting and

At the time of the investigation, Henry attended a day school for deaf children, located in the eastern United States. Henry, who is the only deaf member of the Camillo family, was four years old at the time of this investigation. This work also addresses the fact that Henry views the world in primarily visual ways and explores how he adapts to and lives productively in a home environment that is structured for individuals with an auditory orientation.

The central research questions that guided this investigation were: *How do a deaf child and his hearing family members make sense of each other's worldviews?* and *How are their perspectives demonstrated in their actions?* Therefore the investigation attempted to understand how family members socially and linguistically construct their knowledge and understandings of deafness among themselves and with others.

The story told in professional literature about deaf children and their families often begins with the reality that children who are deaf are most often born into families that possess a hearing identity or an auditorily oriented worldview (Erting 1982, 1994a; Padden and Humphries 1988). Often, hearing parents, siblings, and extended family members of a deaf child have never met or interacted with another individual who is deaf (Garretson 1994; Meadow-Orlans 1990). Padden and Humphries (1988) observed this circumstance and assert that hearing parents possess an auditory (hearing) perspective that can interfere with their ability to understand how their deaf child makes sense of their environment (i.e., visually). Their intrinsically auditory orientation and use of a spoken language are coupled with extensive contacts with members of their social support system, most often composed of hearing educators and professionals, medical experts, and family. Padden and Humphries suggest that the ongoing, prevalent nature of these hearing sociolinguistic interactions may prohibit parents from moving toward "a different [or visual] center" when interacting with their child (1988, 39). In other words, hearing family mem-

------

learning about the Camillos' lives. For ten months of that period (October 1996 to July 1997), I lived in the family's home as a researcher.

I wish to thank the LLCD project director, Dr. Carol J. Erting, as well as my other dissertation committee members (Dr. Barbara Bodner-Johnson, Dr. Jan Hafer, Dr. Jeff Lewis, and Dr. John Caughey), and LLCD team members Ms. Carlene Thumann-Prezioso (who also served as my peer debriefer) and Dr. Charles Reilly for their persistent and unequivocal support throughout the course of my dissertation experience.

bers create their own realities by living their day-to-day lives based on hearing experiences, using a spoken language. Therefore, they may not be able to see the world through their deaf child's eyes as readily as they are able to understand a hearing child's perceptions.

Schlesinger and Meadow (1972) were the first to attest that a medical diagnosis of hearing loss is minute in light of the sociocultural ramifications of growing up deaf in a society in which interactions are built on the experience of hearing. In other words, although hearing family members are often distressed when a child in their family is identified as deaf, the identification of the deaf child's hearing loss, per se, is not necessarily the most significant problem for the child or the family (Meadow-Orlans 1990). Meadow-Orlans elaborates on the early years of child rearing and the challenges that hearing parents of deaf children face:

> They [hearing family members] must face the difficulties of communicating with their child in the absence of a common linguistic system. This is the central feature of the early experiences of deaf children: The language readily available to deaf children is not the language used by their parents. (1990, 285)

Differing communication strategies (both linguistic and modality differences) used by hearing parents and their deaf child frequently create communicative tensions between deaf and hearing relatives. Both lack of access to the primary language of the home and communicative tensions can produce a deleterious effect on the child's and family's interpersonal communication and social interactions, as well as the deaf child's ensuing identity development (Erting 1982, 1994a; Johnson, Liddell, and Erting 1989; Meadow-Orlans 1990). The result is often a young child learning and living on the periphery of activity and interaction in his own home.

Nash and Nash (1981) posit that whereas deafness is framed by the majority of society as an audiological or medical condition, many others define the deaf experience using a sociocultural perspective (Jacobs 1974; Lane, Hoffmeister, and Bahan 1996; Meadow 1980; Padden 1989). As a result, the experience of being hearing while nurturing and raising a child who is deaf is further complicated as parents try to make sense of these divergent understandings of deafness.

Within the field of deaf education, the age-old "oral–manual debate" within the United States reflects both the medical and cultural understandings of deafness, exemplifying the mixed messages that parents receive when faced with the need and desire to make informed decisions about their child's education. During one of the most vulnerable periods for making sense of their child's deafness, parents are frequently presented with dichotomous sets of facts and figures, communication methodologies, and teaching philosophies. Nash and Nash (1981) describe the beliefs of the oral doctrine as always operating from the criteria prescribed for interaction in mainstream society. The worldview of a deaf child from an oral or medical position involves measuring the child's interactive competence by determining "how closely it resembles the speech of hearing people and whether the child can 'talk to anyone'" (Nash and Nash 1981, 48). In other words, the medical perspective of deafness believes that the closer a deaf child can emulate the behaviors of a hearing child, the more successful and productive the child will be as a member of society.

In contrast, Erting (1994a) characterizes the Deaf experience from a sociocultural perspective and describes it as a primarily visual experience (Erting 1994a).[3] In other words, those who view Deafness as a cultural phenomenon acknowledge that individuals who are Deaf learn to organize and make sense of their life experiences using a different (visual) perspective of the world from that of their hearing parents and family members. Although culture and language are distinct phenomena, they are explicitly embedded in one another (Spradley 1979; Woodward 1972). Stokoe (1994) asserts that "sterility is the result of studying a language without studying its use and those who use it" (266). Language serves a variety of purposes in the lives of social beings. Language is typically viewed as a medium for social interaction, but it also serves as a symbol representing linguistic/cultural knowledge and social identity (Markowicz and Woodward 1982). Erting (1994a) suggests that in hearing families with deaf children, the problems that exist are evidenced in the family members' use of dissimilar symbols and behaviors. The symbolic linguistic and behavioral compromises presented within this chapter's stories are characteristic of interactions between hearing parents and their deaf and hearing children.

Linguistic and cultural conflicts within hearing families of deaf children produce increased stress levels for parents and children alike, contributing to the sustained tensions within the family (Meadow-Orlans

3. Woodward (1972) began the practice of distinguishing between a person with an audiological hearing loss (deaf), from individuals who identify themselves as part of a cultural community (Deaf). From this point forward, Deaf will be used to refer to a person or situation that identifies with a cultural worldview.

1990). Hearing family members often do not have the ability to communicate with their deaf child immediately and fluently, nor do they know how to provide a physical environment in the home that is visually accessible (Lane et al. 1996). Because the social systems of hearing families are composed of individuals who hear, supportive social relationships with extended family members and friends are often dismantled or disrupted (Erting 1982, 1994a; Markowicz and Woodward 1982; Meadow-Orlans 1990). Friends may distance themselves from the family or feel uncertain about how to respond to the deaf child or changes in communication. Disruptions in family social support may also occur because of increased stress levels, relationship discord, and feelings of grief and hopelessness among family members (Meadow-Orlans 1990).

Markowicz and Woodward (1982) point out that the early childhood experiences of deaf children raised in a hearing family context are quite different from what is experienced by hearing family members. They indicate that while growing up, "most deaf children do not have any contact with Deaf adults" (4). This phenomenon occurs in part because hearing family members have not had previous social or linguistic experiences with individuals who are Deaf and are less likely to incorporate Deaf people into their family's interactive social context (Erting 1982, 1994a). The absence of culturally Deaf adults is pervasive in the lives of many children who are deaf. The result is that they are denied social access to those who are culturally and linguistically most like themselves.

Lane (1993) theorizes that abundant access to hearing individuals, coupled with the absence of Deaf adults, constructs the "problem of deafness" worldview. Lane suggests that hearing parents of deaf children often perceive their child's deafness as a problem or deficit because they are introduced to their child from a medical or pathological perspective of deafness. McDermott and Varenne (1995) explain that worldviews are socially constructed when individuals are labeled as deaf or hearing. Consequently, a collective social response occurs that strengthens the label or stereotype that has been applied to an individual or community.

ETHNOGRAPHIC METHODS

In response to the problems faced by hearing families with deaf children, most research in the field of deaf education has looked empirically at separate variables related to the deaf child and his or her family; most have not taken a holistic stance (Evans 1994; Nash and Nash 1981). There is also a significant absence of naturalistic research that systematically investigates and describes the environments in which deaf individuals grow and live (Stokoe 1995). In contrast, the ethnographic methods used in this investigation are grounded in the field of anthropology and are used to develop an understanding of the meanings informants make within the context of their environment. The job of the ethnographer, then, is to translate those understandings into writings that can be understood by individuals outside the informant's context or worldview (Erting 1994b). The anthropologist's research is focused on learning about people based on what they say and do. Finally, the anthropologist attempts to determine whether what people say and do makes sense in terms of their behavior in different contexts (Erting 1997).

The theoretical perspective of this work is based on a sociocultural view of deafness. Erting's model of the family members as social actors provided a theoretical framework for the Camillos' experiences (Erting 1982, 1994a). In other words, the theoretical position for this investigation is that cultural behavior and knowledge are learned through interaction using a language or languages within various reciprocal and social environments. Individuals cannot learn about themselves as social beings in isolation. A person's identity development or particular view of reality is developed through various opportunities for interaction with others, as well as the components of others' worldviews. Therefore, linguistic/cultural knowledge and identity development within a family that has deaf and hearing members produce unique kindred circumstances and related issues that need to be addressed when considering the educational needs of the deaf child and his family.

Data Collection and Analysis

Data were collected primarily within the Camillos' home, which served as the main hub of activity and interaction for the family. Participant observation events were documented in the form of condensed and expanded fieldnotes on a daily basis over the ten-month period that I lived with the family. Nineteen ethnographic interviews were recorded on audio- and videotape with Henry's parents and extended family members (see table 1). Interactions among Henry, his siblings, and cousins were captured during the last two weeks of data collection as I accompanied the Camillos on vacation to visit extended family members.

TABLE I. *List of Informants*29

Father's Family		Mother's Family	
Camillo Adults/Ages	Camillo Children/Ages	Medina Adults/Ages	Medina Children/Ages
*Harry, 42 (brother)	Harry Jr., 13	Ernest, 38 (brother)	Maria, 17
*Maura, 36	Joshua, 11	Heather, 34	Arthur, 12
	Becka, 7		Samantha, 10
	Melissa, 5		Roger, 3
*Steve, 27 (brother)	single, no children	*Francis, 33 (brother)	Marie, 5
			Christine, 7
Lila, 31 (sister)	James, 10	Bobbie, 30 (sister)	no children
Ted, 21	George, 3	Jerry, 28	
	Christine, 8 months		
*Bobbi, 43 (sister)	Roberta, 12	*Nannette, 25 (sister)	single, no children
*Michael, 43			
Margaret, 38 (sister)	Karl, 7	Ernest Medina Sr. and Peggy Medina (parents)	
Christopher, 40			
Elaine, 32 (sister)	Bart, 6		
Joe, 35			
*Meg, 44 (sister)	single, no children		
*Mark, 34 (Henry's father)	Daniel, 6		
	Henry, 4		
	Madeline, 2		
*Sara Jane, 36 (Henry's mother)	Mary, 10 months		
	Luke, 10 months		
	John, 10 months		
Steve and Geneva Camillo (parents)			

Note: Asterisks (*) indicate individuals who participated in interviews over the course of data collection.

One of the primary discoveries of this work was that different family members (e.g., the deaf child, parents, siblings, aunts, and uncles) held divergent understandings of deafness. The research design combined three types of analysis that worked in tandem to identify the various perspectives of family members (Agar 1986; Ely et al. 1991; Erickson 1992). The use of three different forms of analysis allowed me to "shine spotlights" into different corners of the Camillo family's life. First, the methods recommended by Ely and her associates organized fieldnotes and interview transcripts by themes that were pertinent to the family's experience. Second, Agar's methods helped to illuminate cultural tensions and social dilemmas that ensued among family members. Finally, Erickson's microanalysis of specific linguistic/social interactions enabled me to capture the diverse perspectives of participants, as well as build connections between (triangulate) the three different types of data: fieldnotes, interview transcripts, and videotaped interactions.[4]

THE THEORETICAL POSITION

As described earlier, Erting (1982, 1994a) developed various models of individual social actors that demonstrate how biological and social environments, as well as personal and interactional influences, structure the

---

4. Three different types of data are presented in this chapter: fieldnotes, transcripts from interviews, and transcripts from interactive video clips. Each type of data was explicitly cited so as not to mislead the reader. There is an important distinction between the information provided in transcripts from audiotapes/videotapes and fieldnotes. Transcripts from interviews and interactive videotape are the *exact words* used by informants and therefore are presented in American Psychological Association (APA) style as direct quotes. Fieldnotes in their condensed and expanded forms are the researcher's way of restructuring the events that occurred during participant observation. My condensed fieldnotes included phrases, single words, and unconnected sentences (Spradley 1979, 75) that I jotted down while conducting fieldwork. Later, expanded notes were created that provided a richer account of events and conversations that transpired among informants. Because the majority of my condensed and expanded fieldnotes contained my recollection of events and not the exact words of informants, they should not be considered exact or quotable representations of what the informants said.

development of each person's unique worldview. Erting recognizes and this research adds evidence to the position that it is possible for individuals to live in the same physical environment or space but perceive and understand the world in totally different ways (Blumer 1969). Identity is developed and demonstrated by each person's biological and experiential contributions to interaction. For example, two people may make sense of deafness in different ways because of their familial relation to the deaf person (e.g., younger sibling versus older cousin). Other factors include biological characteristics (e.g., intelligence or hearing status) and the quality and quantity of social and linguistic interactions the individuals have had with deaf people throughout their life span.

Of the four conceptual models I used to describe the Camillo family members' views of deafness, I borrowed two models from Erting (1982): *model of the hearing parent* and *model of the Deaf child of hearing parents,* and developed two new models to represent other members of Henry's family: *model of the hearing sibling of a Deaf child* and *model of the hearing extended family members of a Deaf child.* It is important to understand that Erting's model of the Deaf child with hearing family members depicted in the next section allows for the consideration of three aspects that influence how individuals construct their worldviews of deafness: opportunity structure, personal characteristics, and interactional spheres.

The component that grounds all aspects of the model is called the individual's *opportunity structure.* Erting borrowed this term from Barth (1981) to refer to characteristics of the larger macrostructure of society and to represent the opportunities available to the social actor within that society. Using the model of the Deaf child (next section) as an example, the Camillo family's socioeconomic status, Mark's career as an officer in the armed forces, and the family's religious affiliations and practices are examples of specific components that build the framework of their family's model.

The second component looks at the personal characteristics of the individual. This center portion schematically represents information regarding the person's biological characteristics (e.g., Deaf person, attends preschool), the person's contact and personal history with deafness (e.g., attends a preschool for Deaf children, has access to Deaf adults who serve as ASL models), and the values, decisions, and choices the deaf child makes as they relate to the Deaf experience. Finally, the model schematically represents the interactional spheres that are available to Deaf children in

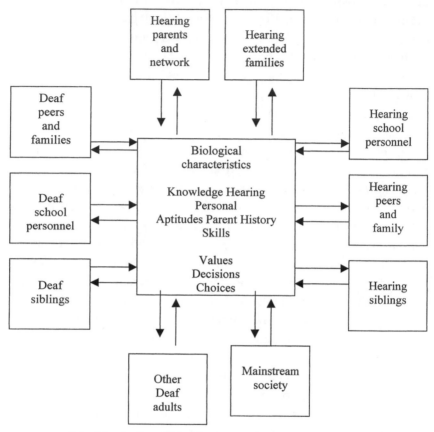

Opportunity Structure

Hearing parents and network

Hearing extended families

Deaf peers and families

Hearing school personnel

Biological characteristics

Knowledge Hearing
Personal
Aptitudes Parent History
Skills

Deaf school personnel

Hearing peers and family

Values
Decisions
Choices

Deaf siblings

Hearing siblings

Other Deaf adults

Mainstream society

FIGURE 1. *Model of a Deaf Child of Hearing Parents*

From *Deafness, communication, social identity: Ethnography in a preschool for deaf children*, by C. J. Erting, 1994, 21. Copyright 1994 by Linstok Press. Reprinted with permission of the author.

hearing families (these are represented by arrows and small squares in figure 1).

My analysis presented four views of deafness that emerged, in part, from the interactions among various family members, immediate and extended: (1) the parents' view, (2) the view of the hearing children, (3) the view of extended family members, and (4) Henry's view. I used Erting's models as a framework for understanding how Henry and his family made sense of deafness. The themes that are described within each view reveal that individuals portray their understanding of deafness in unique ways. This individuality is developed and demonstrated by each person's biological and experiential contributions. This chapter focuses on Henry's worldview.

HENRY'S WORLDVIEW

The findings presented here developed from the contextual analysis of fieldnotes, as well as the microanalysis of selected video clips that showed Henry interacting during visits at the homes of extended family members (June 28–July 15, 1997). The stories and descriptions of interaction described in this section represent typical interactions that occurred among Henry, his siblings, and his cousins. Even though I did not have direct access to Henry's thoughts and feelings, in this section I present the interactions as they apply to the model of the Deaf child of hearing parents, adapted from Erting (1982).

Erting emphasized that her models of individual social actors represent theoretical differences in how individuals construct their worldview in three important ways: "structurally, personally, and interactionally" (Erting 1982, 22). It is important to recognize that because Henry is part of a hearing family system, differences exist in these three aspects that pervade the development of his worldview in profound ways. Structurally, unlike a Deaf child from a Deaf family system, Henry's does not have Deaf adults within his primary family of socialization. Like his parents and siblings, as the model indicates, Henry has regular opportunities to interact with Deaf people at school or during school-related activities. However, the model demonstrates his predicament and the complications of his development as a person who views the world in visual-only ways but is immersed in an environment that is arranged and organized for individuals who manage their environment in both visual and auditory ways.

Consequently, this section describes Henry's interactional spheres within that context. First, I tell a story that describes Henry's typical interactions with his siblings. In the second part of this chapter, I describe four interactive contexts that are typical for Henry when he is with groups of hearing family members: no access to interaction (video clip #1), delayed access to interaction (video clip #1), contingent access to interaction (video clip #2), and comprehensive access to interaction (video clip #3).

It is important to point out that some of Henry's behaviors were evidence of his variable access to communication and interactive activities at home. For example, Henry always knew where his shoes were, and they typically were on his feet from first thing in the morning until it was time for bed at night. Sara explained that Henry wore his shoes habitually to be sure he "didn't miss anything." In other words, there were times when Mark and Sara discussed an outing using spoken English. Perhaps they were in separate rooms saying to one another, "I'm almost ready to go. Have you changed the babies?" and "I'm getting their bottles ready for the road!" In this situation, family members who were not directly involved in the preparations to leave the house (e.g., Daniel and Madeline, the hearing siblings) still had passive access or the ability to "overhear" communication and conversations about the errand or trip. For Henry, family outings may have sometimes had the appearance of the group making a hasty dash for the door. He kept his shoes on to adapt to an environment consisting of primarily hearing people using a spoken language. Because Henry did not have passive access to communication in his home environment, he learned to watch for shifts in patterns of behavior (e.g., packing the diaper bag, changing the babies' diapers), kept his shoes on, and expected to be informed of the decision to leave the house shortly before departure.

Henry's visual worldview and the behavioral adaptations he made in his home environment were evident in many parts of the following story. For example, when Henry was not standing at the front window with Daniel watching the snow fall, he was sitting on the stair landing in the living room (see figure 2 to identify Henry's spot on the stairs). Henry sat on the stairs because it was the one location on the entire main floor of his home where he had almost complete visual access to family interactions. The landing was a popular spot for him to locate himself when he anticipated a special family outing or activity. If the family was expecting company, Henry could see the guests walk up the steps to the front door. If it was almost time for dinner, he could see the food being prepared and watch for his father's arrival at the same time. On Thanksgiving Day, Henry waited at the bottom of the stairs for his father to wake up from a midday nap, which would signal it was time to carve the turkey. Finally, when Henry sat on the stairs on this particular snow day, he could simultaneously watch the snow falling outside and watch for his mother to come down the stairs as he monitored the interactions among his siblings and me.

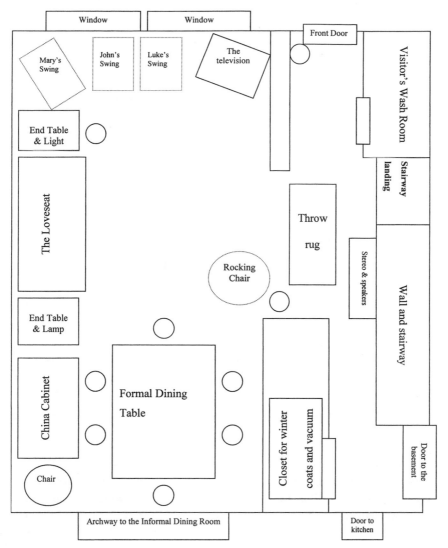

FIGURE 2. *The Camillo family's living room and dining room*

Events on a Snow Day

In early January an overnight snowfall canceled school one morning for Daniel and Henry. At their request I heated up frozen pancakes. Sara went upstairs to catch up on her sleep after she realized school was cancelled (the babies were not sleeping through the night yet, and a snow day for Sara meant an opportunity to catch up on her rest). Before she went upstairs, she reminded the boys not to open the front door. Henry had been opening the front door all morning, letting in the cold air from the outside. From Henry's perspective, peering through the storm door was the best spot to watch the falling snow and see the snow plows in action.

Obeying Sara's request, Daniel and Henry remained at the front windows until midmorning. As they watched the snowfall, the brothers signed to each other endlessly about what sleds they would use and about the snowmen they would build later in the day. Daniel used his voice in a quiet whisper when he signed to Henry.

The rest of the morning, Daniel busied himself building an elaborate castle with discovery blocks and watching cartoons on television. Henry entertained himself from his perch on the stair landing by watching me, even when I thought he was paying no attention. For example, when I moved from floor to floor in the house, Henry repeatedly stopped and asked me where I was going (WHY WALK-WALK? WHY BASEMENT? [5] [FN: 72: 1:22]).[6] On this particular morning, I explained twice why I was going

5. In communication situations described throughout this work, when a deaf person uses ASL or signs without spoken English, I use small capitals to represent the informant's signed intent, rather than English words written in upper- and lowercase letters. Because this research examines the intersections of signed and spoken communication between a deaf child and his hearing family member, the practice of making the written distinction between signed and spoken communication will help the reader see sociolinguistic, communicative, and cultural tensions more clearly within the context of the different stories presented.

6. On the recommendation of Oswald Werner (1998), I have provided a list of pseudonyms for "expert informants" in Table 1. I have cited the location of their contributions in my fieldnotes (FN), interview transcripts (INT), and interactive video clips (VC) (Werner 1998, 29) the same as I cite Werner's expertise and recommendations in this sentence. For example, the following is a statement made by an informant during a videotaped interview: "I really don't think it's much of an issue. You just do it" (INT: 19:42:23). INT means the data are derived from an interview. The numbers that follow INT provide the exact location of the in-

downstairs ("I'm checking the clothes in the dryer") and five times why I had moved my car ("The snowplows are coming and I need to move my car off the street"). Henry was diligent at making sure he understood what was happening next, and he was not bashful about asking me to repeat my responses.

As the morning progressed, Sara called for Daniel to come upstairs several times to help her with chores. Sometimes she called him upstairs to get Madeline out of her crib or to bring the portable telephone. Henry waited and watched everyone move about the house because he did not want to miss a moment of going outside to play in the snow. He was the first child dressed that morning. Every time Sara called Daniel upstairs that morning, Henry followed. He got out his sledding clothes and put them on before anyone else. At one point, Henry could not find his socks and became frantic. He knew it was Mark's job to lay out his clothing in the morning and commented to Sara, "Daddy forgot my socks!" (FN:72:2:17).

When Sara came downstairs later in the morning dressed in her long johns, the children considered it her signal that it was almost time to go outside and play in the snow. Henry asked her where the snowplows were; I assumed he was concerned that the plow had not come into the cul-de-sac yet, and he did not want to miss it. I remembered viewing my parents as all-knowing in my early childhood and wondered if he thought Sara knew the snowplow's schedule.

Even as Daniel and Madeline visibly dressed to go outside, Henry repeatedly asked Sara, PLAY SNOW SOON, RIGHT? ("We're going out to play soon, right?") (FN:72:1:31). Fortunately for Henry, Sara was aware that day that the weather might quickly change to sleet or freezing rain. She decided to take the children outside sooner rather than later. Henry was so excited that as he added more layers of clothing, he stopped to physically shake his mother to ask one more time if they were really going out to play in the snow. Sara told him, STOP SHAKING MOMMY! He immediately kissed her apologetically, and she responded, I KNOW [you are] EXCITED BUT PLEASE DON'T SHAKE MOMMY'S BODY! (FN:72:2:13).

---

formant's statement in the interview transcript in my database. The first number in the sequence (19:42:23) represents the number of the interview, fieldnote, or video clip. The second number (19:42:23) indicates the page number of the transcript, and the third number (19:42:23) labels the line number where the statement begins on the page of the database.

When the time to play in the snow finally arrived, the babies and I watched the older children and Sara romp in front of the house. Each child had a different colored plastic sled, and they slid down the slight hill near the house. Sara was moving sluggishly in the snow with boots and a baseball cap to cover her hair. Everyone was wearing gloves instead of mittens so they could use sign language to communicate. The foursome built a snowman, and Sara sent Daniel in to ask for raisins and carrots.

Later when they came inside, Sara made hot cocoa, and we sat around the dining room table and discussed their sledding adventures. I asked Henry if he had seen any KIDS outside on the sleds. Madeline joined our conversation, signing and speaking she said, KIDS YES-YES (pointing outside) SNOW! ("Yeah! We saw kids outside in the snow!") Henry saw her attempting to imitate the sign KIDS and laughed out loud. He mimicked Madeline's incorrect handshape or "baby sign" to make his point and said, YOU CUTE. He and Madeline giggled over their hot cocoa about her baby sign (FN:72:3:2).

Later Henry helped me feed the babies, and Madeline stepped in to help teach him how (she had spent many days at home with Sara and the babies when Henry and Daniel were at school). When we were feeding the babies, Henry tried to prop Luke's bottle on the edge of the bouncy seat but did not know how. I watched the situation unfold as Henry shrugged in Luke's direction and set the bottle down next to the baby on the floor. Before I could cross the room and show Henry how to prop the bottle, Luke was already wailing in frustration. Madeline quickly came to his rescue, explaining to Henry in ASL, NO NO MORE EAT MORE! ("No! The baby wants to eat more!") (FN:72:3:8).

After Luke finished his bottle, Henry spent about ten minutes chatting with the baby, articulating signs on the baby's body. I was surprised to see Henry using the baby's body space to articulate signs because I was not aware that Henry had ever seen a Deaf adult model that type of early interactive "motherese." Henry told Luke about the snow outside and how he had waited for a long time to go sledding. Luke watched Henry attentively—cooing and waving his hands in response to Henry's signs.

HENRY AND HIS COUSINS: SELECTED INTERACTIONS

Although the Camillo siblings generally accepted their home communication in two languages and several modalities as a matter of fact,

Henry's interactions with his cousins had a different quality. Their responses to using visual communication strategies were naïve but genuine. The older children had the advantage of recollecting previous interactions—the idea of Deafness and Henry as a Deaf person were not new to them. They typically assumed a care-taking or big-brother role with Henry. In contrast, cousins who were Henry's same age or younger reacted with curiosity, confusion, frustration, and in some cases anger. The response of Henry's youngest cousins was clearly one of culture shock.

This section details the results of the videotape microanalysis. I looked at selected social interactions among Henry, his siblings, and his cousins. My findings build upon Evans's (1994) continuum of communication, ranging from inclusion to exclusion. Evans posits that deaf children from large hearing families have numerous opportunities at home to interact in communicative contexts ranging from dyads to small groups to large-group family gatherings. She submits that the quality of access available to deaf children from large hearing families ranges from fully inclusive to exclusive. My analysis found not only the size of interactive groups to be pertinent but also the quality of interactions and the role of actors to be critical to Henry's communicative success.

A *no-access-to-interaction situation* was a social scene in which Henry did not have access to information and communicative messages that were being exchanged in his presence. Individuals participating in the social scene around Henry might have viewed him as being attended to in the field of interaction when he was not actually included. In some instances, family members made overt attempts to include Henry in the activity by signing to or interpreting for him. However, for one reason or another, in a no-access situation, Henry was not focused on the same interaction as other family members. In a no-access situation, he did not attempt to obtain information from family members or to engage himself in the interaction going on around him. In other words, a no-access situation typically appeared as though Henry was isolated among a group of people, entertaining himself "in his own world," attending to entirely different objects and activities in the environment than other family members.

No-access situations generally led to *delayed-access situations*. In delayed-access situations, Henry entered the field of activity "at the tail end" of the social situation that had held the interest of other family members. He either used time upon entering the scene to try to determine what had happened or missed the meaning or importance of the interaction completely. In these situations, Henry sought clarification of the event, asking questions of family members who he considered to be competent communication informants.

Situations of *contingent* or *conditional access* typically occurred within the context of one-to-one and small-group interactive scenes. In other words, Henry had greater access to interactions that occurred when he was with a small group of family members where he could independently monitor interactive exchanges or when he was with one or more family members who were willing and able to interpret for him. This type of access was deemed contingent or conditional because Henry's degree of access to the scene was subject to the communicative competence and attentiveness of the person facilitating interaction. In other words, contingent-access situations can quickly become no-access, delayed-access, or comprehensive-access situations, based on the level of involvement and skill of the facilitator and individuals present in the interactive scene. The only measure of control or independence available to Henry in contingent-access situations was his degree of assertiveness within the social situation. Henry demonstrated his vigilance when obtaining comprehensive access in two ways: (1) by using his voice or body language to state his position and make demands or requests; and (2) by asking questions through an interpreter, as well as redirecting and reminding the person who served as the moderator of interaction.

Comprehensive access occurred when Henry was able to thoroughly interact with a group of individuals who may or may not have been using ASL to communicate. In a comprehensive-access situation, Henry was able to fully contribute to the interactive situation and thoroughly understood the contributions of others. In some comprehensive-access situations, Henry taught others about his visual way of viewing the world during their exchange of information. Comprehensive-access included some lapses in communication, but these scenes were characterized primarily as interactive situations in which Henry was able to participate fully in the field of interaction.

Scene 1: Finding a Frog Poolside at Marble Beach

The following poolside scene demonstrated a no-access situation for Henry that led to a delayed-access situation. The scene opened at the home of Bobbie and Jerry (Henry's aunt and uncle) during the family's vacation immediately after the children (Henry, Daniel, Madeline, and their cousins Marie and Christine) were permitted to enter the pool for a morning swim (video segment #6). It is important to recognize that no one was signing in the first two minutes of this scene. Henry did not have access to the spoken conversations that transpired among the children until halfway into the four-minute segment. See figure 3 for a diagram of the pool area.

Francis (another uncle), Mark, and I were focused on putting sunscreen lotion on the children and blowing up flotation toys for the pool. Henry, Daniel, Marie, and Christine were already playing in the shallow end of the pool. Daniel, Marie, and Christine were bobbing in the water as an interactive triad, passing two flotation devices and a plastic ball among them.

> DANIEL: [growls at Christine] Ha! Ha! I made you drop! I made you drop!
> CHRISTINE: No, you didn't!
> DANIEL: Yes, I did! I went like [growls] and you dropped it!
> CHRISTINE: No, it didn't! I wanted to let go.
> MARIE: Brrrr! [comments on the chilly water] Daddy! You can be the lifeguard! [Francis doesn't respond]
> CHRISTINE: Daddy, you're the lifeguard, okay? [Francis doesn't respond]
> LAURA: [I respond for Francis] You know what? Daddy's going to get the sunblock and we're going to put it on your body. Okay? [Christine and Marie turn to where Laura is talking outside the pool]. (VC:6:1:7)

Henry was standing on the steps in the shallow end, engaged in his most common play activity: maneuvering his toy vehicles on the edge of the pool. Occasionally he glanced over his shoulder to watch the older children bobbing in the water. When he noticed Marie and Christine turning their heads toward the picnic table, he glanced with them to see what was happening. He surveyed the situation (I was putting lotion on Madeline at the picnic table) and returned to pushing and lining up his vehicles. Madeline's and my conversation could be overheard as we sat at the picnic table next to the video camera, set up to capture interactions in the pool. I was saying to Madeline, "You can go in the water as soon as I finish putting on this lotion, ok?"

Daniel pushed the two flotation devices out of the pool and walked past Henry, up the stairs and alongside of the pool toward the deep end,

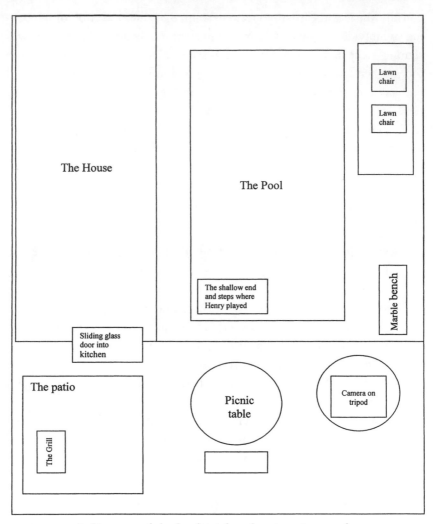

FIGURE 3. *A diagram of the backyard and swimming pool*

where Francis was blowing up toys. Marie and Christine continued talking to Francis:

MARIE: Daddy, can you please give me that thing?
FRANCIS: Ok, but you've got to put suntan lotion on.

At this point, the ball that Marie was playing with floated out of her hands and became inadvertently stuck under Henry's arm as he climbed out of the pool. Henry got out of the pool and walked away with the ball.

MARIE: Give it here! Come here! Come here! Henry! Henry! [talking to his back] Come here! Henry! Henry! Henry! Henry! (VC:6:1:10)

Henry's back was turned, so he did not know that Marie wanted the ball back. His perception of the situation was that the ball had floated to him by chance and he decided to remove it from the pool because no one was playing with it. Henry then decided at the water's edge that he should push all of the floating toys into the water and threw the ball and another floating toy back into the pool. Meanwhile, Daniel had made his way into the deep end of the pool and found a frog floating near the filter flap.

DANIEL: Eww! A frog!
CHRISTINE: Let me see it!
LAURA: Is it in the water?

Marie was still trying to get Henry's attention, and when she heard me ask about the frog ("Is it in the water?"), thought I was asking about the ball.

MARIE: I can't get it [the ball] because he [Henry] threw it over there [in the deep end]!

Christine joined Daniel at the deep end of the pool. Henry continued to throw floating toys into the pool, oblivious to the other children's conversations about the frog and Marie's protests about the ball.

CHRISTINE: It's a toad, Daddy!
FRANCIS: Leave it alone!
MARK: Is it alive?
DANIEL: I'm trying to get it [out of the water] so it could be alive! (VC:6:1:18)

Henry returned to the steps at the shallow end and, after throwing all the floatable toys into the pool, entered the water and picked up his vehicles to begin playing with them again. Marie forgot about the ball floating out of her reach and became interested in Daniel's frog discovery.

MARIE: Where's the toad?

DANIEL: It's down here! I'm trying to get the dumb thing!

Marie got out of the shallow end of the pool and walked to the deep end to see the frog. On her way out of the water, she accidentally bumped Henry at the steps. Henry got out of the water and shook the water off his feet. He was still not aware that the children were talking about a discovery at the other end of the pool.

MARK: Here, Daniel [approaches Daniel with sunblock lotion].

DANIEL: [protesting about getting out of the pool to apply sunscreen] Dad, there's a toad in the pool!

MARK: [shakes his head playfully in disagreement]

DANIEL: Yes, there is! (VC:6:1:26)

Henry finished shaking the water off his feet and began to make his way around the edge of the pool. He was again focused on bumping flotation devices into the pool. On his way to the deep end, where Mark and the children were gathered, he nonchalantly kicked one more floating ring into the water. Henry walked past the group gathered at the edge of the pool and started to pick up other toys to throw into the water. Mark, Daniel, Christine, and Marie huddled closer around the toad.

CHRISTINE: [says to Mark] Look! It's a toad!

At this point, the no-access situation becomes a delayed-access event. Henry recognized that the group of children was looking at something on the edge of the pool. He pointed and spoke to his father, "Da-Da-Da," meaning "What are they looking at Dad?" Mark responded to Henry's question by signing LOOK FROG and then asked Henry to come closer so he could put on sunscreen lotion. Mark signed LITTLE-BIT PRO.1 ("Let's put a little bit of this on you"). Henry did not respond to Mark's request and Mark repeated the original answer to Henry's question, FROG [points to the frog at the side of the pool], meaning, "There's a frog at the side of the pool." Henry's cousin and brother continued to talk about the frog.

CHRISTINE: It's a baby frog! I've never seen one before!

MARIE: What is that thing right there?

Henry moved between Christine and Marie, standing on the edge of the pool. He bent over and looked in the filtration flap at the water's edge. As Henry tried to see the frog, Daniel scooped something into his hand, which might have been the frog, and threw it into the grass at the pool's edge.

Henry turned to look into the grass and started to walk to the grass to find the frog. Mark stopped Henry as he tried to put lotion on Henry's back. The scene dissolved as Christine and Marie jumped in the pool with Daniel. The other children were finished looking at the frog, and Henry's delayed access to the event caused him to miss it entirely. I walked around the edge of the pool to get more lotion from Mark for Madeline. Henry's eyes were still glued to the grass as he strained his body away from Mark's grasp to get a better look. Mark vocalized and signed,

MARK: Henry, Henry. STOP PLEASE WAIT.
LAURA: Can I have some more lotion?

Daniel continued to discuss the frog sighting with his father.

DANIEL: Daddy! I saw it! Daddy, I saw something, Daddy! I saw something and then I saw it was a frog! (VC:6:1:31)

Henry turned and tapped Mark's arm while he put lotion into my hands. As Henry tapped his father's arm, he continued to look in the grass for the frog. Mark returned his attention to putting sunscreen on Henry and tapped him to draw his attention away from the grass. Henry's eyes remained glued to the grassy area, and he raised his outstretched palm for Mark to put lotion in his hand.

MARK: [responding to Daniel] Are you serious?
CHRISTINE: That's the first time I've seen a baby frog!
DANIEL: That's my second! I seen one in Texas!
MARIE: [responding from the shallow end of the pool] You have never been in Texas before!
DANIEL: [talking to Marie] Uh huh!

Mark continued to put lotion on Henry's front and back torso and then lifted his face to him to apply lotion, breaking Henry's line of vision with the grass. Francis was finished blowing up toys for the pool and asked Christine:

FRANCIS: Do you have lotion to use?
CHRISTINE: Why can't we use Uncle Mark's?
FRANCIS: [no response]
CHRISTINE: Why can't we use Uncle Mark's?
FRANCIS: I think Nay-Nay [Aunt Nannette] has some for you to use.
CHRISTINE: I want to use Uncle Mark's, Daddy!
MARIE: I want to use it, too!

MARK: [responding to the girls' requests for his sunscreen lotion] A special blend of herbs and spices!

CHRISTINE: [gets out of the pool to retrieve lotion from Mark] I'm next!

MARIE: I don't need any!

DANIEL: [to Marie] I'll race you to it!

MARIE: I'll still get to be next 'cuz I asked first.

Daniel and Marie got out of the pool in the shallow end and raced to where Mark and Henry were standing near the deep end. Mark finished putting sunscreen on Henry and signed,

MARK: FROG IN GRASS. DANIEL THROW.

Daniel and Christine arrived at the edge of the pool and tried to take the sunscreen from Henry's hands. Mark reprimanded them, signing and talking:

MARK: Well, tell him, don't grab it!

TELL! DON'T GRAB!

The scene ended as another creature at the water's edge distracted Christine:

CHRISTINE: Eww gross spider!

MARIE: Spider!

CHRISTINE: Eww gross! (VC:6:1:34)

SCENE 2: PLAYING WITH CARS AT COUSIN ROGER'S HOUSE

One of the days at Marble Beach was spent visiting Sara's brother Ernest Jr., his wife Heather, and their four children (video segment #7). Ernest Jr. is Henry's godfather—a role conferred on Ernest because Henry's birth and identification as a deaf person affected him notably. Although Henry had seen pictures of Ernest and his family, this was their first face-to-face meeting. In an effort to win Henry's favor and show his affection, Ernest gave Henry a large number of toys, including a large cylinder filled with toy cars and trucks.

Scene 2 began shortly after Henry received his gifts from Ernest. Communication in this scene illustrated Henry's contingent access to interaction in several ways. The clip opened with brief interaction among adults and children. Sara acted as Henry's interpreter and voiced his responses for extended family members. Henry's access to interaction during the beginning of the scene was contingent on Sara's ability to sign and voice interpret effectively, as well as how long she decided to remain in her interpreting role. After Henry had opened his gifts, Sara left the room to visit with her siblings while Daniel and Henry played with their cousin Roger for the first time. At this point, Henry's ability to access interaction was again conditional. His access to effective interaction was dependent on his ability to make his needs and wants understood without using ASL and the degree of his playmates' communicative competence. Although I was present and could have interpreted, Henry understood that he was required to communicate independently with his brother and cousin.

The scene opened as Henry opened his canister of toys. Sara responded to Henry's gift by signing and saying:

SARA: For you only! Wow! Kiss Uncle Ernest!
    WOW. KISS ERNEST [name sign E at the heart]. (VC:7:1:34)

Henry kissed Ernest and returned his attention to the toy in his hand. Sara had taught Henry how to spell the first names of extended family members earlier in the week. Making an effort to bridge the communication gap between Ernest and Henry, Sara said:

SARA: Henry, spell his [Ernest's] name.
    FINGERSPELL NAME PRO.1 [points at Ernest].
HENRY: I-DON'T-KNOW.
SARA: Remember? Tell him!
    REMEMBER? E TELL E. (VC:7:1:37)

Henry's cousin Marie watched Sara and Henry's interaction intently. Marie tried to imitate the signs and fingerspelling they were using to interact. Unknowingly, Marie was making sense of deafness by mirroring interactions in a social setting. Marie was learning that Henry communicated in different ways and required visual rather than auditory interactions.

Henry seemed shy and looked down at one of his new toys. Sara voice interpreted for Henry:

SARA: He says, "I don't know [how to spell Ernest's name]!"

Sara tapped on the new toy in Henry's line of vision to get his attention. Marie continued to watch, learning how to get a deaf person's attention. Sara asked Henry,

> SARA: You like that?
> LIKE THAT?

The next segment of the video clip began as Henry, Daniel, and their three-year-old cousin Roger played with Henry's new cars and trucks on the "traffic carpet" on the floor of Roger's bedroom. Henry was trying to get the lid off the cylinder filled with toy cars. Sara continued to mediate interaction among the children by engaging Henry in conversation. Henry's access to interaction was still contingent on Sara's ability to use spoken English and ASL to interpret for both Henry and hearing extended family members who did not understand sign language. For example, Grandmother Medina (Peggy) was watching as the boys played with cars and chattered about different items in Roger's bedroom that reminded her of when her own children were young. Sara mediated or interpreted part of the interaction that was occurring in the room for Henry. However, Henry was paying attention only to the action that was centered on his new cars.

> SARA: What do you have? Whose is that?
> WHO THAT?
> HENRY: DRIVE DRIVE PRO.1 [points at the cylinder and shows Sara the toys inside the cylinder]! ("There are cars inside this cylinder!")
> PEGGY: He wasn't expecting it. It's a surprise from Uncle Ernest and
> SARA: SURPRISE WHO? [Sara rephrases Peggy's comment in the form of a question for Henry].
> PEGGY: from Arthur [Henry's cousin] and his Daddy [Ernest Jr.]
> SARA: [Sara asks again] And who's it for?
> FOR WHO?
> PEGGY: For Henry! (VC:7:1:40)

Daniel was sitting on the bottom bunk of the bed listening and watching. Cousin Roger was setting up his share of the cars on the bottom bunk next to Daniel. Sara continued to facilitate interaction, speaking and signing simultaneously to set up the parameters of the play session for Daniel, Henry, and Roger. From a mother's perspective, Sara understood that it was important to clearly define what toys belonged to whom in order to stave off arguments and miscommunication after she left the room. Sara explained to Henry,

> SARA: This [car] is for Henry! It's a surprise from Uncle Ernest and Arthur and Aunt Heather.
> THIS FOR HENRY PRO.1 [points to cousin Arthur who is standing off camera]! [Sara moved out of camera range, so her signs were not visible].
> HENRY: [Nods] YES YES YES YES YES ("Yes! I understand the cars are from Arthur.")
> SARA: Okay! He's fine with that. (VC:7:1:41)

Grandmother Medina was learning about deaf and hearing interactions by watching Sara and Henry. She repeated or filled in gaps in their visual and auditory interactions by talking aloud to herself as she followed their conversation:

PEGGY: Okay, he knows that, he says.

Henry vocalized to get his mother's attention. He then pointed into the cylinder containing cars and signed to Sara,

> HENRY: NO MORE CARS ("There are no more cars in here.")

Sara walked over to the bottom bunk to sit between Daniel and Roger and turned her back to Henry briefly to clear a space to sit on the bed. Henry continued to vocalize her name in order to gain her attention. When Sara settled into her spot on the bed, she took the cylinder from Henry, waved her hand to get his attention, and signed/said,

> SARA: Here, pour it out [there's more at the bottom you can't see].
> POUR

Sara poured the contents of the cylinder, at least ten more matchbox vehicles, into the middle of the traffic rug. Grandmother Medina squealed in excitement, and Sara interpreted her response.

> PEGGY: Look, Henry! Wow, Henry! Yeah, Henry! Yeah!
> SARA: Wow!
> WOW!

Henry smiled, surveyed the pleased expressions of his grandmother and mother, and then knelt on the floor to start playing with the cars.

PEGGY: He's so happy! (VC:7:1:42)

Daniel moved to the floor with Henry. The pile of cars was between them. Sara signed silently to Henry and Daniel, reminding them to share.

SARA: LOOK FOR BOTH-OF-YOU.

Grandmother Medina started to talk about items in Roger's bedroom, and Sara chose not to interpret their conversation:

PEGGY: Look, Sara, do you recognize that? [points to the dresser in the room]
SARA: What?
PEGGY: Those pennies? That bowl [pointing at Roger's dresser]?

Daniel looked on top of the dresser.

PEGGY: That [container] was in Ernest's room! It was Ernie's! I brought it here for Roger!

Daniel asked Sara a question, but she did not have the opportunity to respond.

DANIEL: Mommy, do you know what? Can you put that stuff together? [he points to other new toys that are on the bed]
SARA: Yes. I'm going to put this stuff together.
PEGGY: [Grandmother Medina asked me a question from behind the camera.] See this bowl here, Laura?
LAURA: Um hm?
PEGGY: It was Ernest's!
LAURA: Wow, neat!
PEGGY: And we filled it up with pennies and dimes again!
LAURA: Wow!
PEGGY: We brought it here for Roger!
LAURA: Isn't that neat? (VC:7:1:43)

Sara and Peggy left the room, and the boys continued to play with the cars on the rug without looking up. The responsibility for Henry's access fell more heavily on his own shoulders or upon Daniel or me to act as interpreters or mediators at this point. It was interesting to note that as Daniel and Henry began to interact, Daniel initiated interactions using ASL, and Henry responded using his voice. Both boys seemed to understand that adult mediators had left the room, and accessible interaction was now their responsibility. Henry got up from the traffic rug to peer into the cylinder for more cars. Daniel handed Henry a blue tractor-trailer truck and asked using ASL only,

> DANIEL: HENRY PLAY THAT? ("Does Henry want to play with that truck?")

Henry responded to Daniel by speaking and shaking his head, NO! Again, Daniel responded using sign language only, WHAT? Henry signed, NO. Daniel grabbed for the cars Henry was holding in his arms, and Henry turned his body away and refused to give the cars he was holding to Daniel. Henry signed, MINE (VC:7:1:44). By observing Daniel and Henry's interactions, Roger concluded that it was time to claim his share of the toys and establish the pecking order for who got the "best" cars.

What Roger did not fully understand was that Henry did not hear his requests. Roger's exaggerated body language and facial expressions seemed to indicate that he understood on some level that his attempts to communicate with Henry had to be visual. However, his anxiety markedly increased as he attempted to negotiate with Henry but received no response to his requests. It appeared that Henry was aware of what Roger wanted and purposely did not allow Roger the opportunity for visual interactions. Henry's degree of access and success in this interactive situation was contingent upon Roger not fully understanding the "rules" of interacting with a deaf person. When Henry put the car back down by coincidence, Roger grabbed it and held it to his chest—copying Henry's behavior. "I was playing with that," Roger said. "Hey! Those are mine! Give it back! Mine!"

Henry picked up a car and showed it to Daniel. He seemed aware that Roger was irritated but continued to ignore his attempts to interact. Roger and Henry established a competitive environment with their body language (e.g., facial expressions and grabbing and holding the cars). Daniel's head was cocked to the side as he listened and watched Roger and Henry squabble. He chose not to participate in their interaction but was keeping a watchful older-brother lookout. Daniel ignored Henry's car offer, so Henry put the car down right in front of Daniel. Roger persisted, "It's mine! Give it back!"

Grandmother Medina came up behind me at the doorway and commented about the upcoming storm. Roger heard her comment and turned to look at us, apparently unaware that I had been standing in the door-way. Roger smiled for the camera, wiggled his eyebrows, and returned to his power struggle with Henry. Roger tried to take a car out of Henry's hands, but Henry held fast to the vehicle. Roger shouted, "Mine! They're mine!" and tried again to take the cars; this time Henry pushed him away, vocalizing, "No!" Roger tried a third time, and Henry turned his body and shielded the cars, glancing up at me as if to say, "Aren't you going to do something about this?" When Henry realized I was not going to in-tervene, he shook his head, an emphatic NO for Roger. Roger's temper was getting the best of him. He threw a car into the pile in the middle of the rug and screamed, "Share! I *said* share!" (VC:7:2:3).

From behind the camera, I asked Roger, "Do you want to learn how to sign SHARE?" but he ignored my question. Instead, he picked up an-other vehicle that had the ability to open and shut and "clacked" it in front of Henry's face. Henry smiled victoriously. By now Daniel was moni-toring the interaction overtly, ready to step in if necessary and break it up. Roger attempted one more time to strike a preschool deal:

ROGER: You can play with this one, and I can have that back.
HENRY: [vocalizes] No!

Roger looked to Daniel for his reaction and threw down the "clacky" car in disgust, shaking his head from side to side. Daniel looked to me and back to the play situation. Roger got up and walked out of the room. I as-sumed that he was leaving to collect himself when actually he left to tell his father (Ernest) that Henry was refusing to share. In the interim, Daniel and I had a brief spoken conversation about the traffic mat and how it was similar to the mat they had in their basement at home (VC:7:2:9). Moments later, Roger returned with support; Ernest and Sara were now standing behind me at the doorway of Roger's bedroom. Roger jumped across the traffic mat to where Henry had his cars "running." Ernest stayed briefly, long enough to give the boys a cursory reminder, "Be care-ful!" Roger made one last effort to retrieve his car from Henry's arms but was thwarted. Roger's verbal requests were emphatic ("Can I have my car? That's my car! Give me that car! *I said,* 'Give me my car!'"), but each time he reached for the car, Henry avoided his reach and did not respond to Roger's attempts at visual communication (VC:7:2:13).

At the end of the clip, Henry got up and walked away from the traffic mat, and Roger followed him from the room, shaking his index finger and saying, "*I said,* 'Give me my car!' Give me my car!" Henry continued to walk out of the room and did not respond to Roger, seemingly oblivious to his requests.

Scene 3: Sara Leads Group Games

One afternoon near the end of the visit to Bobbie and Jerry's house, the skies were filled with severe late-afternoon storms. The children had been cooped up in the house too long, and to harness their energy and keep them occupied, Sara began to lead them in a series of group games (video segment #10). Henry's cousins Christine and Marie participated in these activities, along with Daniel, Henry, and Madeline. During parts of the third game, the adult onlookers praised even baby John for participating.

Sara called the first game "Mommy Says," an adaptation of the traditional "Simon Says" listening-skills game played by hearing children. The rules of "Mommy Says" involved Sara signing and calling out commands to the children (e.g., Mommy says, take two baby steps; Mommy says, spin three times, take one giant step). The trick was that the only commands the children were permitted to follow were the commands that began with the phrase "Mommy says." Despite the fact that this game was originally designed to include listening strategies, Henry participated and followed Sara's directions along with the other children. The task of listening or watching for "Mommy says" seemed to be equally difficult for all the children. Sara needed to review the directions several times throughout the course of the game (VC:10:1:10).

The second game involved short relay races across the room while performing a special skill (e.g., carrying an egg on a spoon, walking sideways, and crawling like a crab) (VC:10:2:32). During the third game, which Sara called "Act Like an Animal," Henry moved from having contingent access to participation in the games via Sara's moderating techniques to a comprehensive-access situation in which he was able to fully participate and even contribute to the group members' interactions. Sara started the game by explicitly explaining the directions (signing and speaking simultaneously) to the children:

> SARA: Mommy is going to say the name of an animal, and you have to pretend you're that animal."
> MOMMY SAY NAME ANIMAL. HENRY [points to all the other children sitting on the couch] PRACTICE ACT THAT ANIMAL O-K? (VC:10:5:19)

The Worldview of a Deaf Child within His Home Environment : 249

Then Sara checked their understanding by asking them to respond to a sample animal:

> SARA: If Mommy says bird, then you have to pretend you're a bird.
> MOMMY SAY BIRD THEN PRACTICE ACT BIRD
> How does a bird go?
> WHAT-DO BIRD? (VC:10:5:20)

All the children were sitting either on the couch or on the floor in front of the couch. Christine got up off the couch and demonstrated what a bird looks like by flapping her "wings" (arms) across the room. Sara asked Henry and Madeline to show her what a bird does:

> SARA: Show me. Show me
> SHOW ME. SHOW ME.

Madeline and Henry followed Sara's directions, flapping their arms all around the living room. After these trial runs, Sara officially began the game.[7]

> SARA: Okay, you understand. Okay, Mommy is thinking about a fish.
> Show Mommy a fish! (VC:10:5:21)

Daniel, Christine, Marie, and Madeline immediately launched into their own "fish" portrayals. They bent at the waist and moved their arms in a swimming motion that resembled the breaststroke. Henry paused for a moment, obviously thinking about how a fish behaves. Rather than copying the behavior of his siblings and cousins, his mouth was the first body part that we saw in motion. He showed us his interpretation of a fish by sucking in his cheeks, pursing his lips, and wiggling his raised eyebrows. Then he raised his hands to his waist and suddenly sprouted "fins" as he "swam" through the imaginary water in the living room. Sara was excited to see his response:

> SARA: Good! Good!

As Henry-the-fish swam back to the couch, he moved his hands from his waist to the sides of his face, creating a gill effect with his cupped hands. Again, Sara responded enthusiastically:

7. Sara was not in view of the camera and so not all of her signs were recorded, although she signed and spoke simultaneously throughout the game.

SARA: Oh that's right! That's right!

Sara's remarks drew Madeline's attention. She turned to look at Henry and copied his version of a fish. Sara continued,

SARA: Okay, Mommy's thinking of a dog. Show Mommy a dog. (VC:10:5:26)

Daniel and Christine immediately moved to their hands and knees and began to bark. Henry and the rest of the children joined them. All were crawling on the floor making barking noises. Even Bobbie's dog Murphy abandoned his bone and joined the children with his tail wagging as if to say "Hey! I can do this one!"

The third animal Sara suggested was an elephant (VC:10:5:29). Henry puffed out his chest and began to move his body in a lumbering motion, swaying side to side, and moving his head up and down. As he made his way across the living room floor, he stopped occasionally to put his hands at the side of his head and flap his oversized ears. Meanwhile, Daniel was making a high-pitched sound, imitating the sound of an elephant roaring through its trunk. Cousin Marie, who had been carefully watching Henry's previous animals, placed her forearm in front of her face and pretended that her arm was an elephant's trunk. Sara continued with the fourth animal, "Mommy's thinking about a duck." Immediately the hearing children began to "quack," and this time Henry chose to imitate their actions. Henry used his voice ("Ahhhhh—Ahhhhh") to imitate a quacking sound.

"Mommy's thinking about a cow!" (VC:10:5:32). Because of our prior conversations about Henry recognizing and producing the animal sounds, I was particularly interested in how he would mimic a mooing cow. Christine and Daniel began to moo immediately, and again Henry paused to think. He bent over as though he were going to crawl on the floor and placed one of his hands on his stomach, fingers dangling down to represent the cow's udders. I asked Sara, "That's a cow?" and Sara responded, "Aren't those his udders?"

The game continued through horses, snakes, rabbits, lions, and bears. Eventually all the children grew tired of the game, and one animal became difficult to distinguish from the next. The children were enjoying crawling on the floor and making loud noises—details for them became secondary to burning off energy. The event ended after Sara suggested "Mommy's thinking of a cat" (VC:10:6:7). Henry immediately put his hands to his face so that his fingers were splayed to resemble a cat's whiskers. As the other children purred and meowed, Henry-the-cat's body twisted and roamed slinkily around the living room. On the way back to the couch and as the game ended, Henry-the-cat stopped for a lengthy period to lick his "paws" and clean his face.

This video segment illustrates a good example of a comprehensive-access situation because Henry was fully engaged in the activity and was able to contribute to the activity without changing or adapting his particular visual orientation. It was particularly interesting to see how the other children responded to Henry's ideas during this game and how all the children modeled and learned from each other's behavior. In other words, learning and interacting among the children during this activity was reciprocal and mutually enjoyable.

IMPLICATIONS AND CONCLUSIONS

Henry's actions and interactions give us a better understanding of how a four-year-old is capable of orienting himself as a deaf person in an environment that is grounded in a spoken language. We see that his efforts to navigate and understand family life were persistent, practical, and efficient. Henry sat on the steps to visually access activity in the home, always knew where his shoes were, and asked for repeated clarification of communication in the home. He functioned efficiently in his home by using a visual–gestural language that he learned at school from Deaf adults and peers. He corrected the sign language use of those around him and even chose to interact for longer periods with individuals who responded with that same efficiency.

The stories about Henry Camillo and his family contained a significant feature shared by all families with Deaf and hearing members: the use of combined visual-only and visual-auditory ways of accessing and sharing linguistic and behavioral information. Keeping in mind the complexities of mixing these worldviews, communication modalities, and languages, we are reminded that there are no easy recipes for making sense of deafness. Regardless of their personal experiences and understandings of the Deaf experience, family members, including the Deaf child, need guidance in the complex learning process related to the Deaf experience utilizing sociolinguistic and sociocultural perspectives.

REFERENCES

Agar, M. H. 1986. *Speaking of ethnography*. Beverly Hills, Calif.: Sage Publications.

Barth, F. 1981. *Selected essays of Fredrik Barth: Process and form in social life*. Boston: Routledge and Kegan Paul.

Blackburn, L. A. 1999. Linguistic and cultural interactions among deaf/hearing family members: Implications for family partnerships in early education. Ph.D. diss., Gallaudet University, Washington, D.C.

Blumer, H. 1969. *Symbolic interactionism: Perspective and method*. Englewood Cliffs, N.J.: Prentice-Hall.

Ely, M., M. Anzul, T. Friedman, D. Garner, and A. M. Steinmetz. 1991. *Doing qualitative research: Circles within circles*. New York: Falmer Press.

Erickson, F. 1992. Ethnographic microanalysis of interaction. In *Handbook of qualitative research in education*, ed. M. D. LeCompte, W. L. Millroy, and J. Preissle, 201–25. San Diego: Academic Press.

Erting, C. 1982. Deafness, communication, and social identity: An anthropological analysis of interaction among parents, teachers, and deaf children in a preschool. Ph.D. diss., American University, Washington, D.C.

———. 1994a. *Deafness, communication, social identity: Ethnography in a preschool for deaf children*. Burtonsville, Md.: Linstok Press.

———. 1994b. An anthropological approach to the study of the communicative competence of deaf children. In *The acquisition of American Sign Language by Deaf children*, ed. M. McIntire, 173–95. Burtonsville, Md.: Linstok Press.

———. 1997. Personal communication, November 3.

Evans, J. F. 1994. Conversation at home: A case study of the communication experiences of a young deaf child in a large hearing family. Ph.D. diss., New York University, New York.

Garretson, M. 1994. Foreword. In *The Deaf Way: Perspectives from the international conference on Deaf culture*, ed. C. J. Erting, R. C. Johnson, D. L. Smith, and B. D. Snider, xvii–xix. Washington, D.C.: Gallaudet University Press.

Jacobs, L. M. 1974. *A Deaf adult speaks out*. Washington, D.C.: Gallaudet University Press.

Johnson, R. E., S. K. Liddell, and C. J. Erting. 1989. Unlocking the curriculum: Principles for achieving access in deaf education. Gallaudet Research Institute Working Paper 89–3. Washington, D.C.: Gallaudet University.

Lane, H. 1993. Constructions of deafness. In *A Deaf American monograph: Deafness: 1993–2013*, 43, 73–81. Silver Spring, Md.: National Association of the Deaf.

Lane, H. L., R. Hoffmeister, and B. Bahan. 1996. *A journey into the DEAF-WORLD*. San Diego: DawnSignPress.

Markowicz, H., and J. Woodward. 1982. Language and the maintenance of ethnic boundaries in the Deaf community. In *How you gonna get to heaven if you can't talk to Jesus: On depathologizing deafness,* ed. J. Woodward, 3–10. Silver Spring, Md.: T. J. Publishers.

McDermott, R., and H. Varenne. 1995. Culture *as* disability. *Anthropology and Education Quarterly* 26 (3):324–48.

Meadow, K. P. 1980. *Deafness and child development.* Los Angeles: University of California Press.

Meadow-Orlans, K. P. 1990. Research on developmental aspects of deafness. In *Educational and developmental aspects of deafness,* ed. D. F. Moores and K. P. Meadow-Orlans, 283–98. Washington, D.C.: Gallaudet University Press.

Nash, J. E., and A. Nash. 1981. *Deafness in society.* Lexington, Mass.: D. C. Heath and Company.

Padden, C. 1989. The Deaf community and the culture of Deaf people. In *American deaf culture: An anthology,* ed. S. Wilcox, 1–16. Silver Spring, Md.: Linstok Press.

Padden, C., and T. Humphries. 1988. *Deaf in America: Voices from a culture.* Cambridge, Mass.: Harvard University Press.

Schlesinger, H. S., and K. P. Meadow. 1972. *Sound and sign: Childhood deafness and mental health.* Berkeley: University of California Press.

Schwartz, S., ed. 1996. *Choices in deafness: A parents' guide to communication options.* Bethesda, Md.: Woodbine House.

Spradley, J. P. 1979. *The ethnographic interview.* New York: Holt, Rinehart, and Winston.

———. 1980. *Participant observation.* New York: Holt, Rinehart, and Winston.

Stewart, D. A., and B. Luetke-Stahlman. 1998. *The signing family: What every parent should know about sign communication.* Washington, D.C.: Gallaudet University Press.

Stokoe, W. C. 1994. Comment on Turner. *Sign Language Studies* 83: 265–70.

———. 1995. Review article: Deaf culture working. *Sign Language Studies* 86: 81–94.

Werner, O. 1998. Short take 25: Referencing native consultants. *Cultural Anthropology Methods* 10(2): 29–30.

Woodward, J. 1972. Implications for sociolinguistic research among the deaf. *Sign Language Studies* 1: 1–17.

The Search for Proto-NSL: Looking for the

Roots of the Nicaraguan Deaf Community

Laura Polich

It was mid-July, and nearly impossible to breathe in the small office without air conditioning in the deaf association in Managua. Because both audio and video were being recorded, it had been necessary to close the outside windows to shut out the traffic noise from the street, but the blare of television and laughter from the adjoining room meant the door also had to be shut. In this ovenlike atmosphere, Mariana (pseudonym), a deaf woman approximately thirty years old, had been responding for about an hour to questions about her experiences growing up and her present life. But now we were all exhausted, and I moved to bring the interview to a close.

"Just one last question before I turn off the camera," I told Yolanda, the Nicaraguan Sign Language interpreter with whom I was working. Looking at Mariana, I asked in Spanish: "What is it like to be deaf?" Yolanda's hands went immediately to work, translating my words, and after gravely following Yolanda's motions, Mariana turned to me and signed her reply.

"I am content. I feel contented to be deaf."

Curious, I continued: "If you could change anything, what would you change?"

"I'm deaf, that's all," Mariana answered. "I would be fine always being this way, being deaf. I feel like myself. I don't know what to say, but I would be deaf, even if I could be born again, I would be born deaf the second time. It is what I am meant to be. It is the same as for you being hearing."

I persisted. "But what if you would be reborn the only deaf person in Nicaragua – everyone else would be hearing – would you still choose to be born deaf?"

This manuscript is based upon fieldwork I did in Nicaragua in 1997 supported by a Fulbright Foundation Dissertation Fellowship. Additional support to

"Me the only deaf one? No way. I remember being little and how lonesome I felt, and it wasn't until I went to school that I felt happy — I met other deaf children — what a wonderful surprise! It's true that they didn't use sign language, just gestures without meaning like sign language has. But I was so happy to find myself with other deaf people. If I were the only deaf person, I just know I would have no hearing friends — I wouldn't be able to understand them!"

There was something more here, I thought: "And what if you could be reborn and there would be many, many deaf people — thousands and thousands — but there was no sign language. What if there were deaf people all over the place, but all of them only spoke with their mouths, orally, none ever used their hands — would you still choose to be born deaf?"

"No, not that way. If there was sign language, yes, I would still choose to be deaf. It is impossible to understand only through speaking. With writing, you can get a little, but it is only so-so. But with sign language you can learn so much."

When Mariana was born in 1968, Nicaragua reportedly had no deaf community nor any commonly accepted form of sign language used by groups of deaf people in that country. Until she went to school, Mariana believed she was the only deaf person in the world and the only one shut out from understanding the mouth movements that served her parents, relatives, and neighbors so well. On that first school day, the realization that others like her existed was such a high point that even as she narrated the discovery twenty-five years later, her joy was apparent. Still, until she was a teenager, Mariana's prognosis for participation in society depended upon her ability to master oral communication — a skill with which she, like many other people born with profound congenital hearing loss, has never had any success. But in her teenage years, Mariana began to participate actively in a group in which the language modality was completely accessible to her — this was when the present deaf community in Nicaragua began to form.

———
underwrite research costs was received from a National Security Education Program fellowship and a graduate fellowship from the Pan-American Roundtables of Texas. A Multicultural Leadership Grant doctoral fellowship through the University of Texas at Austin supported me while I wrote the dissertation. I wish to express my gratitude to all the informants who generously gave me their time and took pains to explain the Nicaraguan situation to me.

Participation in the Nicaraguan deaf association and the use of sign language opened a new world for her—one of unhindered communication and full participation. Today Mariana helps to support her family by sewing in the assembly plants in the free-trade zone. She lives with her husband, who is also deaf, and her seven-year-old hearing daughter. She taught her daughter sign language at the same time that the child learned spoken Spanish; Mariana is now able to attend Mass, and, with her daughter interpreting, understand what is happening. This is a ritual that she says was a complete mystery to her when her parents took her to church as a child. Mariana's family participates in weekly social activities at the deaf association and maintains social contacts with other deaf families. The one bleak spot that Mariana mentions is that her own mother has refused to learn any sign language, so that face-to-face communication when Mariana returns home is fragmentary and labored. Mariana, therefore, leads a life nearly identical to that of other thirty-year-old women in Nicaragua. The major difference is that she uses a non-oral language.

In 1968 there was no deaf community in Nicaragua, but in 1997, when I did the fieldwork for my doctoral dissertation, there was.[1] The Nicaraguan

1. Nicaragua is a country that has destroyed or lost the archival portion of its collective memory more than once during the twentieth century. Devastating earthquakes in 1931 and 1972 meant that all major libraries, as well as all repositories of governmental and institutional records, were lost forever. Internal warfare played havoc with record keeping early in the century and had an even worse effect in the turmoil of the 1970s, which resulted in the 1979 Sandinista Revolution. Political bickering and machinations have meant that at each transition of government power (e.g., 1979, 1990, and 1996) more records were destroyed or "lost" because each new government chose to begin with a clean slate. I searched as assiduously as I could, but many documents, which would be most helpful to substantiate the history that is recounted here, simply no longer exist or are unofficially stored where I could not reach them.

Thus, this chapter relies heavily upon interviews and personal reminiscences for its historical documentation. I am well aware that memories deteriorate over time and that subsequent events color one's remembrances of past happenings. And, of course, personal agendas can intrude on how a story is told or remembered. I have made an effort to corroborate the stories and triangulate my sources. For my dissertation I interviewed more than 135 sources; 76 of these people provided the information and views most relevant to this chapter. Twenty-two of those 76 interviewees are deaf, including almost all of the "elders" present in the contemporary Deaf community (e.g., the members of the deaf association who were 36 years of age or older in 1997).

deaf community thus formed less than thirty years ago. In 1968 no one sat around conversing in Nicaraguan Sign Language because that language did not exist, but in 1997 the language was in daily use by deaf people in cities and towns in large parts of Nicaragua. This development is within such recent memory that ethnographic and historical information about the period before the community existed can still be collected, and the main actors involved in the community's formation are available for interview. The Nicaraguan example, then, provides an excellent case study to examine the development and formation of sign languages and deaf communities.

There is no reason to believe that deafness is a recent phenomenon in Nicaragua, and education for the deaf has been available since 1946 (Ministerio de Educación 1980, 1981, 1984). Yet, the use of a communally adopted sign language (e.g., manual communication beyond homesigns) was first documented only in 1986 (by Judy Kegl and her student, Cyndi Norman), and the first organization of deaf people claims 1986 as their founding year (ANSNIC 1997). Naturally, the development of a sign language predates its first documentation, and a formal organization implies prior informal organization. But the evidence indicates that the current sign language began to develop only in the early 1980s, at approximately the same time that the deaf community began to coalesce.

Before 1946, Nicaraguan children born deaf or with a hearing loss that prevented them from acquiring speech and language were generally considered incapable of education or growing to independence in adulthood. Such children, along with those having blindness, mental retardation, or motoric difficulties, were considered sources of shame for their families and were kept isolated in their family homes, out of society's sight.[2]

Parents with adequate financial means were known to set aside a suite of rooms for the child and hire a full-time nurse to care for the child's needs, and support was provided throughout the child's lifetime. Even as

2. Gregorio Mercado, the father of a deaf adolescent, explained to me how children with disabilities had traditionally been perceived in his country: "People see the child as a punishment from God *(Diós castigandoles)* or a judgment from God, and they don't want it known publicly that they have this child. So they never take him out or let other people outside the family see the child. Many people say that a child has a disability because the father sinned too much or had too many women, or because he beat the mother too much. They say 'look, because of how much you have sinned, God has punished your child with this disease *(enfermedad)*.' They see the child as sick *(enfermo)*." (personal communication)

these children became teenagers and adults, they were still considered to need protection. Other cases were not so fortunate, however. As these children became stronger and less amenable, some wished to roam, and cases of physical restraint were also known. Ana Laura Gutierrez[3] remembers visiting a childhood friend whom she knew had a daughter with Down syndrome. After the first day of her visit, Gutierrez asked about the girl, who had not been introduced to her and was told that she was kept in a back room chained to a bed because she had become "unmanageable" since becoming a teenager.

Other informants stated that they learned of the existence of relatives who had children with handicaps only when they were informed, after the fact, that the person had died. Silvia Ayón remembers that she learned that her husband's cousin had a son with a handicap when other relatives shared the news with them that the "boy" *(el niño)* had died. "That night my husband and I were sitting there talking, and we started putting things together that we had heard before, and we realized that the 'boy' was probably in his 40s when he died." The *eternal children model* views people born with disabilities as destined to live out isolated lives, sheltered and fed, but never considered capable of functioning in the wider society.

Deaf Education History

In 1946 the Escuela de Enseñanza Especial No. 1, located in Managua's Barrio San Sebastián, opened with twenty pupils, ten of whom were deaf.[4] The first curriculum was strongly influenced by Montessori principles, and instruction for the deaf class was oralist in focus. Because none of the first teachers for the deaf had formal training in deafness, all learned empirically on the job.

The school—which later became known as the "Berríos" school—moved to a new location, and the enrollment of deaf students probably

3. Ana Laura Gutierrez is a pseudonym.

4. The details about the first special education school in Managua are drawn from multiple personal interviews with Olga Tenorio Hernández, who began as a teacher at that school in 1948. She remained on the staff until 1974, when she was named principal of the school. Her tenure ended when the school was closed at the end of the 1976 school year and all of the pupils transferred to the new Centro Nacional de Educación Especial (CNEE).

reached an average of fifty per year before the 1972 earthquake. Also enrolled at the school were a few blind students and a number of students with mental retardation.

Although the methodology for teaching deaf students was always oral, from the beginning, the students used manual means to communicate with their teachers and peers. This probably was a pooling by the children of homesigns combined with gestures and iconic references. Manual communication was heavily discouraged by the teachers but persisted outside of the classroom. Olga Tenorio Hernández, who was a staff member of the school from 1948 to 1976, stated that, although teachers were generally successful in maintaining oral classrooms, "It was a waste of time to try to stop the children using their hands during breaks and after school. From the beginning, the deaf children were always waving their hands and making faces. I gave up worrying about it. That's just the way deaf children are. Among themselves they seemed to get a lot across."

There is no evidence of the existence of any deaf community in Nicaragua between 1946 and 1977. Tenorio said that she did not remember the deaf students having much contact outside of school sessions in the earlier years of the school, and she was unaware of any socialization group for deaf persons or informal group that met to socialize during the time that she was at that school. Three of the teachers who taught at the Berríos school in the 1950s and 1960s stated that they were unaware of any socialization groups for the deaf either during or after school hours.[5] This is naturally not proof that such groups did not exist, but if they did exist, they are likely to have been small and restrained in their activities.

Noel Rocha, a deaf man who works on road crews for the city of Managua, attended the Berríos School from the early 1960s until the earthquake of 1972. He was adamant that visiting among the students after classes in their homes was not common while he was in school but became more usual in the late 1970s. From that time until the early 1980s, he joined some activities at the homes of friends he had known from the school even though he was then employed and not part of a school at-

5. None of these three teachers had maintained contact with any of their deaf students from the 1940s through the 1960s. The few names they could remember were salient because the former students had either died or emigrated. It is puzzling that I was unable to locate any of the school's former deaf pupils from this period, although I did inquire extensively about them, asking others besides these teachers.

mosphere. He said that he acquired sign language basics at these gatherings of school chums. He emphasized that the shared homesigns that the pupils had used in the 1960s and early 1970s were "not a language like they have now at the deaf association." He was in his late twenties when he joined the activities and began to learn sign language, and he attributed his inability to acquire fluency to the fact that he was about ten years older than his friends who learned the sign language so well "they can say whatever they want in it." [6]

Professionals Trained

In the early 1960s, three Nicaraguan teachers went to Mexico to study speech and language therapy at the Instituto Mexicano de la Audición y del Lenguaje (IMAL). One of them was Olga Tenorio Hernández, who received a degree as a speech therapist. She returned to the Berríos school and continued to teach there, ultimately assuming the directorship of the school in 1974. The other two teachers, Silvia Ruiz de Ayón and Antonio Ayón, also received speech therapy degrees. They then set up a private school in their home in which they worked with children who had learning disabilities and who were deaf. They taught twenty-eight children annually, fourteen in a morning session and fourteen in an afternoon session.

In 1967 Dr. Eloy Isabá, an otolaryngologist, and his wife, Dr. Alma Acuña de Isabá, an audiologist and speech therapist, returned from Mexico, where Isabá had also received her training at IMAL. She set up a small program that annually enrolled six to fourteen children with speech and language problems, including children who were deaf or hard of hearing.

6. I interviewed Noel Rocha with the aid of Yolanda Mendieta, an excellent interpreter of NSL who has taken a particular interest in adults with limited signing skills. She stated that this man's sign language productions were nonstandard and included many productions that may have been homesigns and for which she had to request clarification. Fingerspelled and written Spanish words were used extensively throughout the interview to supplement understanding. We were introduced to this man by one of his "younger" deaf friends, a member of the group who had learned to sign as a teenager. This friend participated actively in the interview, providing clarifications (in NSL) and helping to bring out the older man's meaning. The linguistic gymnastics required in this interview are a striking contrast to the straightforward interviews (in which Mendieta also served as interpreter) I had with other members of that early cohort who learned to sign as teenagers.

In 1965 the Escuela Especial No. 2 was founded through the efforts of Dr. Gonzalo Meneses Ocón with Isaura García as the principal. Some deaf children appear to have been accepted at that school, but it is difficult to obtain information on the school's history or present functioning.

The Earthquake

The earthquake that destroyed Managua on December 23, 1972, had an impact upon all of these educational options for deaf children by destroying the buildings in which they were housed. The Berríos school closed for a period but reopened in another location; it was closed definitively in 1976, and the students transferred to the new Centro National de Educación Especial (CNEE), which opened in 1977. The Ayónes relocated to Altamira, a nearly undeveloped suburb at the time, and reopened their school in their new home.

The Escuela Especial No. 2 was relocated to a private building and ultimately renamed the Escuela Manolo Morales. Immediately after the 1979 Sandinista Revolution, it was included in the national special education system as a subsidized school, but it ultimately lost that subsidy for failing to follow the required curriculum.[7] The school still existed in 1997, but it was very difficult to get any information on it. Isabá reopened her program and ran it until the revolution, when she closed it to concentrate on her audiological practice.

Outside the Capital

Until 1974 education for the deaf was available only in the capital, Managua, in these four schools. Deaf children from other areas of the country either moved to the capital or went without education. Early in the 1970s, however, groups of professionals and parents began the work necessary to found schools for children with handicaps in cities outside the capital. Like the previous schools, these new schools accepted children who were blind, deaf, or mentally retarded. Classes were grouped according to disability.

7. The cancellation was published in the *Gaceta,* May 23, 1983, p. 324. (The *Gaceta* is the official publication of the Nicaraguan government, equivalent to the *Congressional Record* in the United States.)

LEÓN AND CHINANDEGA

Under the inspiration of Jilma Balladares de Herdocia and with the support of the Club 20–30,[8] a special education school was founded in 1974 in León (the second largest city in Nicaragua). In the first year of operation there were twenty deaf pupils divided into two classes. At the same time Zela Porras lent her support to the founding of a special education school in nearby Chinandega, in which ten deaf students were enrolled.

PUERTO CABEZAS AND CIUDAD DARÍO

For two years, a church missionary from the United States, Paul Wallace, worked with a small group of children with handicaps, including some who were deaf, in his home in Puerto Cabezas. Wallace left the country as the Revolution approached, however, and did not return. In 1978 the pastor of the Roman Catholic church in Ciudad Darío, Monseñor Santi, raised the funds to build the Escuela Hogar para Niños Minusvalidos (Residential School for Handicapped Children), intending that the school would educate children with motoric problems, such as those caused by polio and cerebral palsy. Later, in 1982, when the necessary physical therapists could not be found, the focus of the school changed toward educating children with mental retardation (day students only) and children with hearing impairments (who came from all over the country and were boarded at the school).

Centro Nacional de Educación Especial

In the mid-1970s Hope Somoza, the wife of then-dictator Anastasio Somoza, was head of the Junta Nacional de Asistencia y Previsión Social (National Board for Assistance and Social Planning, or JNAPS), a Nicaraguan institution that administered and funded various social welfare projects from 1955 to 1979 (JNAPS 1975). Somoza became interested in the area of special education, and JNAPS, along with the Institute for Social Welfare, submitted a joint proposal to the U.S. Association for International Development (AID) for funding to build a new and expanded special education school in Managua.[9] In 1976 ground was broken for

8. Club 20–30 was a group that supported civic improvements.

9. It appears that a member of the extended Somoza family had a disabled child who was attended by a nurse and never presented in public. Although there are rumors that Hope herself had such a child whom she kept hidden, I can find no support for that rumor. Some people state that it was Luis Somoza, the brother

the school in an isolated part of the capital.[10] Rosemary Boehmer de Selva, at that time head of the psychology department at the Jesuit Universidad Centroamericana (University of Central America [UCA]) was named principal of the school. The decision was made to close the Escuela Apolónio Berríos and to absorb those students into the new school.

In June 1977 the Centro National de Educación Especial (CNEE) opened with a total of 120 pupils, including 32 deaf students. Ruthy Durán, who had studied deaf education in Panama and Uruguay and who had taught at León's special education school and at the Escuela Apolónio Berríos, was named head teacher for the deaf section. Olga Tenorio Hernández, the former principal of the Escuela Apolónio Berríos, took over as the speech therapist.

Like the other special education schools previously established in Nicaragua, the CNEE accepted children with mental retardation, blindness, deafness, and motoric disabilities. In addition to the children who were transferred from the Escuela Apolónio Berríos, students were recruited from lists prepared in anticipation by JNAPS. According to de Selva, there were no financial or social prerequisites for acceptance. The school's funding was provided by funds from the lottery, and there was never any need to charge tuition or other fees. Some parents who could afford to do so were encouraged to contribute to the school in order to encourage their sense of participation, but no child was required to pay anything. Children came to the school from all areas of Managua and from all social strata. A set of school buses, each with a driver and an attendant, made the rounds twice a day to pick up and drop off the children.

The school had an evaluation team of social workers and child psychologists who placed the children. It also had access to a team of physicians (pediatricians, neurologist, physiatrist, and audiologist) for referral of any children needing medical care. There were eight pavilions of classrooms.[11] Each pavilion had an attendant who attended to the children's

---

of Hope's husband, who had a child with motoric problems and that Hope knew about Luis's child. Others believe that Hope Somoza had had contact with the people from the Kennedy Foundation and had been inspired by them to improve education for the handicapped in Nicaragua.

10. The school today is still isolated, although public transportation does pass by the school, something that was not available until the 1980s. On all sides of the school, very low income housing has appeared.

11. In Spanish, *pabellón*. A pavilion is a building consisting of a row of classrooms set side by side in strips. It is the typical architectural plan for schools in

personal needs and acted as a teacher's aide as needed. The teaching staff included the classroom teachers, as well as a speech therapist, and two physical education teachers. In the deaf section, one room was set aside to house a group auditory trainer. There were also prevocational workshops with training available in carpentry and manual crafts for the boys and in sewing and handwork for the girls. In total, the school employed 80 staff members and served 120 students in 1977.

CNEE's two physical education teachers found a group of very enthusiastic adolescents, most of whom were deaf and interested in individual sports events, an option not open to them at their previous school. The group took part in practices during and after school. They also competed successfully against "regular" Managua schools in various track and field events, and the team was sent to a meet in Costa Rica in 1978, as well as to meets in Venezuela and Honduras in 1980. Another group of students learned to perform folkdances, and they accompanied the athletic group to Venezuela. Ruthy Durán, the teacher of the older deaf students at CNEE, served as one of the chaperones. She remembers that the long-distance trips involved groups of twenty to thirty students who were gone for a week to ten days. While in each of the foreign countries, the group met with representatives from the various local deaf associations. In all of these countries, the representatives of the deaf association used sign language, and the adolescents were introduced to it, although at the time they neither signed nor had a very clear idea of what signing was.[12]

Outside Influences

In the late 1970s the first challenges to a strictly oralist methodology began to enter Nicaragua. In 1974 Gilbert Delgado, then dean of the graduate school of Gallaudet College and director of the college's International Center, did a study of deaf education in Costa Rica that was

---

Nicaragua, often with four pavilions connected in a square, with the enclosed school yard (known as the *plaza cívica*) used for school assemblies and drills.

12. Durán remembered: "In every country to which we went there was always a meeting set up with a representative [of the local deaf association], usually in the evening. At all of the meetings I remember the person welcoming the students used sign language. The kids were just fascinated. They wanted the evening to go on and on. It was very difficult to get them to leave. We had to literally drag them away because it got to be so late, and they had activities the next morning."

sponsored by the Organization of American States. The study's recommendations resulted in the establishment a few years later of two outreach centers, one in Puerto Rico to focus upon the Caribbean, and a second in Costa Rica to focus upon Central America.

In an agreement with the University of Costa Rica, the outreach center was located on the university's campus in San José and named Progreso. Progreso championed the use of a Total Communication methodology for educating deaf children. Total Communication, which originally meant use of whatever communication system or modality would work, whether voice or sign or writing, came to be identified with what is now more often referred to as Simultaneous Communication, in which speaking and signing are performed at the same time (Maxwell and Bernstein 1985). The hope in the 1970s was that this combination of speech and signs would provide a better way for deaf children to learn the spoken language through a visual medium more salient to them than speech.

Progreso sponsored workshops in Total Communication methodology in San José to which educators and administrators from throughout Central America came. The center also sent trainers to other Central American countries, including Nicaragua, to provide workshops.[13]

In addition to training teachers of the deaf, Progreso promoted the use of sign language by the adult population. In the late 1970s Francisco Montoya, one of the students at CNEE, acquired a dictionary of Costa Rican Sign Language (Infante 1995) and began to teach himself and some of his classmates the signs illustrated in it.[14]

Although Total Communication was never officially adopted as a methodology in Nicaraguan schools for the deaf, it did introduce the novel concept that sign language might have a linguistic content, rather than being nothing more than pantomime or rudimentary gestures. For the pupils, the combination of seeing adults in other countries communicating with their hands (behavior they had assumed to be childish because they had seen only children doing it and which their parents and teachers had char-

13. Delgado also acquired the funding necessary to underwrite the expenses of a month-long intensive summer workshop in Total Communication conducted in Spanish that was held annually for various years on the Gallaudet College campus in Washington, D.C., and attended by invitees from Central America. (personal communication, October 1998)

14. Francisco Montoya is a pseudonym.

acterized as "behaving like monkeys") and of having a printed dictionary were the first steps in their reification of sign language.

PEACE CORPS WORKER

Thomas Gibson, a Peace Corps volunteer, was assigned to teach sign language to the teachers at the CNEE.[15] He arrived in April 1979 and had only just begun to teach before the imminence of the Sandinista Revolution encouraged his superiors to withdraw him from Nicaragua and send him to Costa Rica to finish out his assignment. Ruthy Durán remembers that Gibson gave one of the older deaf pupils a sign language dictionary from the United States and that the older students were abuzz with enthusiasm about the sign language and trying to learn it from whatever source they could encounter. Gibson told me that even his short time in Nicaragua emphasized to him what a challenge he faced because "the sign language I witnessed in Nicaragua consisted of home signs. There was very little contact and communication between members of the deaf population. . . . The faculty at the [CNEE] was a dedicated group but lacked even the basic knowledge of sign language."

Gibson remembered that, during his 1979 stay in Managua, he was invited to "a deaf gathering" that took place at a student's home. All those who attended were adolescents, and communication was via gestures, homesigns, speech, and fingerspelling. Only one young man, Francisco Montoya, was able to string ASL-like signs together well enough to carry on a coherent conversation. Montoya had learned to sign from a dictionary of Costa Rican Sign Language, and Gibson was able to make out with minimal difficulty what Montoya was signing because the signs closely resembled ASL.[16]

Not until the mid-1980s was there proof of out-of-school interaction among the deaf students or a communally accepted sign language. In 1986 Judy Kegl and her assistants documented the everyday use of sign language at the Centro Ocupacional para los Discapacitados (Vocational

15. I interviewed Gibson by telephone on March 30, 1998, from his present home in Florida.

16. Gibson had previously worked for five years as a teacher of the deaf in North Carolina and during that time had socialized with the adult Deaf community. He characterized his American Sign Language skills in 1979 as "comfortable with normal conversations, but not interpreter level."

Center for the Handicapped, or COD).[17] Cyndi Norman, one of Kegl's students, spent an extended period as a volunteer at the COD collecting sign language examples. Norman stated that, during her stay, the students at the COD definitely used a common sign language at the school and certainly socialized with each other outside of classes, but there was no organized deaf group or anything that could be called a deaf community. Thus it appears that there was a limited amount of interaction among deaf students in the mid-1980s, although there was no evidence of a deaf community at that time. At about the same time, Kegl and some of her students further documented the everyday use of sign language at COD. So for the period up to the late 1970s, there is little substantiation of out-of-school interaction among the deaf students or a communally accepted sign language, but in the mid-1980s such proof exists, although there is no evidence for the existence of a deaf community.

SITUATION IN 1979

Prior to the Sandinista Revolution in 1979, there were seven special education schools in Nicaragua, five of which accepted pupils with hearing problems.[18] There were 512 children enrolled in these schools (MED 1980, 1981), of whom about 100 were deaf, and there were 33 teachers, probably 9 of whom taught students with hearing impairments. In addition, some deaf students (approximately 20 annually) received speech and language training. All of the teachers for the deaf used oral methods of instruction, and all of the teachers had the common goal of "restoring the deaf to society" by teaching the children oral Spanish. For all of the educational institutions, the most important goal for teachers of the deaf was to "make the children talk."

A NATIONAL SYSTEM

This goal did not change with the new government that entered in 1979, although the coverage of special education was broadened to the

17. For information regarding COD, see the section "The Beginning of a Change."

18. Specifically, the Special Education Schools No. 1 and No. 2 in Managua, as well as the special education schools in León and Chinandega and the program in Puerto Cabezas. The school in the Barrío Candelaria (Managua) accepted only blind students, and the residential school in Ciudad Darío at that time accepted only children with motoric handicaps.

countryside and teaching methodology was made consistent across institutions. Education for deaf students took place only within a strict oral framework, and the Total Communication influences from the 1970s were banned.

The Sandinista philosophy included a dedication to universal education. All of the schools within the republic were incorporated into one national system under the supervision of the Ministry of Education. Private schools were allowed to continue to teach special subjects, such as religion, but they were required to follow the national curriculum for the academic courses. All of the special education schools were also incorporated into the national system. In addition, the decision was made to set up at least one special education school in each of the fifteen *departamentos* (administrative districts, similar to the states in the United States), with the result that the number of special education schools increased from seven in 1979 to twenty-four in 1981.

Special Education

A division of special education was created within the Ministry of Education, and Natalia Popova, who had received her university degree in Moscow, was appointed the first coordinator of deaf education. Popova had been trained to emphasize the development of speech and to use fingerspelling as a teaching adjunct. No sign language was allowed and gestures were kept to a minimum. At the CNEE the number of classrooms for the deaf increased from five in 1979 to ten in 1980, and the deaf students increased from a little over 40 to 120. In the next four years (1981–1984) the number of deaf students at CNEE increased gradually to 200 (MED 1984), where the average enrollment has remained for the past thirteen years (MED 1997a, 1997b).

Outside Managua, twenty-three special education schools were functioning in 1981, but throughout the 1980s there was some fluctuation in those numbers. The system has averaged approximately twenty special education schools with classrooms for hard of hearing and deaf students over the years, with the overwhelming majority located in the Pacific portion of Nicaragua. From one to three of the schools have been located in the central area, and from one to three on the Atlantic coast. Nationally, the enrollment of deaf and hard of hearing students has fluctuated between 350 and 500 since 1980.

Although the teachers and administrators were careful to prohibit the use of any sign language in the national special education classrooms, the children, during recess and away from school, seemed oblivious to the prohibition, just as they had failed to heed earlier prohibitions at the Berríos school.[19]

Just how much of the manual communication that went on outside the classroom was sign *language* as opposed to gestures and pantomime is impossible to tell. No one recorded it, and no one capable of categorizing it was there watching. Still, the reports from the few teachers who began to imitate the children and learn their communication systems, and from the children themselves, when they remember back as adults, is that at this point, it was at most a very rudimentary language system. The children pooled the invented home signs used to communicate with their families, they incorporated common Nicaraguan manual gestures, and they invented new signs for events happening at school that did not have a counterpart at home.[20] Most of the now-adults, who were children at the time, and the teachers I talked with, say that this communication system was not a "real" language because according to these informants, the language of that time "wasn't anything like the sign language now used at the deaf association." The system was dependent upon shared background knowledge and was very iconic in form.

The Beginning of a Change

Around 1983 a few of the teachers of the deaf (especially those who had deaf children of their own and who noted how difficult speech was for their children and how little progress they seemed to be making) became discontented with the strict oral methodology required of them. A

19. As Elena Salazar (pseudonym), a teacher of the deaf in the early 1980s remembered, "We made sure that, in the classroom, we taught the classes orally, but the kids outside were using signs among themselves. During recess, at the snack bar, everywhere. Some of us used our hands, too, to communicate with the kids but only in private or where no one could see. In the classroom it was us emphasizing the oral and the fingerspelling, but outside, it was another matter." (personal communication, September 1997)

20. There are many gestures commonly used in Nicaraguan discourse (see Aguirre Heredía 1995). Also, some of the most "Nicaraguan" words in the 1997 NSL dictionary are based upon nonverbal gestures common in the discourse of hearing Nicaraguans (example: *caro* "expensive," p. 14).

training program at a Costa Rican school for the deaf in 1983 was an eye-opening experience for Yadira Miranda, a teacher with a deaf daughter:

I was shocked to see how much success they were having with the kids. They had oral classrooms, of course, but they also had non-oral classrooms, too. It was the first time I began to see what a resource sign language could be for the deaf, and it really changed my ideas. I began to see that forbidding the use of sign language was limiting the deaf. I had been very definite before about the need of the deaf to assimilate to hearing society, but slowly it dawned on me that it might be easier for us to assimilate to the deaf.

Three teachers had gone together to the training. One continued her dedication to the official methodology, but the third teacher, like Miranda, began to reconsider her teaching methods. At home they recounted their experiences to another teacher, Gloria Minero, a Salvadoran woman who also had a deaf daughter. The three teachers subsequently began quietly to modify their teaching methods. One result was that they consulted with Maria Lourdes Palacios, a secretary at the school and herself a deaf adult, about what she would have liked to see in her own schooling — possibly the first time that any deaf person in Nicaragua was asked to give an opinion on education for the deaf. Through one of the teachers' contacts with former deaf students, some of the young deaf adults were also invited to "demonstration" classes and asked to comment about what they would like to see.

Vocational Training

Until 1980 the only institutions accepting deaf pupils were the schools mentioned previously. They provided an elementary curriculum with the goal of turning out youths able to read, write, and hopefully, speak enough to gain employment in manual trades. At the Escuela Apolónio Berríos, classes in manual arts *(manualidades),* including crochet and embroidery, had been included for the girls, and probably some beginning carpentry was included for the boys. All the students took drawing lessons, at which the deaf students were said to excel.

But upon finishing their schooling at fourteen or fifteen years of age, the students had few "real world" skills. Dr. Berríos took it upon himself to find placements for the boys in workshops where they could be employed as carpenter's helpers, construction helpers, mechanics' helpers, and so on. The deaf youths, then, were typically placed in positions in which they had to function as the only deaf person among hearing people. There was no expectation that deaf students would necessarily learn the trade well enough to function independently at it because most of them continued to have severe difficulties communicating with hearing people. But simply to be able to earn a salary, even if it was only the minimum wage, was considered a great step forward over the pre-1946 view that considered deaf people incapable of ever leaving home.

In 1977 when the CNEE was built, it included well-furnished workshops in carpentry and horticulture for the boys and sewing and hairdressing for the girls. The goal of the school was that upon graduation, the students would have some marketable skills. For a few this evidently worked. Two members of the older deaf class in 1977 stayed at the school. They left in 1981 and found work as carpenter's helpers. One subsequently learned a great deal about repairing engines and ultimately emigrated from Nicaragua. The other has worked at a succession of different jobs over the years and is presently employed in a factory in the *Zona Franca* (assembly plants).

In 1980, after the Revolution, when the expansion of the educational system was envisioned, administrators realized that the CNEE would not have the capacity to retain the older pupils if it were to admit more younger pupils. The government board that had administered the CNEE ceased to exist when the Sandinista government assumed power. It was decided that the CNEE would be incorporated into the public school system under the direction of the Ministry of Education and would be responsible for the elementary academic education of children seven to fourteen years of age (ultimately grades one to six, although, at the beginning, fewer grades were offered as the curricula were revised). Administrators also decided that the older pupils (over the age of fifteen) would be sent to one of three vocational schools that would be set up. During the transition period in 1980, it appears that the older pupils continued to come to CNEE for classes in the workshops, but they came in the afternoon after the younger pupils had gone home.

Expanded Vocational Education

Three vocational schools were set up in 1980 to meet the needs of disabled youth: the Centro Gaspar Garcia Liviana, which targeted vocational training for youths with motoric problems;[21] the Centro Carlos Fonseca Amador, which was a training center for blind youths; and the Centro Ocupacional para los Discapacitados (COD),[22] which was established to provide vocational training for mentally retarded and deaf youths.

THE COD IN VILLA LIBERTAD

The COD staff included administrators, psychologists, social workers, a speech therapist, and teachers of workshops in manual arts, tailoring, sewing, carpentry, cabinetry, hairdressing, horticulture, commercial baking, and daily living activities. The workshops were typically gender segregated, with the males learning carpentry and cabinetry and the females studying sewing and hairdressing. According to a former social worker at the school, Nancy Guadamuz, the classes in horticulture and daily living activities were geared mainly to the students with mental retardation, and few deaf students participated. Likewise, the carpentry, cabinetry, sewing, and baking classes demanded the ability to do arithmetic calculations, and it was mainly the deaf students who were in these classes. Still, the classes were not separated by disability, so some classes included both deaf students as well as hearing students classified as mentally retarded.[23]

About fifteen students who had been at CNEE who were fifteen or older were transferred to the COD. These students obviously had received

21. Remember that this is immediately after the Revolution, and there were many young men who had sustained injuries that left them paraplegic or hemiplegic. Such disabilities were the focus of this center, not the more traditional motoric problems (such as those associated with polio or cerebral palsy) that special education schools had seen before, although youths with those problems were certainly included. This center continued to receive an influx of new para- and hemiplegic students throughout the 1980s as a result of the Contra War.

22. The COD took over the unused Casa Comunal, a community center, in Villa Libertad, a suburb in the eastern section of Managua. Thus, the center came to be known as the "school in Villa Libertad." All of the deaf people I interviewed seemed to think that the center's name was "Villa Libertad." Only hearing people referred to it as the COD, its official name.

23. This area is still a problem in Nicaragua. There are a large number of students who, because of low test scores or inability to progress academically, have been labeled "mentally retarded" when in other places or times they might simply be called "slow learners" or "learning disabled." Educational psychologists are few in Nicaragua, and educational testing is still in its infancy.

education in oral Spanish and had experience communicating with hearing teachers. In addition to these students, the center also accepted adolescents who had previously received no education. These students presented more difficulties because most of them entered with only the most rudimentary, if any, language skills. To the consternation of the staff, the communication methods that had worked at CNEE did not do any good with the new arrivals. The new students had some homesigns, and in time they adopted the communal gesture-pantomime-homesign system that the older students had brought with them from CNEE. Approximately 40 of the 150 students at the center were deaf. In the first few years, then, the previously educated deaf students were outnumbered by those just entering the educational system, and all of the deaf students were outnumbered by students categorized by the Ministry of Education as "mentally retarded" (Grooteman 1990).

Within the COD, the gesture-pantomime-homesign system became a major and basic form of communication.[24] According to several teachers who worked there, communication at the COD was a multimodality affair. Teachers and students used whatever means were possible to communicate. These included oral speech and speechreading, fingerspelling, gestures, signs, pantomime, writing, and pointing to pictures. The emphasis was on effective delivery, not purity of performance. The students entering from CNEE had a common vocabulary of signs that they had previously used at that school. When a common sign was lacking, signs from Costa Rica (learned by the speech therapist during her course, which was probably a course in Total Communication given at Progreso) were added. If no sign was available from those sources, and fingerspelling the Span-

24. Nancy Guadamuz, who worked as a psychologist from 1981 to 1985 at the COD, remembers: "In Villa Libertad, almost everything that one did with the deaf was done with signs *(casi todo lo que se hacía con los sordos era seña)*. Let me tell you that only kids over fourteen came to Villa Libertad, and the emphasis was on making these kids employable. So some had been to the special education school (CNEE), but the majority had not. We used a mixture. Even though I know a little bit of fingerspelling and speechreading and working on articulation, we didn't emphasize that at the center. We used signs *(se utilizaba señas)*, something we learned from the speech therapist who had gone to Costa Rica for a sign language course. When we would have group meetings with the kids, usually one of the teachers was talking, but there was always another teacher signing *(haciendo mímicas)* to translate for the other kids." (personal communication)

ish word or speechreading it would not do, a form was created at COD to fill the need.

At the beginning many students entered with no educational background at all. It was important that they be able to communicate with classmates as soon as possible in order to be integrated into the group. The speech therapist, then, gave individual sessions to teach newcomers a basic "survival" vocabulary of signs, but as soon as possible, the newcomers were integrated into a language group to learn enough signing to be able to function in one of the workshops. According to Nancy Guadamuz, most of the teachers became functional in signing. Besides the speech therapist (who often acted as interpreter), the sewing and manual arts teachers, the social workers, and the psychologists were able to communicate fluidly in signs. The instructors for carpentry and horticulture, however, never seemed to be comfortable with using their hands to communicate.

When the students had completed a level of training that indicated they could be employed, the COD sought placements for them with small area businesses sympathetic to the goal of employing people with disabilities. In those years, the most successful placements were in hairdressing establishments, but only a few of the deaf women trained at the COD are still working in hairdressing. Some of those who are employed at the *Zona Franca* (assembly plants) are graduates of the COD in sewing and tailoring.

The personal ties formed among the students at the COD were, without doubt, very important. Asked if there was a deaf community at the time that the COD came into existence, Guadamuz replied:

> I wouldn't call it a "community." There wasn't anything organized or identified as such, but something like that was in the making. The students who came from the CNEE had their ties to each other, and they had their own signs that they used with each other, but it wasn't consolidated in any way. That came later. The signs and the way of using them then are nothing like they are now, which I understand is a real language. But at the time it was a way that a very heterogeneous group was able to learn enough so that everyone could understand.

Early in 1985 personnel in all of the vocational centers were consolidated, resulting in a high turnover of positions. The COD went from two social workers and two psychologists to one of each. Many of the teachers most fluent in signing appear to have left at this time to take other jobs and were replaced by others who were not familiar with sign language.

Changes in Special Education

Late in 1984, Popova left her position as coordinator of deaf education to return to Moscow, where she resumed her studies and later received her doctorate in deaf education. When she returned to Nicaragua in 1989, she did not resume her post at the Ministry of Education but began to work with the Asociación de Padres con Niños Discapacitados (Association of Parents of Handicapped Children) — "Los Pipitos" — an organization that had been founded in 1987.[25]

From 1980 to 1984 teachers of the deaf were required to follow strictly a standard curriculum and methodology for teaching, but under the subsequent coordinators of deaf education, more leeway was allowed, and teachers were encouraged to seek individual solutions to teaching problems and to take the initiative in enhancing the curriculum's content. Additionally, in the latter half of the 1980s, various foreigners teaching as volunteers in Ministry of Education programs advocated the inclusion of signing (usually some form of Total Communication or Simultaneous Communication) in the deaf curriculum.

Two U.S. citizens working as volunteers with the León/Minnesota Project ran an experimental kindergarten using a Total Communication approach in León (Hougan 1993). Their success favorably impressed the Ministry of Education and paved the way for more use of signing in classrooms. The volunteers also worked with members of the deaf association in Managua in the production of an early hand-drawn and mimeographed dictionary of Nicaraguan Sign Language.

Anna Scott, a retired teacher of the deaf from Sweden, worked as a volunteer teacher in Nicaragua several times between 1987 through 1997. Scott spearheaded a campaign to encourage sign language use in classrooms in San Marcos and Managua. At the same time she encouraged the formation of a San Marcos chapter of the deaf association. Tuula Jaaskelainem, an educator of the deaf from Finland, worked as a volunteer in the Ministry of Education's main office in 1992 and 1993. She also encouraged the use of sign language in both the formal and the nonformal (home visitor) educational programs, participated in activities with the

---

25. This is a Nicaraguan term of affection referring to small children, perhaps translatable as "the kids." The name of the association is significant in that it is definitely an association *for* kids with disabilities. The "kids" themselves have no voice in the organization's agenda.

deaf association, and provided in-services to teachers of students with hearing disabilities encouraging the use of sign language.

Officially, sign language had been banned in special education schools from 1980 to 1988. From 1988 to 1992 selected teachers were allowed to experiment with signing as an adjunct methodology. Since 1992 any teacher of the deaf has been allowed to incorporate sign language into her or his teaching.[26] The official goal of the Ministry of Education, however, remains assimilationist, with the ultimate aim of teaching deaf children to speak well enough to function adequately within an oral society. Teachers, overwhelmingly, rationalize the use of signing in the classroom as a means of moving toward competence in Spanish and ultimately oral competence. Most teachers sign only at a basic level, and sign language ability is not, and never has been, a prerequisite to employment as a teacher of the deaf.

The Beginning of a Core Deaf Group

When the CNEE was established in 1977, special education students usually studied with the same teacher for multiple years. Ruthy Durán taught the oldest deaf group at CNEE from 1977 to 1980. Many of those pupils had also been her students when she had taught two years earlier at the Escuela Apolónio Berríos. She took a special interest in her students and invited them to her house to celebrate their birthdays and other special occasions. When the sports team and the dance ensemble went on trips to Costa Rica, Venezuela, and Honduras, Durán was one of the chaperones. Most of these students were among the first group transferred to the COD in Villa Libertad.

In 1981 Durán assumed responsibility for the youngest deaf class at CNEE, but she maintained social ties with the older group and was instrumental in encouraging them to form a folkdance troupe with other hearing students under the direction of Haydeé Palacios, a famous dance teacher in Nicaragua. The troupe performed widely, and some of the deaf students were the outstanding dancers. Palacios or an assistant gave them visual cues so that they could remain in synchrony with the music, and depending on the surface on which they were dancing, they could feel some of the vibrations of the music and stay in time.

26. Over 90 percent of teachers of the deaf are female.

By this time the group ranged from eighteen to twenty-one years of age and were very competent at riding the buses of Managua to get to their desired destination. It was not unusual, according to Durán, for three or four of her former students to stop by on Sunday afternoons to visit. The communication mode was similar to that used in the COD—anything that worked.[27]

In 1984, after a disagreement at the CNEE, Durán resigned and took a job in the Ministry of Education's newly created preschool program. Toward the end of the school year, a CNEE teacher named Gloria Minero suggested to Durán that if the young deaf adults wanted to have an impact on anything or improve their futures, they would need to organize themselves into a self-help group that could advocate for areas that would improve the lives of deaf people. With a background in special education, Minero worked as a teacher of the deaf at the CNEE from 1980 to 1985. A forceful personality, she was undaunted by obstacles in her path and was willing to take charge when a leader was needed. Her dedication to her deaf daughter was legendary among educational professionals.[28]

Because Durán had a close relationship to many of the young adults and because Minero was interested in the formation of the organization for the sake of her own teenage daughter, she suggested to Durán that the two of them collaborate in encouraging and helping the young people to organize and that the two women should help them in the process.

Durán agreed, and the two of them began to seek out the young deaf adults and adolescents to invite them to meetings that took place on weekends, usually at either the Minero or the Durán home. From the beginning the meetings had multiple purposes. Socialization was always a major part of each meeting, and basketball games were routine. Festivities around holidays and birthdays were an excuse for parties. But Minero

27. "There wasn't a sign language at the time, not like there is now. But we were able to understand one another. We would talk for part of the time and use a lot of the gestures that everyone around here [in Nicaragua] uses, and we had a set of some signs that the students had made up – they aren't used now – like, for the days of the week, we had special signs that we had used with each other for years, and at Villa Libertad they had learned new signs that they taught me, and when everything else failed, we would write words down or else act it out. I don't remember there being any big barriers. We always managed to figure each other out."

28. In order that her daughter might successfully attend secondary school, Minero attended the classes at her daughter's side, took notes for her, and later reviewed the material with her so that her daughter could study it for examinations.

insisted that the young people had to think of their futures and improving their job skills, so basic literacy and arithmetic classes were also included. Although sign language soon became a popular form of communication, it was seen only as an auxiliary form of communication, with oral proficiency still the goal to strive for. The first group to attend the meetings consisted mainly of Durán's former students from 1977–1980 at CNEE as well as Minero's daughter. They were soon joined by Yadira Miranda and her daughter, Lisbeth.

ORGANIZING THE ASSOCIATION

Minero found that she could not teach during the 1985 school year because, as a refugee, her legal papers were not in order. She spent most of that year regularizing her legal status, but as she recalled later, "not being able to work that year was what gave me the time that year to devote to organizing the association." Minero convinced Durán that if the organization was to be useful in the long run, it needed to be registered with legal standing as an official organization. That required a written constitution and bylaws and presented a daunting set of legal paperwork requirements. All of that seemed well beyond the capability of the students, so Durán and Minero, joined at times by Miranda, set out to compose the organization's constitution and bylaws. Durán remembers that they worked on the documents for hours, often finishing so late at night that she slept at Minero's house because it was too late to find transportation home.

The young people found the meetings and the chance to socialize with other young deaf adults to be stimulating, and they began to invite other deaf friends and acquaintances to the Saturday and Sunday gatherings. The group started with eleven young people but soon grew. In April 1986 a vote was taken to adopt the name Asociación Pro-Integración y Ayuda al Sordo (Association to Integrate and Help the Deaf), or APRIAS.

APPLICATION FOR LEGAL RECOGNITION

The statutes were finished in 1987 and were ratified by the members in a December 1987 meeting. The whole certification process took another few years, and in 1990 the organization was officially registered at the Ministerio de Gobernación (the ministry responsible for administration of the country's internal affairs).

The original statutes envisioned an executive council of five officers, each with a given area of responsibility: General Secretary (now commonly referred to as "president"); Organizational Secretary; Secretary of Archives ("secretary"); Secretary of Finances ("treasurer"); and Secretary for Information, Education, and Culture. The officers were to be advised by five hearing people "sensitized to the problems of deafness." The first advisory committee included Ruthy Durán, Gloria Minero, Yadira Miranda, Mario López, and Esperanza Acevedo, all parents of deaf children except for Durán. Meetings were to be held at least every three months, and the day-to-day functioning was to be carried out by the executive council, which was to meet at least every fifteen days.

The official slogan was "Together Let Us Break This Wall of Silence" (Estatuos de APRIAS 1989). The structure of the deaf association mirrored that of many other Nicaraguan organizations, with an executive body responsible for policy and the daily conduct of affairs but with periodic meetings at which members would vote upon issues presented to them by the executive council. At this point the model of deafness underlying the formal organization of APRIAS was assimilationist, premised on the need for deaf people to be part of society, but the attainment of that goal was something still viewed as possible only within the mainstream hearing society. Only deaf or hard of hearing people were allowed to be members, but an advisory board of hearing people was available for consultation.[29]

DOMESTIC AND FOREIGN ASSISTANCE

In 1987 Socorro Carvajal, a high official of the Instituto Nicaraguense de Seguridad Social y Bienestar (INSSBI; the social welfare arm of the government), who had learned of the organization and progress of APRIAS, went to Sweden. There she met with the heads of various organizations that were providing material aid to Nicaragua. One official with whom she spoke put her in touch with a representative of the Swedish Association of the Deaf (SDR), who took an interest in the possibility of aiding the fledgling group. The SDR soon approved a funding request from APRIAS, and a grant of $50,000 was made in 1989 for the purpose of buying and equipping a permanent meeting place in Managua. A suitable location was found and purchased in a central area of Managua near mul-

29. The youth and social inexperience of the majority of the founding members in 1986–1989 is probably responsible for the addition of the *Comité de Apoyo* in the original statutes.

tiple bus routes. The house was inaugurated on November 18, 1989, and the membership list at that time included fifty names.

Sign Language Use

The use of sign language continued to grow among the members of APRIAS. When the first church wedding in the group took place in 1989, it was interpreted into sign language so that the deaf participants and their guests could understand (R. Senghas 1997).

According to Minero, before 1987 the deaf students exhibited great diversity in the signs they used. "There was a lot of use of *gestos rusticos* [rudimentary gestures] and ASL signs and *mímicas* [homesigns], which are not "signs" but more *signos icónicos* [iconic signs]. There wasn't much structure—that came later." After a series of weekend workshops to standardize sign language usage among the young adults, the association, in conjunction with various foreign volunteer workers, published a mimeographed dictionary of signs in 1989.

In the early 1990s, a Canadian social worker, Scott Sorrell, used his own videocamera to record members of the association demonstrating a lexicon of common signs and compiled a "video dictionary" that was distributed among interested family members and teachers of the deaf. Work on a more comprehensive dictionary continued. In March 1997, with the financial backing of the Swedish Deaf Association, the first commercially printed dictionary of Nicaraguan Sign Language was presented to the public.

DEAF COMMUNITY FORMATION IN LIGHT
OF NICARAGUAN DEAF HISTORY

Before extracting some conclusions about deaf community formation from the Nicaraguan history just presented, it will be useful to examine what other authors have written on the topic. The bulk of works have concentrated on how deaf people should be, were, or are educated. There is also a large corpus of works on what it means to be deaf and on deaf people's experiences. But there are very few works detailing deaf communities historically or ethnographically, and the ones that exist (e.g.,

Erting et al. 1994; Fischer and Lane 1993) have rarely examined how or why deaf communities come to form. Thus, only a few authors have theorized about the factors that bring deaf communities into existence. I will consider three works by authors who have treated this theme.

Alexander Graham Bell

In the nineteenth century, individuals such as Alexander Graham Bell attributed the formation of deaf communities and social groupings to segregated education and activities (Bell 1888). Bell believed that routine and custom were at the heart of deaf communities. If deaf children went to school together and played together after school, they would naturally prefer to socialize together as adults. Bell, a eugenicist, feared that deaf socialization would result in a higher incidence of deafness in the overall population (a scientifically unfounded conclusion, by the way). He therefore proposed that deaf children be educated in the most oral environment possible and discouraged from socializing with other deaf people. If deaf children grew up only in oral environments, Bell hypothesized that they would prefer oral social interaction as adults, and no deaf communities would form because they would not be needed.

Van Cleve and Crouch

In their 1989 book, *A Place of Their Own: Creating the Deaf Community in America,* Van Cleve and Crouch presented the premise that the various deaf communities in the United States originated when enough deaf people were brought together in residential schools. This theory is a combination of two hypotheses: that the proximity of a sufficient number of deaf people results in the formation of a community, and that the community forms out of the shared experiences of growing up in a residential school among others who also use sign language. This theory implies that simply bringing enough deaf people together (even if they are children) should be enough to spur community formation and that the community forms at the residential school when the children are acculturated into the community and simply continues as the members become adults. It also implies that the deaf residential experience is/was so uniform that the communities formed in all the schools were basically identical. This explains how a person can grow up in one state at one residential school but later join a deaf community geographically far away and yet fit right in.

Schein

Schein (1989) hypothesized that there are five factors necessary for a deaf community to form: demography, alienation, affiliation, education, and milieu (199). By *demography* Schein meant the same proximity factor discussed by Van Cleve and Crouch. The deaf population in a given area must reach critical mass before a community forms. How "critical mass" is determined is not defined—more than one, certainly, but exactly how many or how few make a community possible is unknown. Schein suggests that a pool of 1,000 deaf people may be the point of critical mass. He points out that Wyoming did not have a chapter of the National Association of the Deaf until the state's deaf population reached this number, and the Union League was formed in New York when the city's deaf population was approximately 1,000, but Schein admits that that number is only a suggestion and that empirical research is needed to prove or deny the hypothesis.

Gathering enough deaf people in proximity, however, is not sufficient to induce a deaf community to form, according to Schein. The other factors must also be present. *Alienation* is "the motor that drives the deaf community" (204). Deaf communities are based on the fact that potential members are estranged from their hearing families and suffer discrimination in the larger society. Schein wrote that *affiliation* is "the counterforce to alienation" (207). The shared feature of deafness creates a commonness that is the foundation for a sense of belonging to the deaf community. Schein refutes that *education* per se engenders deaf communities (he cites the example of the Paris deaf community, which formed before any education for deaf people, residential or otherwise, was available), but he finds that the shared experiences of deaf education (not the content) are another necessary factor in triggering deaf communities.

Finally, Schein targets "milieu" as a necessary condition for deaf communities to form. In the case of the United States, Schein notes that the country has many minority members and tolerates and encourages them

(214); thus, deaf communities are seen as just one more example of diversity. Schein finds that is not true in other countries, and thus there are places in which deaf communities have been discouraged from forming.

FORMATION THEORIES IN LIGHT
OF THE NICARAGUAN HISTORY

Bell's hypothesis that routine and simple custom is the basis for deaf community formation receives no support from the Nicaraguan example. Education for deaf and hard of hearing children has been available in Nicaragua since 1946. From the 1960s up to the 1972 earthquake, it is probable that an average of fifty deaf children and early adolescents were in daily contact at the largest special education school in Managua for approximately eight hours a day over multiple years. According to the school's former teachers, there is no evidence that the students formed any socialization groups outside of school hours or made any effort to remain in contact with each other or their teachers once they had left the school. They did not appear to form any kind of group identity that was retained after their schooling was over, and they do not appear to have made any effort to seek each other out as adults in order to live in proximity to each other or socialize regularly. In other words, there is no evidence for deaf community formation either when the pupils routinely spent large blocks of time together during schooling or afterward as adults.

Alternatively, I interviewed three deaf adults who had been educated in oral environments before the present deaf community of Nicaragua formed. Each of these three came from families willing to sacrifice generous amounts of time and resources to provide intensive private tutoring so that their children could attend "regular" (not special education) schools in which all of their classmates were normally hearing. These three did not grow up with any regular contact with others who were deaf, and they were never allowed to sign as children.

When, as teenagers (two) or young adults (one), they came into contact with other deaf peers and saw them using sign language, they all immediately took steps to learn the sign language and participate in activities with other deaf people. Two of these people were among the founding members of the Nicaraguan Deaf Association. The third followed a similar path upon his first acquaintance with sign language in the United States at age seventeen. He begged his parents to send him to a "manual" school, and he now considers ASL to be his strongest language, although he is also competent in Spanish, English, and Nicaraguan Sign Language. If Bell's hypothesis about routine and custom explained deaf community formation, we would have expected these three, who grew up in strictly oral environments until at least their late teenage years, to have chosen only oral environments as adults. Yet all three have chosen to form significant social ties with various deaf communities.

The first part of the Van Cleve and Crouch hypothesis that proximity results in deaf community formation is also not substantiated by the Nicaraguan case. Groups of deaf children spent significant amounts of time together daily beginning in 1946, but there is no report of any deaf community formation before the early 1980s. Van Cleve and Crouch, however, emphasize that they believe that residential schools incite the formation of deaf communities because the children essentially spend all of their waking hours together and develop a common socialization that leads them to seek out each others' company when they reach adulthood. Sharing the similarity of boarding school life and sign language accounts for participants' ability to easily join a deaf community geographically removed from the area in which they grew up.

But when a deaf community did form in Nicaragua, probably in the early to mid-1980s, it formed among a group of adolescents who had had no experience with residential schools and among some who had very little experience with schools at all. All of the founding members of the deaf association were educated in day schools in Managua, which they attended for four to eight hours a day, and they spent the remainder of their time living among their hearing relatives. Similarly, the members from Masaya and San Marcos, who took the initiative to begin attending deaf association events in Managua and then recruited enough members in their hometowns to form local chapters of the deaf association, were uniformly educated in day schools. The founding members of these subchapters had fewer overall years of schooling and had been introduced to other deaf people at a later age than those who founded the Managua chapter.

Further, Nicaragua has had a boarding school for the deaf since 1982. The enrollment for deaf students has averaged fifty for the past fifteen years. Yet there is no evidence of a deaf community in Ciudad Darío, the town where the school is located. I found no instance in which a deaf graduate of the boarding school chose to move back to Darío after graduating in order to be close to a deaf community or to participate in any town activities. Instead I have listened to descriptions of graduates who have chosen to return to very remote, rural sites and face a future as the only deaf person for miles.

Five former students of the boarding school at Ciudad Darío returned to Estelí (the third largest town in Nicaragua) after graduation and made no attempt to contact former schoolmates for three to five years. Brought together by a deaf shoemaker (who, by the way, never received any education), an extraordinary personality who seeks out and invites deaf people to gather at his home on Sunday afternoons, they have become reacquainted and in 1997 began to form a deaf group in Estelí. Experience with residential school is coincidental; seven of the group's members never attended residential school, and, in fact, two of them never attended any school whatsoever.

Similarly, four former students who attended the residential school concurrently returned to their homes in Jinotega and Matagalpa (towns about twenty miles apart) but made no attempt to gather. Each of them independently heard about activities at the deaf association in Managua and began to make the four-hour trip regularly. The four became reacquainted in Managua and later began to plan activities in Matagalpa. Spurred by the example of organization they witnessed in the capital, they sought out other deaf people and in 1996 formally organized the third local chapter of the deaf association in Matagalpa. Only a minority of the Matagalpa chapter attended residential school. The Matagalpa chapter, in fact, has a large group of older adults who never received any formal schooling. Neither proximity nor experience with residential schooling can explain, at least in the Nicaraguan case, why deaf communities form.

Yet if Schein's critical mass is a necessary factor, it must be significantly less than the 1,000 people he suggested, or else the Nicaraguan deaf community would never have formed. From interviews about the late 1970s in Managua with deaf adults as well as several teachers who taught at the Berríos school from 1948 to 1976, only about fifty names of deaf adults who had been educated before 1980 could be gathered. Approximately sixty children were enrolled in the capital in classrooms for students with hearing disabilities in 1979. This number was not enough for Schein's critical mass, yet the available evidence indicates that it was exactly in this period that the first steps toward the formation of a deaf community were taken. In 1986, a date when the presence of a deaf organization in Managua is documented, the number of deaf adults known to each other probably was no higher than 200, the elementary school had reached an enrollment of 200 deaf children, and the vocational school served approximately 50 deaf adolescents—still significantly short of a deaf population of 1,000.

The group that formed the deaf association started with 11 members (probably in 1985), grew to at least 50 by 1989, and in 1997 had 358 enrolled members, although the president estimates the actual total membership to be closer to 600. The Masaya, San Marcos, and Matagalpa chapters all formed with approximately 10 early members and formally became chapters of the national association when local membership reached approximately 50. The Esteli group, which meets regularly on Sundays, presently numbers 15. Deaf communities are not necessarily identical to formally organized associations, but the Nicaraguan example gives us evidence that the regular gathering of a group of 50 *children* does not result in a deaf community (e.g., the situation in 1971), but a gathering of 11 *young adults* (e.g., 1986) is sufficient for early formation of a community. Critical mass per se may not be as important as what the group offers potential members.

In addition to critical mass, Schein hypothesized that alienation is a factor in deaf community formation. Because the majority of people born with severe to profound deafness have a very difficult time mastering the oral language of the hearing majority, it is not difficult to find alienation from hearing family members in any deaf group. Alienation has certainly been present throughout the history of deafness in Nicaragua. Likewise, affiliation based on the commonality of deafness is a characteristic of nearly any group of deaf people who come together. And deaf children have shared educational experiences since 1946. All these factors were present for nearly forty years before a deaf community formed.

Finally, Schein cited milieu as important. By this term he seemed to imply some form of societal acceptance of diversity. The milieu in regard to deafness (and all disabilities) was probably excruciatingly negative for most of Nicaraguan history and in many ways continues to be so today (Ramos 1997). The first significant change, however, probably took place in the early 1940s— at a point before the first special education school was founded—when the topic of whether children with disabilities should be educated was debated and decided in the affirmative. Before this time, the prevailing societal attitude had presumably been that children with handicaps could not benefit enough from education to make the effort and expense worthwhile. The decision to initiate fund-raising and planning for such a school implies that at least a core group had modified its perceptions, deciding that the targeted children could learn and progress enough to justify the necessary work.

But even with this major turn toward increased acceptance, another forty years elapsed before a deaf community formed. No equivalent attitude shift occurred in the late 1970s or early 1980s that favored another shift in the perception of deafness (or other handicaps) that could be interpreted as an equivalent change in milieu. From the 1940s on, people who could learn to talk and function orally were accepted as members of society, and those who could not, were not. The Sandinista Revolution did not change this societal perspective. In fact, this attitude was enshrined even more dogmatically in the official curriculum of the new government's Division of Special Education. Teachers in the pre-Revolutionary CNEE were free to take workshops in the Total Communication methodology and apply it in their classrooms if they wished, but teachers at the post-Revolutionary CNEE feared losing their jobs if they expressed any sympathy for sign language. This dominance of the oralist orientation did not change until about 1990, and the presence of the by-then-formed deaf community was probably one of the reasons that the attitude was modified.

Thus, the Nicaraguan example provides little support for previous theories about how and why deaf communities form. Even though a group of fifty students were in daily proximity in the 1940s, 1950s, 1960s, and 1970s, with presumably sufficient alienation and affiliation, with common education, and with a more accepting milieu from the 1940s, nothing that could be identified as a deaf community formed. But in the 1980s a group of fifty or fewer young adults with the same levels of alienation, affiliation, common education, and milieu formed a group that was recognized even by outsiders as a community. There seems to be a need to look further.

NO EARLIER SIGN LANGUAGE

Language is the medium through which community is built and maintained. The glaring absence, then, of a sign language during the 1946–1980 period supports informants' remembrances that a deaf community

Age Range	Number (N = 356)	Percentage of Total
40+ years (birthdate before 12/31/57)	22	6%
30–39 years (1/1/58 to 12/31/67)	85	24%
20–29 years (1/1/68 to 12/31/77)	195	55%
15–19 years (1/1/78 to 12/31/82)	44	12%
Unknown birth dates	10	3%

Note: Age ranges are from birth dates listed in ANSNIC files.

did not form during this period even though education was being provided to deaf people.[30] It becomes interesting at this point to ask whether there is any substantiation for this claim of the absence of a prior sign language beyond the remembrances of informants. Could it be that there was such a language (or languages), but it was not passed down directly and present informants are unaware of it? The deaf association's membership statistics provide some useful guidance in attempting to answer this question.

The Search for a Proto-NSL

The present Nicaraguan deaf community has very few people in their forties, but some in their thirties, many in their twenties, and a large number now in their teens (see table 1). What accounts for this skewing? The graph of the birthdates of the membership of the deaf association is not even across all years (see figure 1). The decided peaks probably represent cyclical rubella epidemics.[31]

30. I base this statement upon interviews with six former teachers and thirteen of the older members of the Deaf community.

31. Even today there is no universal vaccination for rubella in Nicaragua, although limited vaccination began in 1997. The same cyclical variation is seen when the birthdates of the children enrolled in classrooms for the hearing impaired in special education schools in 1997 are graphed, indicating that rubella epidemics are continuing in six-to-eight-year cycles. Rubella is a disease that, if

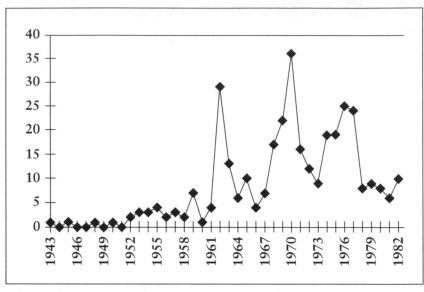

FIGURE 1. *Birthdates (1943–1982) of Members of the National Nicaraguan Association of the Deaf (n = 321)*

Figure 1 key
x-axis = Year of Birth
y-axis = Number of Enrolled Members*

*These figures include only official "members" of
 the National Nicaraguan Association of the Deaf
 (i.e., those persons who submitted an application).

Note the peaks for birth years 1962, 1970, and 1976. Not all of the members born in these years are deaf due to rubella, but because other common causes of deafness (e.g., heredity or meningitis) occur at a constant, not cyclical, rate over time, we can conclude that the variation obvious in the graph reflects the long-term effects of recurring rubella epidemics. The graph is striking in that the first upswing in 1959 leads to the 1962 peak. There is no reason to believe that rubella cycles began in Nicaragua only in the late 1950s. But where is the peak that would have been expected in 1956? Or the one that should be there in 1950? Or those that should have been exhibited in the 1940s or 1930s?

---

contracted by a pregnant woman, results in the child being born with severe-to-profound hearing loss or visual abnormalities (Johnson and Whitehead 1989).

There is only *one* organization for deaf people in Nicaragua, so it is not possible to attribute the lack of older people in the membership rolls to their participation in rival associations. But the older people are not in the deaf association either. One explanation given to me for this sudden occurrence of deaf people born around 1959, and nearly none before, was that previously all disabilities in children were very stigmatized. Parents simply did not bring deaf children out into the light of day to be seen as members of society if they were handicapped in any way (this is the *eternal child* model). Such children were kept at home and either treated well with their own private nurse or mistreated horribly by being chained in a back room, depending on individual circumstances. Thus, the deaf people who would now be in their seventies and sixties and fifties were kept at home and never allowed to become part of society, and that is where they are today. This may be true, but the deaf association figures by themselves are simply not enough to explain the puzzle completely.

The Blind Association

Looking for a parallel group in Nicaraguan society, I went to the Marisela Toledo Association for the Blind. Blind people were just as stigmatized as deaf people. Blind children were just as much seen as punishment for their parents' sins. They were also kept at home and not educated. The first school to accept blind children was the same school set up in 1946 that was the first to accept deaf children. Thus, if a history of being kept at home, not socialized to the larger society, or not allowed to go out was what was keeping older deaf adults out of the deaf association, then we should see this same pattern in the membership list of the blind association (table 2). But what is striking is the number of people who are now in their seventies, sixties, fifties, and forties along with the younger members who are listed. The Blind Association has elders! And the deaf association simply does not. Perhaps language is the cause of this discrepancy.

A Hypothetical Case

Consider the case of a blind person, male or female, whose first sixty years of life were hypothetically spent shut up at home and who was not allowed to go to school, not allowed to go out on the streets, not allowed

TABLE 2. *Comparison of Membership by Birth Years for Nicaragua's Blind Association and Deaf Association*

Birth Years of Members	Marisela Toledo Association for the Blind, Managua Chapter only (N = 253)*		Nicaraguan National Association for the Deaf Membership list (N = 315)	
	Males	Females	Males	Females
1966–1979	60	36	127	95
1936–1965**	89	29	57	36
before 1935	29	10	0	0

*The count for the Managua Chapter was made by the Marisela Toledo Association for the Blind in May 1995.

**The earliest birth year for the Deaf Association is 1943.

to work, but was kept at home being a member of society only through the stories overheard from other family members. Finally, in 1989, the year that the Marisela Toledo Association for the Blind was formed, a friend or a relative offers to take this previously isolated person to the association. That person arrives and finds a group of people with similar stories, sits down to chat and share and, if offered the chance, probably is happy to fulfill the membership requirements to become a part of the group.

Another Hypothetical Case

Now consider a hypothetical deaf contemporary of sixty years of age who has also always lived at home. Overhearing stories is not in that person's repertoire. (That person probably managed to devise a common code for basic functions with one or two family members, but I have yet to find a hearing family of a deaf person who has evolved a family code that could talk in depth about abstract concepts or displaced events, such as those in the past or the future.) The language skills of a sixty-year-old deaf person who has never received any schooling and has always lived at home are rudimentary. Even if a relative or friend offered to take that person to the association, the isolated deaf person's ability to enter that group and communicate would be nearly nil. One certainly *can* learn language beyond the critical period for language learning, which is agreed to taper off around puberty, but it becomes harder and harder to do so.[32] And when one has not had a functioning first language by some time in one's twenties or thirties, only the rarest of individuals manages to learn one later. Thus, the older deaf Managuans (who I am certain do exist, although I have met very few of them), even if they had arrived at the meetings of the deaf association, without language would not have been able to communicate and would have had little reason to continue to visit the association and even less reason to sign up. In that case the membership rolls of the deaf association would have a decided scarcity of older members, exactly the situation encountered.

Another Possibility

Or consider an alternative hypothesis. What if there *were* a sign language that *did* form among the schoolmates of the 1950s, 1960s, and early 1970s, but it wasn't *passed down* to the generation of those who are now in their thirties? What if we posited the existence of a sign language *then* that *differed* from the one used now? That might explain the lack of older people in the membership rolls because, even if they had arrived at the deaf association, if they did not understand the newer sign language, they might have felt uncomfortable and chosen not to join.

But again there is *no* other organization for deaf people. Yes, there are private homes where deaf people meet, but I was unable to find an older person who was not already on the membership rolls who went to those homes to socialize. If older deaf people do come out of their homes and participate in private socializing, they would certainly be known to the members of the present deaf association because—by their age—they would stand out glaringly. So, because there is *no other place* to go, even if these older people had arrived at the deaf association with a different sign language—that is, with a linguistic base—they would have everything to gain by learning the new sign language and nothing to lose. Becoming bilingual means that one adds another language, not that the first is lost. So a little effort put into learning a second language would open up the *only* socialization opportunity that presently exists in Managua for

32. Compare the report of the interview with Noel Rocha in the "First School" section.

deaf people. And *not* learning the new sign language would mean that unique opportunity would be closed to them.

Anyone who has observed the elation that two signers experience when, each having been mired in a hearing world, they meet up and are able, even if only for a while, to communicate freely with their hands, would not doubt that any older deaf person capable of learning the new sign language would not have hesitated to do so. Furthermore, the members of the present deaf association are extremely adept at communicating with signers of other sign languages. They have received signing visitors from the United States, Canada, Sweden, Germany, Japan, and many other places, and a sense of camaraderie has always been present even if not everything is immediately understood.

The present deaf association regrets its lack of elders. In a conversation with the president of the association, this was a point that he mentioned as difficult for the community: They had no role models to follow. If there had been older deaf people who had used a different sign language and who arrived at the association, they would certainly have been welcomed, and ultimately linguistic differences would have been overcome.

An older signing population is conspicuous by its excruciating absence. With one exception, the oldest fluent signers are now thirty-four to thirty-eight years old. The exception is a woman who is now forty-three. She was a secretary at the CNEE and remained in contact with the students who had been in the oldest class in 1977; she participated as one of the founding members of the deaf association and probably learned the sign language through that contact. The other three older deaf men over the age of forty who occasionally come to the deaf association for activities sign with great difficulty and must often supplement their meanings with writing or fingerspelling in Spanish. Other members over the age of forty are also on the membership rolls, but they come to activities only rarely. One suspects that they are not fluent enough to enjoy unhindered communication at the deaf association.

FIRST GENERATION OF SIGNERS

Thus, the evidence implies that the group born around the 1962 rubella outbreak is the first generation of signers in Nicaragua and that the sign language emerged only in their lifetime. Most members of this group, and some members born earlier, are available to interview today in Nicaragua, and they have told me that although they used gestural forms to communicate among themselves when they went to school, the sign language that they now use as their preferred mode of communication did not develop until they were young adults.

We have no evidence of significant contact of deaf people outside of school hours during the 1950s, 1960s, and early 1970s, or of the development of a sign language during this time. But at approximately the time that the CNEE opened in 1977, socialization among the deaf students outside of school seemed to increase, and the interest in sign language, wherever it could be found, also expanded. The opening of the COD in 1981 seemed to encourage even more contact, so that out-of-school contact among the young deaf adults was common by 1986.

The extracurricular sports and folkdance programs begun in 1977 provided a significant increase in social contact among the deaf students, as did the social activities planned by Ruthy Durán. Whereas the deaf students seemed to have little extracurricular contact prior to 1977, this changed when the CNEE opened. At about the same time that extracurricular contact increased, more information about signed languages began to enter Nicaragua. This development made an impression upon the older students at CNEE, especially upon Francisco Montoya.[33]

At this time Progreso was founded in Costa Rica and began to give seminars and workshops in Costa Rica and other countries, including Nicaragua, on Total Communication methodology. The first dictionary of Costa Rican Sign Language was also published around this time. Mayra and Axel Mena were a sister and brother who had attended the Berríos school and who had many relatives in Costa Rica. Axel transferred with the others to the CNEE, but at some point between 1976 and 1980 Mayra was sent to a school in Costa Rica that used sign language, at which she evidently became rather fluent. During her vacations she returned to Nicaragua, visited former classmates, including Francisco Montoya, who took a special interest in learning as many signs as he could from her.

Montoya stated that his interest in sign language had begun in the late 1970s when he was given a sign-language dictionary during an athletic trip to Costa Rica. He had studied the dictionary and thus was interested in practicing what he had learned with Mayra as well as learning even more sign language from her. Mayra later returned to live in Nicaragua, although she and her brother ultimately emigrated to Costa Rica. Both

33. A pseudonym has been used to reflect the individual's wish for privacy.

were members of the Nicaraguan Deaf Association and had very low identification card numbers (indicating that they were early members).

Another Nicaraguan deaf student, Alejandro Castillo[34] was sent on scholarship to a residential school for the deaf in Spain, where the classes were evidently oral in focus, but where sign language was commonly used among the students. He left the country in 1974 but returned twice to visit. Alejandro had not attended the Berríos school, but Ruthy Durán — his cousin — introduced him to her students at CNEE during his 1976 and 1980 vacations. He shared his knowledge of Spanish sign language and began to pick up the shared homesign system that was common in Nicaragua at that time, and he sought out this group in 1982 when he returned home to Nicaragua.

Through his early enthusiasm for sign language, his dedication to making it a functional communication system for himself and his friends, and his commitment to share his knowledge with other deaf people in Nicaragua, Francisco Montoya must be considered a catalytic personality for the nascent deaf community in regard to sign language use. Other students at CNEE were exposed to sign language (they went on the same trips that Montoya did and met with the same representatives of deaf organizations in other countries), but they did not seem to experience the same spark of enthusiasm or curiosity that Montoya did. Remember that Thomas Gibson found only one young man (this was Montoya) capable of holding a nonhomesign conversation at the deaf gathering in 1979. Montoya was famous among his contemporaries for seeking out anyone who knew sign language or had access to a dictionary of any kind.

It appears, however, that it was only *after* APRIAS formed (probably not until 1989 or 1990) that the idea that sign language could become the major medium of communication among the deaf (rather than being used as a secondary system while placing primary emphasis upon oral communication) occurred to Montoya. He was a founding member of APRIAS and designed the group's logo, which was adopted in 1986. The logo, which illustrates a hearing voice breaking down the isolating wall of deafness, is integrationist in perspective. Montoya was an officer of the group from the beginning, meaning that he participated in discussions on the writing of the bylaws and was well aware of and evidently approved the assimilationist goals of the association, at least at the earlier stages. Any

34. Pseudonym.

APRIAS project in any way connected to sign language found Montoya an enthusiastic participant (e.g., the sign standardization workshops in the late 1980s), and he was one of APRIAS's first "sign language teachers." He became both the core leader behind the group's post-1990 move away from the integrationist perspective and a fervent champion of NSL.

CONTACT THROUGH THE COD

Finally, the founding of the COD in 1981 increased contact, not just among the previously acquainted students from the Berríos school or the CNEE, but also among the previously uneducated deaf students whose first experience with education was after 1981. Approximately fifteen deaf students transferred from the CNEE to the COD the first year, but they were outnumbered by approximately twenty-five other deaf students who had had no previous schooling. According to Nancy Guadamuz, an early social worker at the training institution, there had been concern during the planning phase that the COD had no funds for a school bus. It was decided, however, that use of the public transportation system could be made a component of the curriculum—one of the "daily living activities"—integral to a vocational training program. The older students who transferred from CNEE evidently did not need much training in this area, but within a short period all of the students at the COD had memorized all of the different bus routes and were very comfortable moving independently around the city.

The heterogeneous system of communication adopted in 1981 at the COD was an early fusion point in which the typical gestures of Nicaraguan oral conversation were combined with various systems of homesigns that students brought with them, along with the shared homesign pool and signs invented at the Berríos school and at the CNEE, as well as the Spanish, Costa Rican, and American signs learned from dictionaries or courses at Progreso or from Mayra Mena or Alejandro Castillo. All of these components were melded into a language in common use at the COD, which Judy Kegl and Cyndi Norman were able to document in 1986.

A FRIENDSHIP CIRCLE

It is doubtful, however, that a deaf community existed at this point. What is more likely is that between 1977 and 1986 a group of friends and classmates coalesced. Participation in activities was by invitation only and restricted to one's friends. The focus for activities was upon socialization and having a good time. The participants were uniformly of the same age group, from similar economic circumstances, and were without dependents. They possessed neither a wider perspective nor a vision of the future. What formed during these years was a friendship circle—undoubtedly an important preliminary phase, but not yet a deaf community. Significantly, at this point, only a few of the participants were functioning in societal "adult" roles. By definition, those who were enrolled at COD were still "in training" and not yet employed. Another group had received certificates from the COD and were employed at various low-paying jobs but were not yet independent in terms of providing for or contributing significantly to the expenses of a home or caring for children. They were still functioning as adolescents, even if some of them were in their twenties, and social agency (Giddens 1984) was not yet a crucial question for them.

However, in the period between 1985 and 1987, an entity that could be called a "deaf community" began to form. In Nicaragua, at least, another catalytic personality seems to have played a key role. Gloria Minero appears to have been the driving force behind the organization and envisaging that resulted in the formation of a deaf community.

Minero drew inspiration from the encouragement given to grassroots organizing by the then-Sandinista government. The "mass organizations" *(organizaciones de masa)* were basic building blocks of the Revolutionary program.[35] Among the first mass organizations to form after the 1979 Sandinista Revolution was the Organización de Revolucionarios Discapacitados (ORD), the Organization of Handicapped Revolutionaries. Its members had participated in the insurrection against the Somoza dictatorship and been wounded in action and left with permanently handicapping conditions. This group was eminently vocal in lobbying for the long-term welfare of its members, including agitating for medical care, rehabilitation, and pensions. The ORD, and its stance as protector of its members' rights, was a model available when the APRIAS statutes were written.

35. The official encouragement and approval that deaf people received in their efforts to organize would probably not have been there ten years earlier. During the late Somoza years in the 1970s, organizing by young adults or teenagers was considered subversive and heavily repressed. As many people told me, "To be young [in the late 1970s in Nicaragua] was a crime *(ser joven era crimen)*."

The exact point at which the friendship circle expanded to become a community is not clear-cut. By the time the first constitution was written in 1987, the group was described as a national organization, and its purpose extended beyond socialization. Significantly, membership was made available to any deaf person in Nicaragua, a significant departure from the earlier group of friends that gathered in each others' homes in 1979. Still, until the group obtained its permanent meeting house in 1989, it met at Durán's and Minero's houses or other locales they could arrange. To participate, one had to be invited by an active member in order to know where to go. After 1989, however, news of the meeting house spread throughout Managua, and by asking for the *casa de los sordos* ("Deaf House"), one could ultimately be directed to the meeting house without needing prior acquaintanceship with other deaf people. Personal invitation continued to be an important recruitment method, but this reification of the deaf association through the presence of a permanent location was an important step in becoming a community.

Although socialization remained a key activity for the deaf association, Minero insisted from the beginning that the organization's perspective be broader and include the goal of improving the social, educational, and economic circumstances of all of Nicaragua's deaf. The early perspective was certainly integrationist; that is, that the members, through self-improvement, would ultimately find their rightful space in the larger (oral) mainstream society. This attitude is illustrated through the official slogan and logo adopted in 1986 and the manner in which official events were orchestrated. For example, when the permanent meeting house was inaugurated in 1989, the association's president (a deaf secretary, one of the few people truly bilingual in Spanish and Nicaraguan Sign Language), someone very capable of signing her remarks to the crowd, instead read her welcoming speech aloud while at her side Minero translated it into sign language for the benefit of the majority of the association members who could not follow the spoken Spanish (R. Senghas 1997).[36] The integrationist perspective expressed in the 1986 logo, therefore, was still dominant in 1989. Only later would it change.

36. Her speech is very intelligible in one-to-one situations but not as clear in this kind of large-group situation, in which she was probably shouting in order to project her voice to all of the onlookers.

Some authors have written that Nicaraguan Sign Language developed among the elementary pupils at the CNEE in the post-Revolutionary period and that the deaf community formed among the same students (Kegl 1994; A. Senghas 1995; R. Senghas 1997). I do not find that this explanation fits the available evidence. It seems more fruitful to look elsewhere.

The pre-Revolutionary enrollment at the Berríos school, as we have seen, probably reached an annual average of fifty deaf students from the 1960s up to the earthquake in 1972, when the enrollment fell. By 1976 there were twenty-five deaf students enrolled in two classes. When the new CNEE opened in 1977, there were thirty-two students in four classes, and the enrollment climbed to forty in 1978 but remained stagnant in 1979 because of the civil strife that culminated in the final insurrection ending in July 1979. By August 1979 the teachers had returned to the school, and some classes were held. Yet the overwhelming reorganization throughout the country, as well as the nationwide Literacy Crusade, which took place in the early months of 1980, prevented routine classes from resuming until June 1980. By that time five new teachers for the deaf had been hired, and maximum class size had increased to twelve per classroom (rather than the pre-Revolutionary eight). Thus, in 1980 the enrollment of deaf students was 120 at the CNEE. In the transition period before the COD was ready, some of the older deaf students came to the CNEE for classes in the vocational shops, but they came when the younger pupils had been dismissed.

We have evidence from the time that school for the deaf began in Nicaragua that the children communicated among themselves manually — sharing their own homesigns, using iconic references, and making up shared terms particular to the school environment. But there is no evidence for the development of a standardized sign language. Thus, even in the period in the 1950s and 1960s when the enrollment at the Berríos school finally reached 50 annually, there is no basis to believe a sign language developed. In 1977 the enrollment at CNEE was 32 deaf pupils, not a significantly different number from the preearthquake enrollment at the Berríos school. In 1979 the enrollment had increased to only 40, yet this is when we have the first evidence of sign language, as opposed to homesign usage, when Montoya was able to string together a conversation using standardized signs recognizable by a stranger. After the Revolution, when the school enrollment was expanded, it was increased to only 120, a number that grew slowly to 200 over the next four years, with the enrollment then remaining constant for the following twelve years. A threefold increase in enrollment is a definite change, but is it significant enough to explain how a group of 50 students interacting over a period of a decade was unable to develop a sign language, but a group of 120 interacting within a year or two could?

It is important also to remember the attitudes toward manual communication that prevailed in the two eras. In pre-Revolutionary Nicaragua the use of one's hands for communication might have been cause for ridicule, disapproval, and teasing by the teachers, but it was generally ignored as long as it was left outside the classroom. The pre-Revolutionary CNEE teaching staff evidently had flexible enough attitudes that they welcomed Thomas Gibson in 1979 to a planned two-year stint demonstrating Total Communication and ASL. (He carried out only a few weeks of teaching, though, because of the imminence of the Revolution.) On the other hand, in the post-Revolutionary CNEE the curriculum and teaching methodology were made uniform, strict, and consistently oral through official policy. Use of one's hands to communicate was not tolerated at all. Students were publicly reprimanded for any use of sign language, and even use of gestures was discouraged. Teachers were publicly and privately reprimanded for using their hands too much, even if they were not using signs. Teachers of the post-Revolutionary years tell of fearing to lose their jobs if they or their students were caught signing.

The education available to deaf children in Nicaragua actually remained very consistent in the period from 1946 to 1992. Class size was always small, the methodology was always oralist, and the teachers were usually empirically trained. What did change in the late 1970s and early 1980s was the education given to adolescents. In the early period (1946–1976) schooling for deaf children routinely ended when they reached approximately fifteen years of age, after which time the pupils either were apprenticed or simply stayed home.[37] The first general relaxation of this norm came when the older students transferred from the Berríos school

37. It is important to point out that children with disabilities were not being singled out here. At this time it was common for most Nicaraguans to have only an elementary education or often less. Handicapped children in special education schools probably had more years of education than most Nicaraguans because they often took longer to complete the elementary curriculum. Nicaragua remains

to the CNEE in 1977. The elementary curriculum for the deaf was standardized after the Revolution, but its focus did not change.

During this period three new vocational schools were opened for youths with disabilities. These centers were not repeating the past but were treading on new ground. The centers had to be constructed and furnished, the curriculum had to be written, and new goals had to be prepared. The teachers were striving to produce not only youths capable of being eternal apprentices but also adults who could earn a living and support a family. The result was that the COD had no official policy against sign language, manual communication, or any other kind of communication. Anything that worked was encouraged. Both teachers and students were free to use their hands to gesture, pantomime, or sign as much as they knew how.

In this atmosphere the signing became more standardized and made significant steps toward becoming a communally adopted sign language. The students contributed a rich system of shared homesigns that they had used at CNEE. A few of the teachers had access to standardized signs from other countries (through Progreso in Costa Rica). The teachers learned from the students, and teachers and students collaborated to invent specialized signs not otherwise available. From 1981 Nicaraguan Sign Language was forming, although it appears to have been in flux for some years. But by 1986 both Cyndi Norman and Judy Kegl could document the presence of the language at the COD.

CONCLUSIONS

The evidence from Nicaraguan history presented here indicates that simple routine, proximity, critical mass, residential schools (or schooling per se), alienation, affiliation, or common education are not sufficient explanations for why or how a deaf community might form. All of these factors were present in Nicaragua from at least the 1940s; yet we have no evidence of deaf community formation until the early 1980s. And when we do see deaf community formation, there is no indication of any change in these factors that would adequately explain the transformation.

---

today one of the countries with the highest illiteracy rates and lowest rates of school achievement in the Americas (IDB 1998).

The Nicaraguan example underscores the previously noted close relationship between deaf community formation and development of a communally adopted sign language. In the period of Nicaraguan history in which no sign language developed, no deaf community developed either. When a sign language began to appear, the first community organizing soon followed. In the Nicaraguan case, the community and the sign language developed at approximately the same time, but there was a "lead" of a few years (1979–1986) in the development of the language before the community developed soon after (1984–1986). This is not an unexpected situation, for as social scientists have noted, language is the means by which humans participate in a society or a community (Giddens 1984).

The deaf community of Nicaragua formed concurrently with the organization of the deaf association, and today the two remain nearly identical in members' minds. Members of the deaf association routinely use "deaf association" and "deaf community" as interchangeable terms. I found no deaf person characterized as a leader, well known, or acclaimed in any way socially prominent (among the deaf) who was not also a member of the deaf association. There is only one deaf association in Nicaragua, and there are no rival organizations to tempt its members to split their allegiance. I am told that this pattern of development is not universal and that in other areas of the world, there are definable boundaries between a deaf community and organizations that the members of the deaf community belong to. In this regard the Nicaraguan example merits further investigation to determine why it developed this way.

Finally, the Nicaraguan example points to the adolescent/young adult influence that may be crucial in deaf community formation. The use of homesigns among deaf children who otherwise do not have access to standardized sign language is well documented (Morford 1996), and it is probable that a shared system of homesigns has been present among deaf students in Nicaragua since schooling started in 1946. But education for deaf adolescents and young adults was expanded only in the late 1970s. An increase in independence and self-esteem (through participation in sports) coincided with an increase in exposure to information about sign language. Nicaraguan history provides an example of how an adolescent circle of friends, through the encouragement and advice of sympathetic teachers and parents, with the flowering of a communally adopted sign language, developed into a national organization that is now the "voice of the deaf" in Nicaragua.

REFERENCES

Aguirre Heredía, O. 1995. Los gestos como forma de comunicación [Gestures as a form of communication]. Master's thesis, School of Journalism, Central American University, Managua, Nicaragua.

Asociación Nacional de Sordos de Nicaragua (ANSNIC) [National Nicaraguan Association of the Deaf]. 1997. *Diccionario del idioma de señas de Nicaragua.* Managua, Nicaragua: Copy Fast.

Bell, A. G. 1888. *Facts and opinions relating to the deaf, from America.* London: Spottiswoode.

Erting, C., R. Johnson, D. Smith, and B. Snider, eds. 1994. *The Deaf Way: Perspectives from the international conference on Deaf culture.* Washington, D.C.: Gallaudet University Press.

Estatuos de APRIAS, *La Gaceta,* No. 211, 7 Nov. 1989, p. 1514.

Fischer, R., and H. Lane, eds. 1993. *Looking back: A reader on the history of deaf communities and their sign languages.* Hamburg: Signum Press.

La Gaceta. 1989a. Personería Jurídica, Decreto A. N. No. 046, Año XCIII [Legal Standing, Decree No. 46, Year 93], No. 113, June 15, 1989, p. 821.

———. 1989b. Apruebanse Estatutos APRIAS, Año XCIII [Let the statutes of APRIAS be approved, Year 93], No. 211, November 7, 1989, p. 1511.

Giddens, A. 1984. *The constitution of society.* Berkeley: University of California Press.

Grooteman, B. 1990. Informe sobre el Centro Ocupacional para Discapacitados (COD) periodo 1981–1990 [Report on the Vocational Center for the Handicapped (COD) for the period 1981–1990]. Unpublished. Villa Libertad, Nicaragua: Werkgroep COD Villa Libertad/Holanda [The COD Villa Libertad/Holland Committee].

Hougen, S. 1993. *Deaf education in Nicaragua, Nicaragua through our eyes: The bulletin of the U.S. Solidarity Community Benjamin Linder,* vol. VII (6):7–12.

Infante, M. 1995/1998. *Sordera: Mitos y realidades [Deafness: Myths and realities].* San Jose: Editorial Technologica de Costa Rica.

Interamerican Development Bank, Statistics and Quantitative Analysis Unit. 1998. Available: http://www.iadb.org/int/sta/ENGLISH/staweb/statshp.htm.

Johnson, D., and R. Whitehead. 1989. Effect of maternal rubella on hearing and vision: A twenty year postepidemic study. *American Annals of the Deaf* 37:232–42.

Junta Nacional de Asistencia y Previsión Social [National Committee on Assistance and Social Concern]. 1975. *Memorias [Official reports].* Managua, Nicaragua: Instituto Nicaraguense de Seguridad Social.

Kegl, J. 1994. The Nicaraguan sign language project: An overview. *Signpost* 7 (1): 40–46.

———. 1998. Personal communication.

Maxwell, M., and M. Bernstein. 1985. The synergy of sign and speech in simultaneous communication. *Applied Psycholinguistics* 6:63–81.

Ministry of Education (MED). 1980. *La educación en el primer año de la revolución popular sandinista [Education during the first year of the People's Sandinista Revolution]*. Managua, Nicaragua, Ministerio de Educación.

———. 1981. *Principales logros alcanzados por el ministerio de educación dentro del contexto de la nueva educación [Principal successes achieved by the Ministry of Education within the context of the new educational policy]*. Managua, Nicaragua, Ministerio de Educación.

———. 1984. *Cinco años de educación en la revolución [Five years of revolutionary education]*. Managua, Nicaragua, Ministerio de Educación.

———. 1997a. *Boletín informativo educación especial 1989–1996 [Statistical bulletin for Special Education for the period 1989–1996]*. Managua, Nicaragua, Ministerio de Educación.

———. 1997b. *Cobertura de atención, servicios educativos especiales 1990–1997 [Educational coverage of special education services for the period 1990–1997]*. Managua, Nicaragua, Ministerio de Educación.

Morford, J. 1996. Insights to language from the study of gesture: A review of research on the gestural communication of nonsigning deaf people. *Language and Communication* 16:165–78.

Norman, C. 1998. Personal communication.

Ramos, H. 1997. Cuando la sordera no es un destino [When deafness is not a destiny]. *El País* (October): 55–57.

Schein, J. 1989. *At home among strangers*. Washington, D.C.: Gallaudet University Press.

Senghas, A. 1995. Children's contribution to the birth of Nicaraguan Sign Language. Ph.D. diss., Massachusetts Institute of Technology, Cambridge, Mass.

Senghas, R. 1997. An "unspeakable, unwriteable" language: Deaf identity, language, and personhood among the first cohort of Nicaraguan signers. Ph.D. diss., University of Rochester, Rochester, N.Y.

Van Cleve, J., and B. Crouch. 1989. *A place of their own: Creating the deaf community in America*. Washington, D.C.: Gallaudet University Press.

Index

German-Slovenian bilinguals, 46
Gibson, T., 267, 301
Goffman, E., 215
Grosjean, F., 45
Gumperz, J. J., 46–47, 48, 49, 51,
    68

Hammes, D. M., 56, 59
Hayes, L., 168–69
He, J., 14
Healers in Mexico, 121–22. *See also*
    Mexico
Hearing families of deaf child
    linguistic and cultural conflicts
        within, 222–23
    research about, 220–23
    worldview of deaf child, 219–
        54 *(see also* Deaf child of
        hearing family, life experi-
        ences of)
Hernandez-Chavez, E., 46–47
Hindi-English bilinguals, 47, 66
Howitt, R., 146, 149, 153
Huet, F., 124
Humor in miracle cures of Deaf chil-
    dren in Mexico, 136–38
Humphrey, J., 80
Humphries, T., 220

Identity
    development of, 224
    name signs and, 3, 4, 9, 36
Individuals with Disabilities Educa-
    tion Act (PL 94–142), 163
Initials used in NZSL name signs, 7,
    15–16, 29
Integration of Deaf children
    aim of, 117–18, 120
    Barcelona schools, 101, 105–6
    Mexican schools, 123–24
Interpreters
    educational policy and, 161–83
        (see also Educational signed
        language interpretation)
    NZSL name signs for, 21

RID *(see* Registry of Interpreters for
    the Deaf)
Sweden, 79, 84
    transliteration and, 79–82
Interviews
    videotaped interview, 204–16
        (see also Videotaped inter-
        view using Argentine Sign
        Language)

Jäger, L., 147
Jones, B., 169

Kachru, B. B., 47, 66
Kegl, J., 267–68, 302
Kerbrat-Orecchioni, 213
Krupnik-Goldman, B., 56

Labov, W., 205
La Bue, M. A., 166
Lane, H., 223
Larson, M., 80, 81
Legislation
    Nicaraguan, 279–280
    United States, for disabled persons,
        162–63
Levy-Bruhl, L., 22
Linguistic Human Rights and Euro-
    pean Union, 142
Locker numbers as name signs, 7–8
LSA. *See* Argentine Sign Language
LSC. *See* Catalán Sign Language
LSE. *See* Spanish Sign Language
LSM. *See* Mexican Sign Language
Lucas, C., 53, 80–81

Mainstreaming of Deaf children, 161
    increase in, 162
    interpreters for Deaf students and,
        163, 178
    spoken English as source language,
        164
Manually coded English (MCE), 52–
    53, 61
Markowicz, H., 223

Videotaped interview using Argentine Sign Language, 204–16
  attitudes toward Deaf persons in Argentina, 207, 213, 214
  discussion of interview, 209–15
  formal register of interviewee, 211–12
  images meant to empathize with interviewee, 213–14
  interviewer's role, 210–12
  introduction of interviewee, 207
  lack of interviewee's communication problems as point of video, 209
  metafunctional nature of discourse in, 214
  metamessage of, 215
  methodology of study, 206
  narrative nature of LSA signing in, 214
  turn taking during, 210
visual sequences, 206–8
"White Noise" as title of video, 206, 207, 209
world of interviewee, 208

Wandel, J. E., 56
Wesemann, J., 157
Winston, E., 79, 82, 86–90, 166
Woodward, J., 223
World Federation of the Deaf (WFD), 157
Worldview of Deaf child in hearing family, 219–54. *See also* Deaf child of hearing family, life experiences of

Yau, S., 14

Zentella, A. C., 44–49, 51–52, 64, 66, 70, 72